SOVEREIGN

WRITER
CHRIS ROBERSON

ARTIST
PAUL MAYBURY

COLOR CREDITS
PAUL MAYBURY
ISSUES 1-4

JORDAN GIBSON
ISSUE 1-2

BRAD SIMPSON
ISSUE 2-3

AFU CHAN
ISSUE 4

MARISSA LOUISE
ISSUE 5

FLATS/SPECIAL THANKS
DEE CUNNIFFE, VICTORIA GRACE ELLIOTT, WILL MENDEZ, RICKY VALENZUELA.

LETTERER
JOHN J. HILL

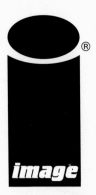

IMAGE COMICS, INC.
Robert Kirkman – Chief Operating Officer
Erik Larsen – Chief Financial Officer
Todd McFarlane – President
Marc Silvestri – Chief Executive Officer
Jim Valentino – Vice-President

Eric Stephenson – Publisher
Ron Richards – Director of Business Development
Jennifer de Guzman – Director of Trade Book Sales
Kat Salazar – Director of PR & Marketing
Corey Murphy – Director of Retail Sales
Jeremy Sullivan – Director of Digital Sales
Emilio Bautista – Sales Assistant
Branwyn Bigglestone – Senior Accounts Manager
Emily Miller – Accounts Manager
Jessica Ambriz – Administrative Assistant
Tyler Shainline – Events Coordinator
David Brothers – Content Manager
Jonathan Chan – Production Manager
Drew Gill – Art Director
Meredith Wallace – Print Manager
Monica Garcia – Senior Production Artist
Jenna Savage – Production Artist
Addison Duke – Production Artist
Tricia Ramos – Production Assistant
IMAGECOMICS.COM

SOVEREIGN. COPYRIGHT © 2014
STORY © MONKEYBRAIN, INC. • ART © PAUL MAYBURY.
DECEMBER 2014.

Published by Image Comics, Inc. Office of publication: 2001 Center Street, 6th Floor, Berkeley, CA 94704. © 2014. Image Comics® and its logos are registered trademarks of Image Comics, Inc.

Leaving Silence

The Luminari cannot simply sit behind
the walls of Silence, ignoring the world
around us. We must venture down into
the lowlands and carry out our sacred
duties, even if it means our death.

—Sant Koel, on the eve of
his execution by Raghir Rhan

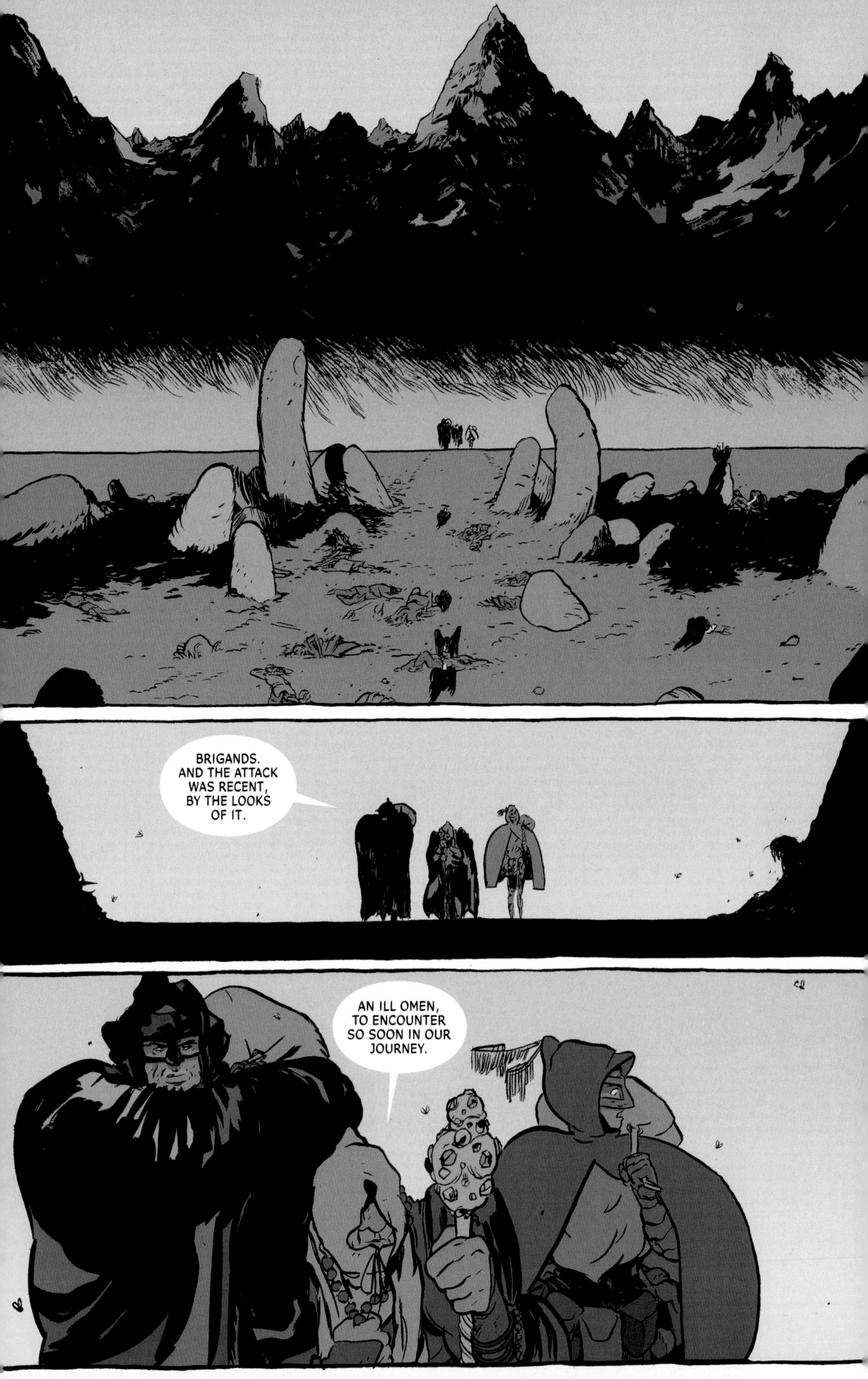
BRIGANDS. AND THE ATTACK WAS RECENT, BY THE LOOKS OF IT.
AN ILL OMEN, TO ENCOUNTER SO SOON IN OUR JOURNEY.

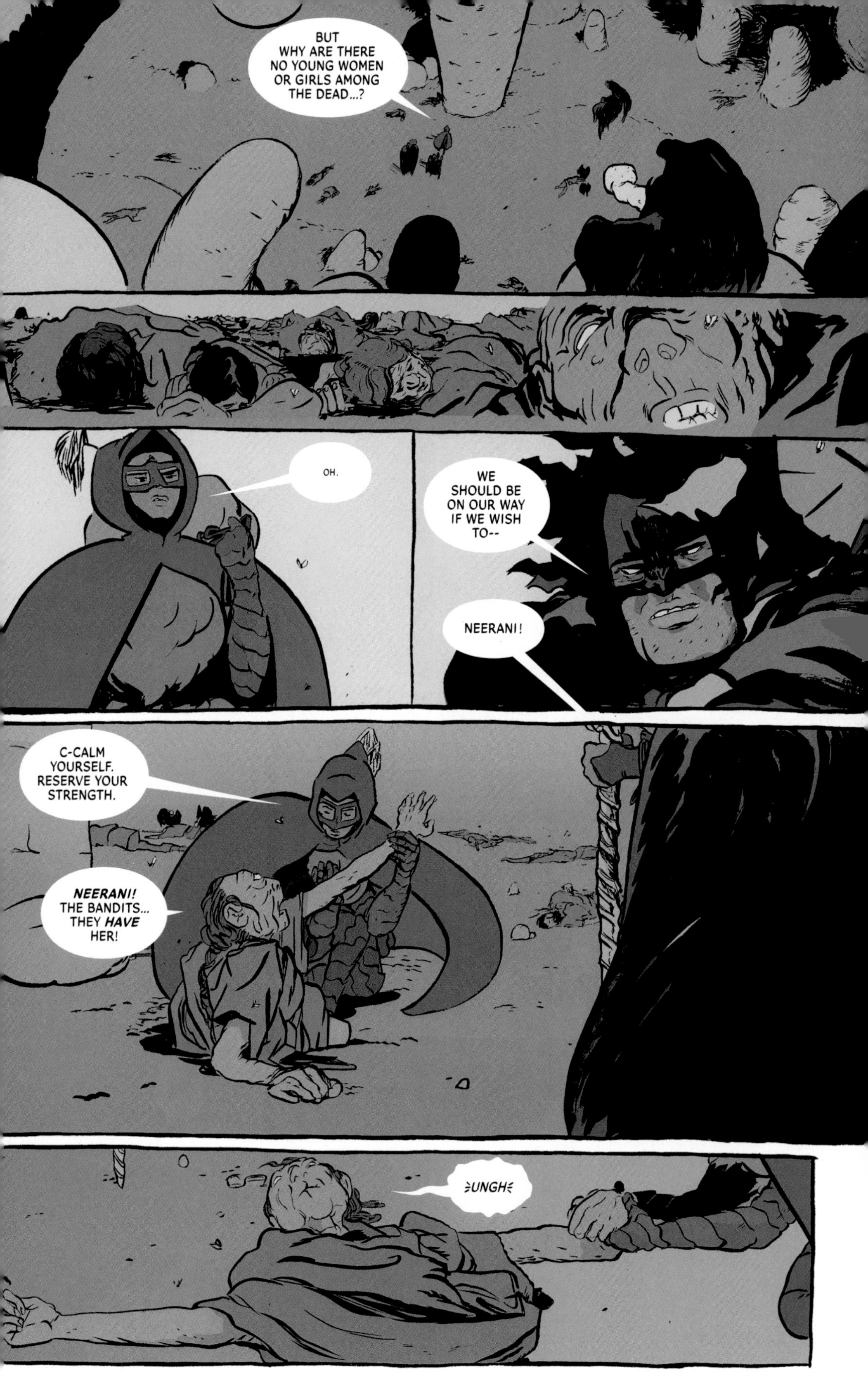
BUT WHY ARE THERE NO YOUNG WOMEN OR GIRLS AMONG THE DEAD...?
OH.
WE SHOULD BE ON OUR WAY IF WE WISH TO--
NEERANI!
C-CALM YOURSELF. RESERVE YOUR STRENGTH.
NEERANI! THE BANDITS... THEY *HAVE* HER!
UNGH

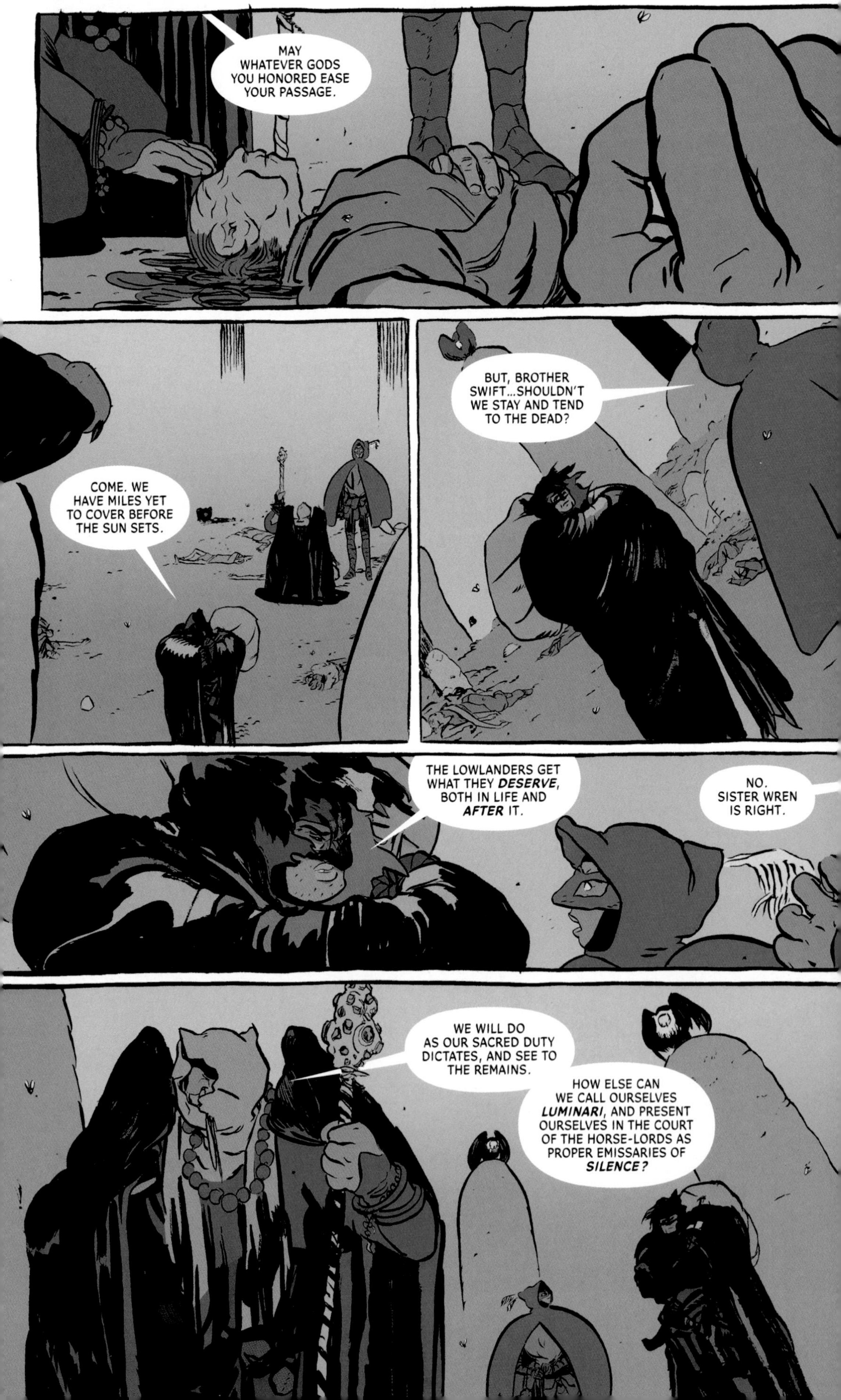
MAY WHATEVER GODS YOU HONORED EASE YOUR PASSAGE.
COME. WE HAVE MILES YET TO COVER BEFORE THE SUN SETS.
BUT, BROTHER SWIFT...SHOULDN'T WE STAY AND TEND TO THE DEAD?
THE LOWLANDERS GET WHAT THEY *DESERVE*, BOTH IN LIFE AND *AFTER* IT.
NO. SISTER WREN IS RIGHT.
WE WILL DO AS OUR SACRED DUTY DICTATES, AND SEE TO THE REMAINS.
HOW ELSE CAN WE CALL OURSELVES *LUMINARI*, AND PRESENT OURSELVES IN THE COURT OF THE HORSE-LORDS AS PROPER EMISSARIES OF *SILENCE?*

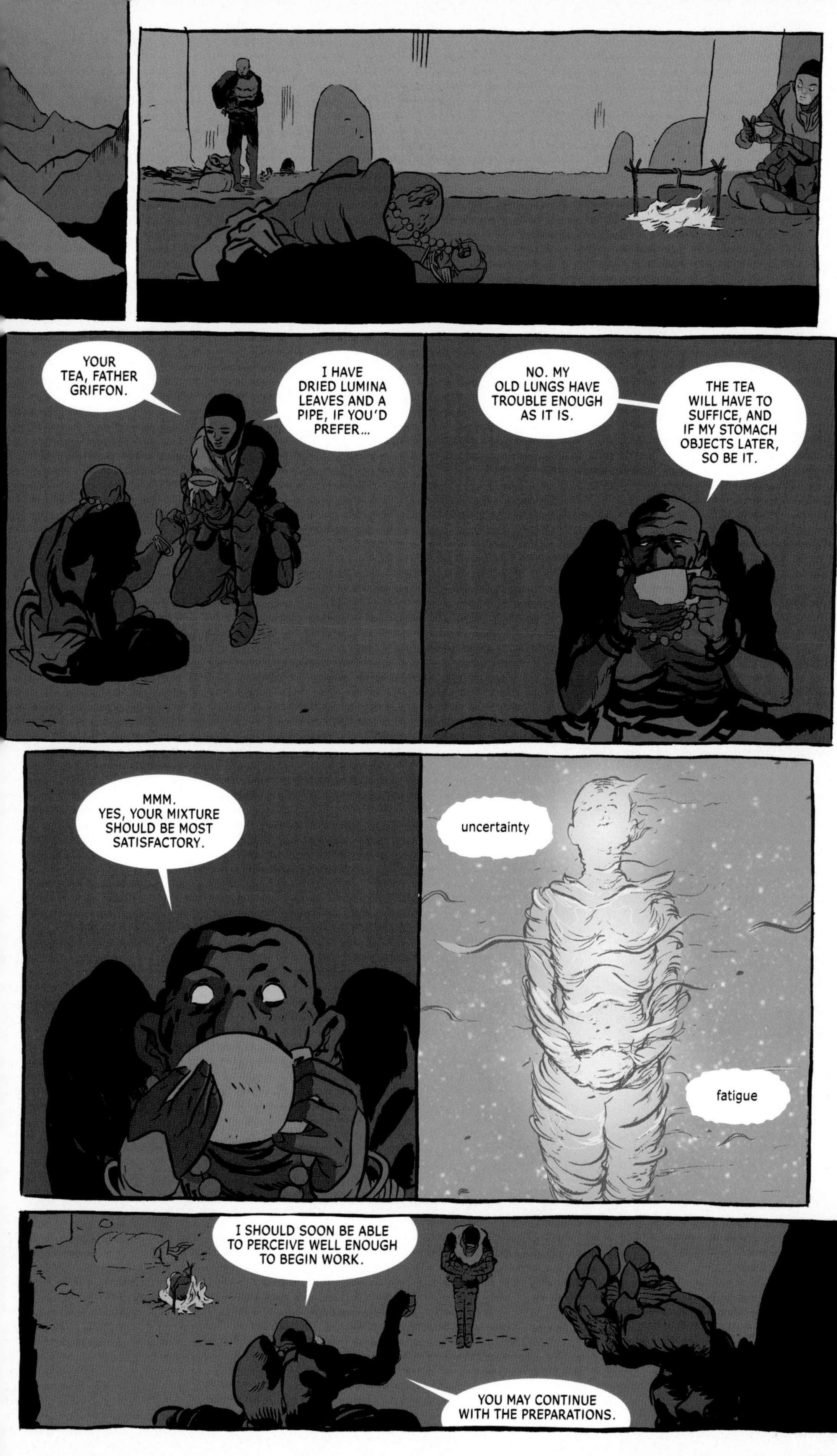
YOUR TEA, FATHER GRIFFON.
I HAVE DRIED LUMINA LEAVES AND A PIPE, IF YOU'D PREFER...
NO. MY OLD LUNGS HAVE TROUBLE ENOUGH AS IT IS.
THE TEA WILL HAVE TO SUFFICE, AND IF MY STOMACH OBJECTS LATER, SO BE IT.
MMM. YES, YOUR MIXTURE SHOULD BE MOST SATISFACTORY.
uncertainty
fatigue
I SHOULD SOON BE ABLE TO PERCEIVE WELL ENOUGH TO BEGIN WORK.
YOU MAY CONTINUE WITH THE PREPARATIONS.

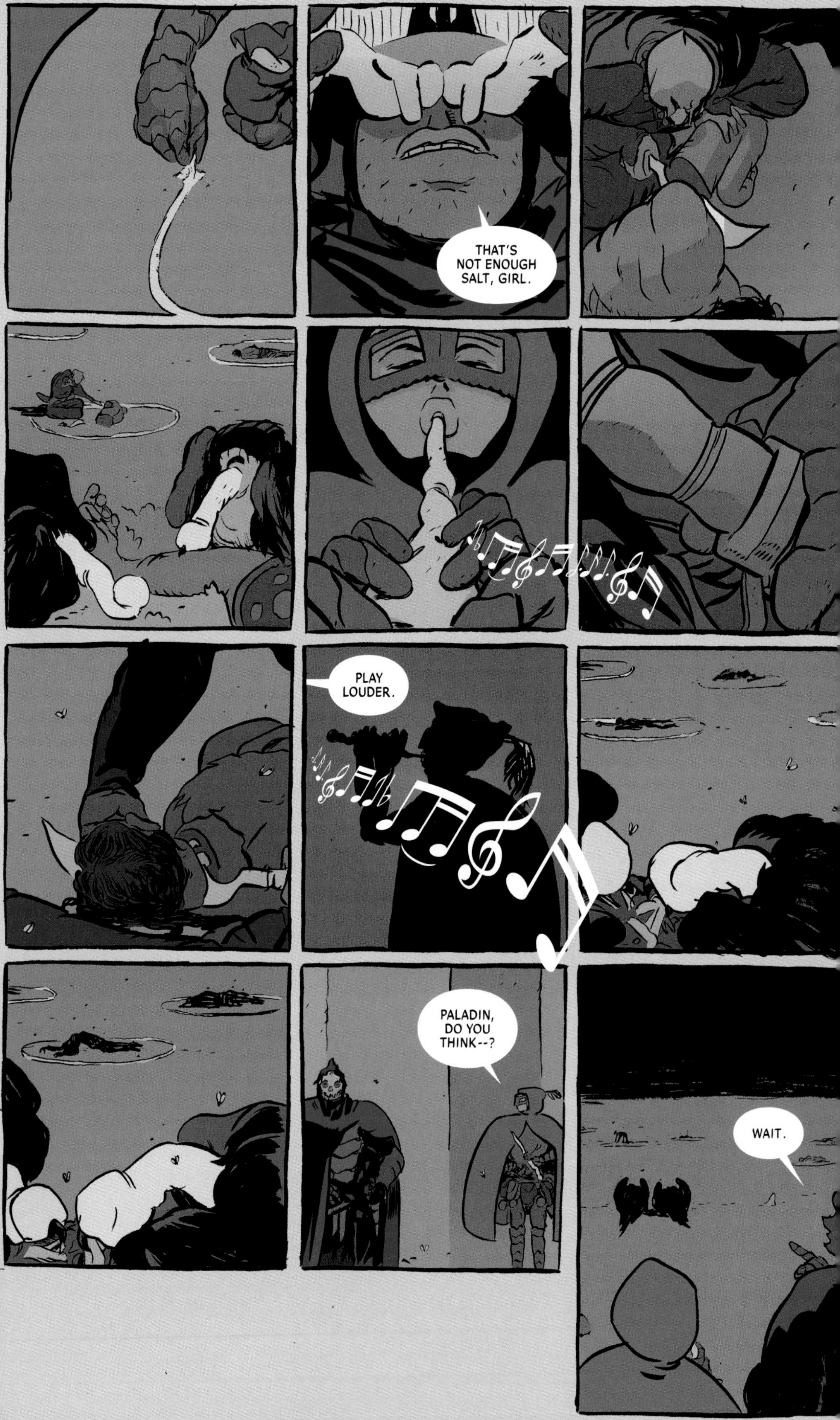
THAT'S NOT ENOUGH SALT, GIRL.
PLAY LOUDER.
PALADIN, DO YOU THINK--?
WAIT.

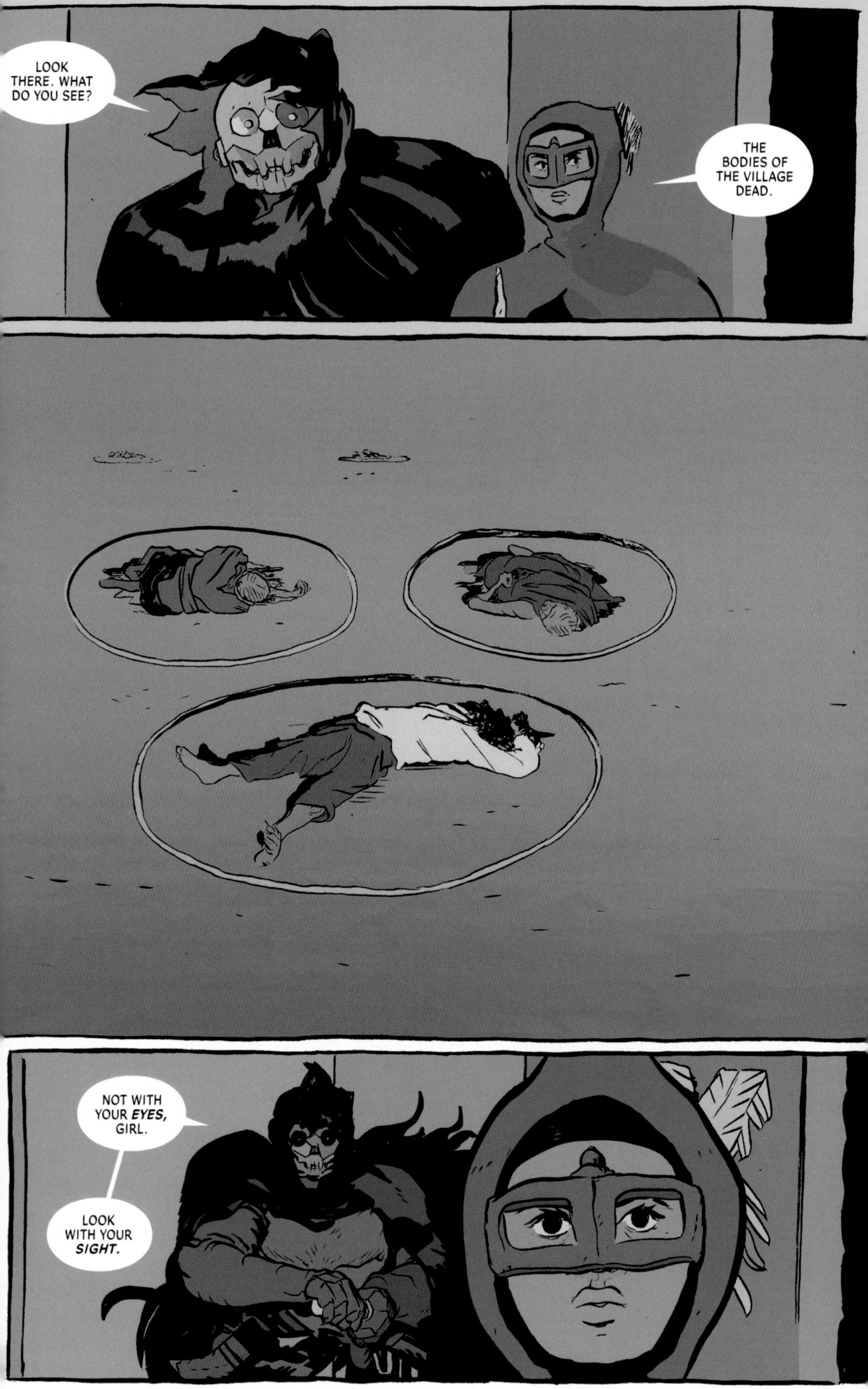
LOOK THERE. WHAT DO YOU SEE?
THE BODIES OF THE VILLAGE DEAD.
NOT WITH YOUR *EYES,* GIRL.
LOOK WITH YOUR *SIGHT.*

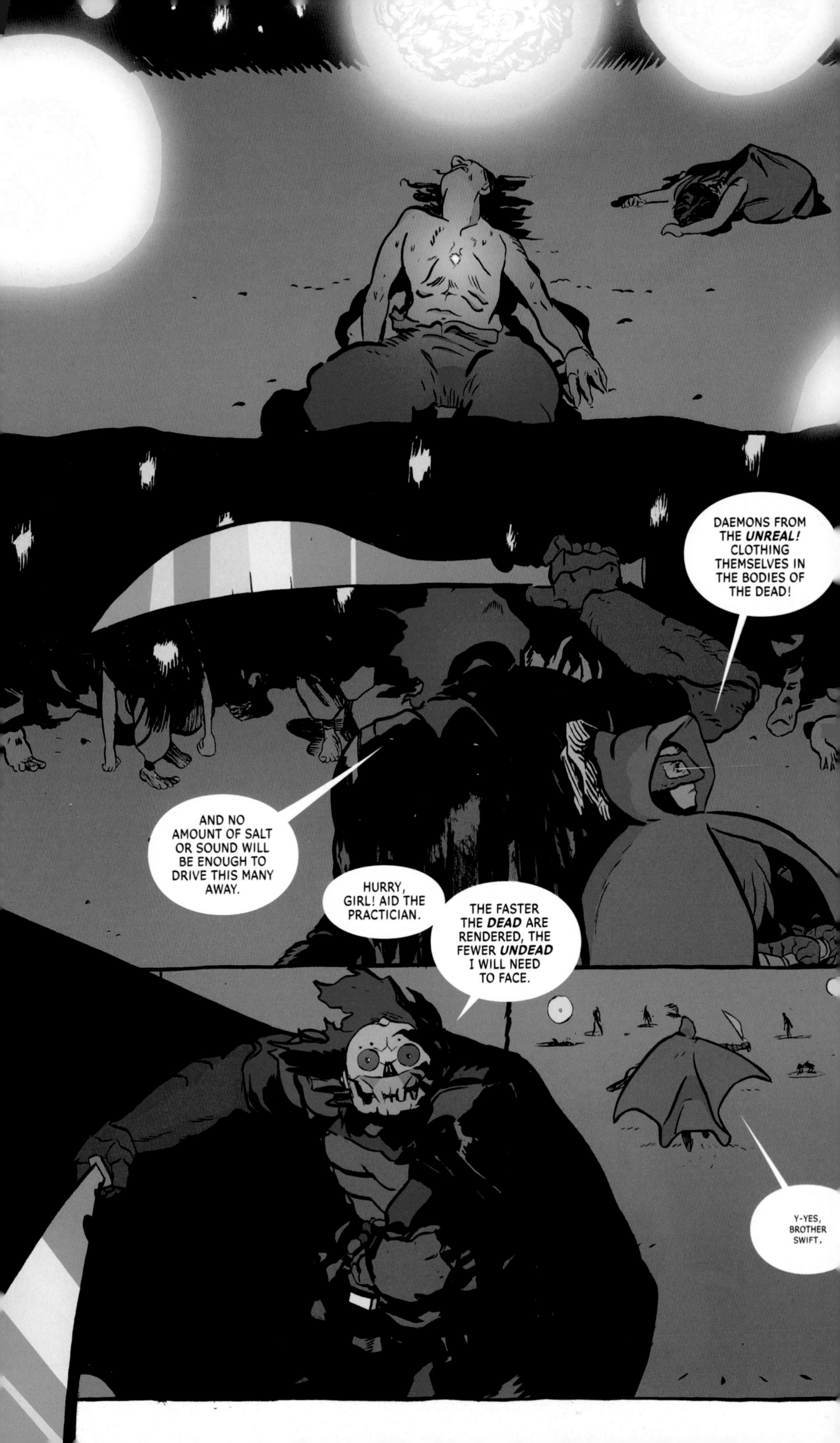
DAEMONS FROM THE UNREAL! CLOTHING THEMSELVES IN THE BODIES OF THE DEAD!
AND NO AMOUNT OF SALT OR SOUND WILL BE ENOUGH TO DRIVE THIS MANY AWAY.
HURRY, GIRL! AID THE PRACTICIAN.
THE FASTER THE DEAD ARE RENDERED, THE FEWER UNDEAD I WILL NEED TO FACE.
Y-YES, BROTHER SWIFT.

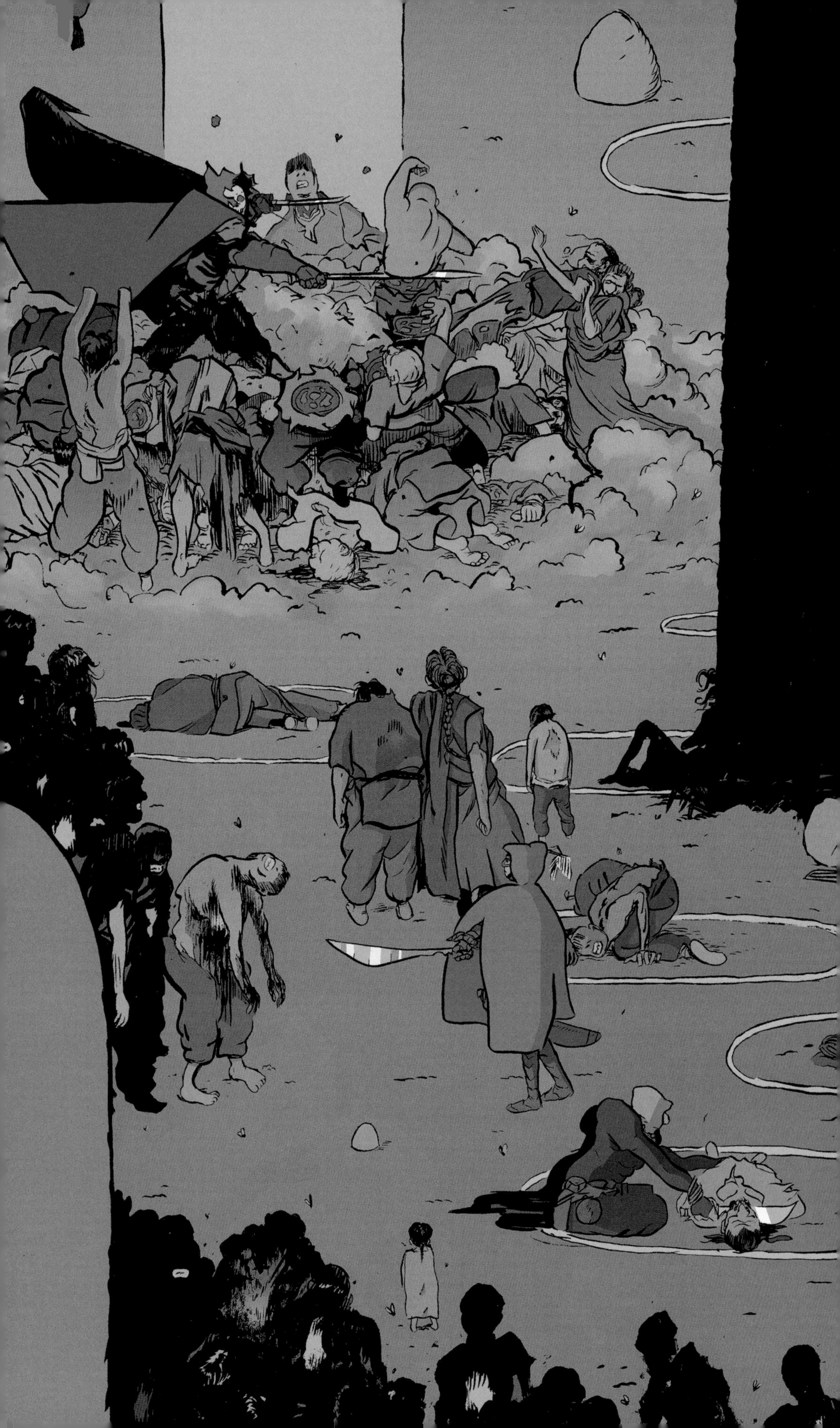

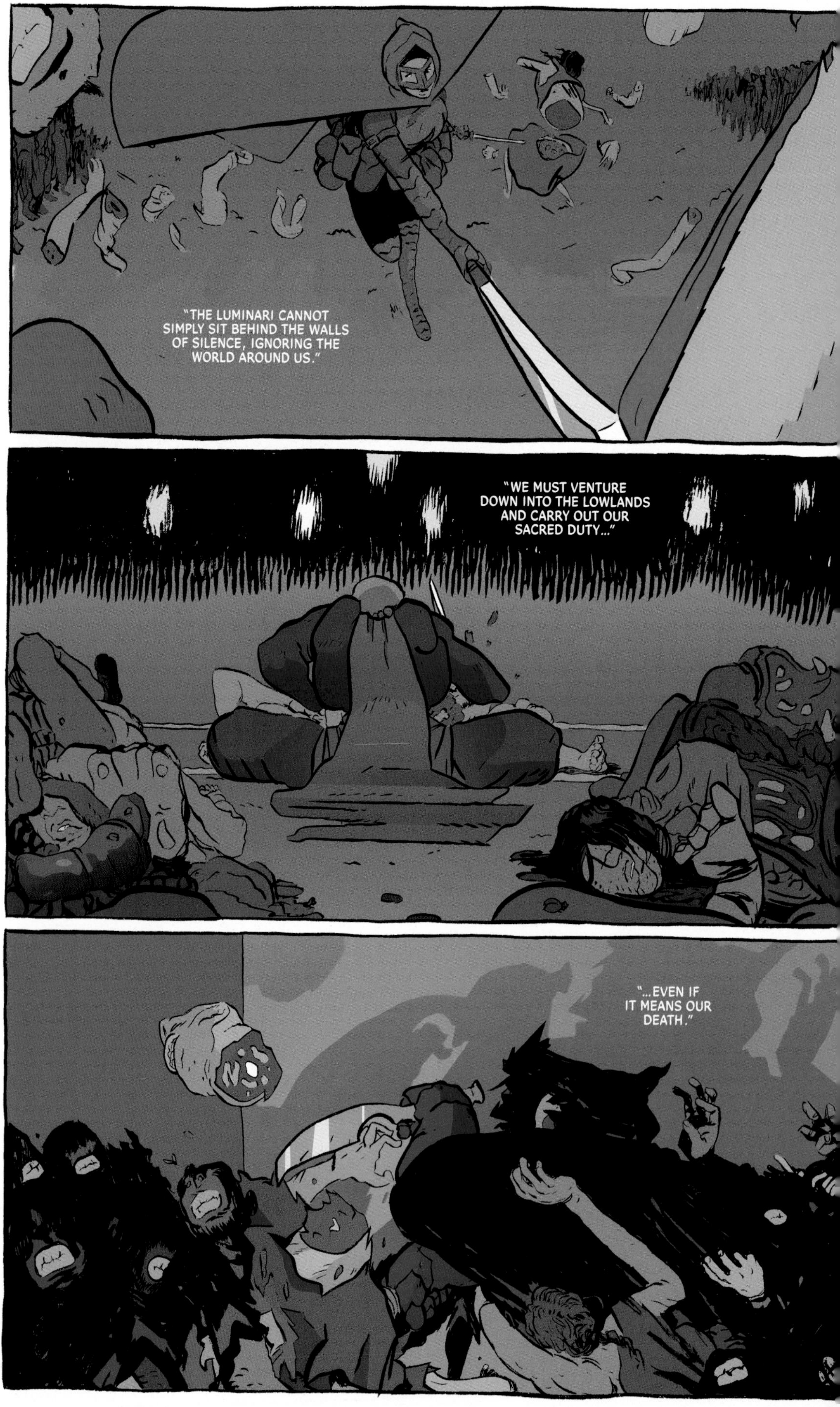
"THE LUMINARI CANNOT SIMPLY SIT BEHIND THE WALLS OF SILENCE, IGNORING THE WORLD AROUND US."
"WE MUST VENTURE DOWN INTO THE LOWLANDS AND CARRY OUT OUR SACRED DUTY..."
"...EVEN IF IT MEANS OUR DEATH."

blade and bow

Vorghiz Rhan, the first and greatest
of the horselords, lived and died in
the saddle. His spirit weeps if death
ever finds a Tamurid sleeping in bed.

—Sanram Rhan

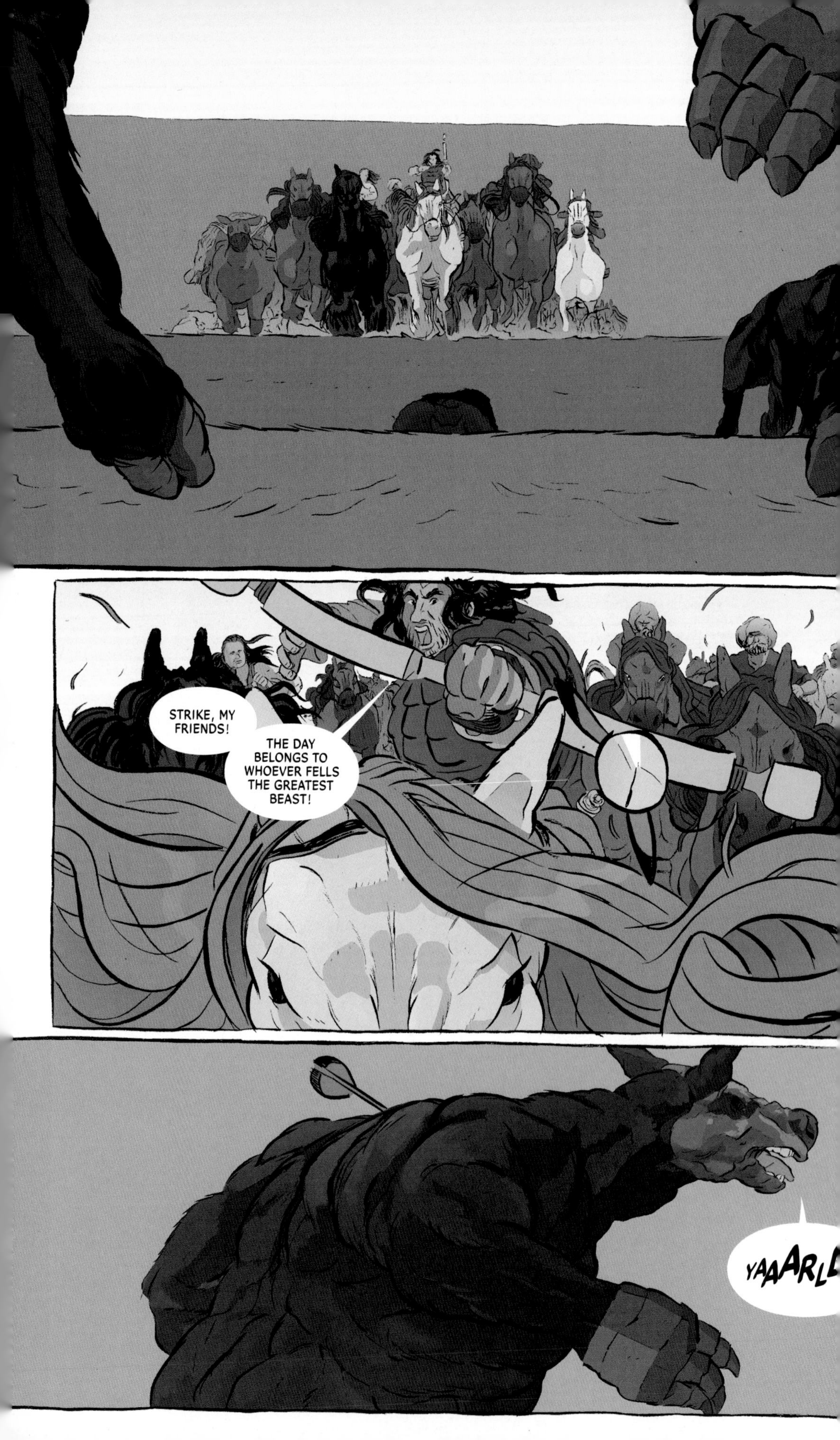
STRIKE, MY FRIENDS!
THE DAY BELONGS TO WHOEVER FELLS THE GREATEST BEAST!
YAAARL

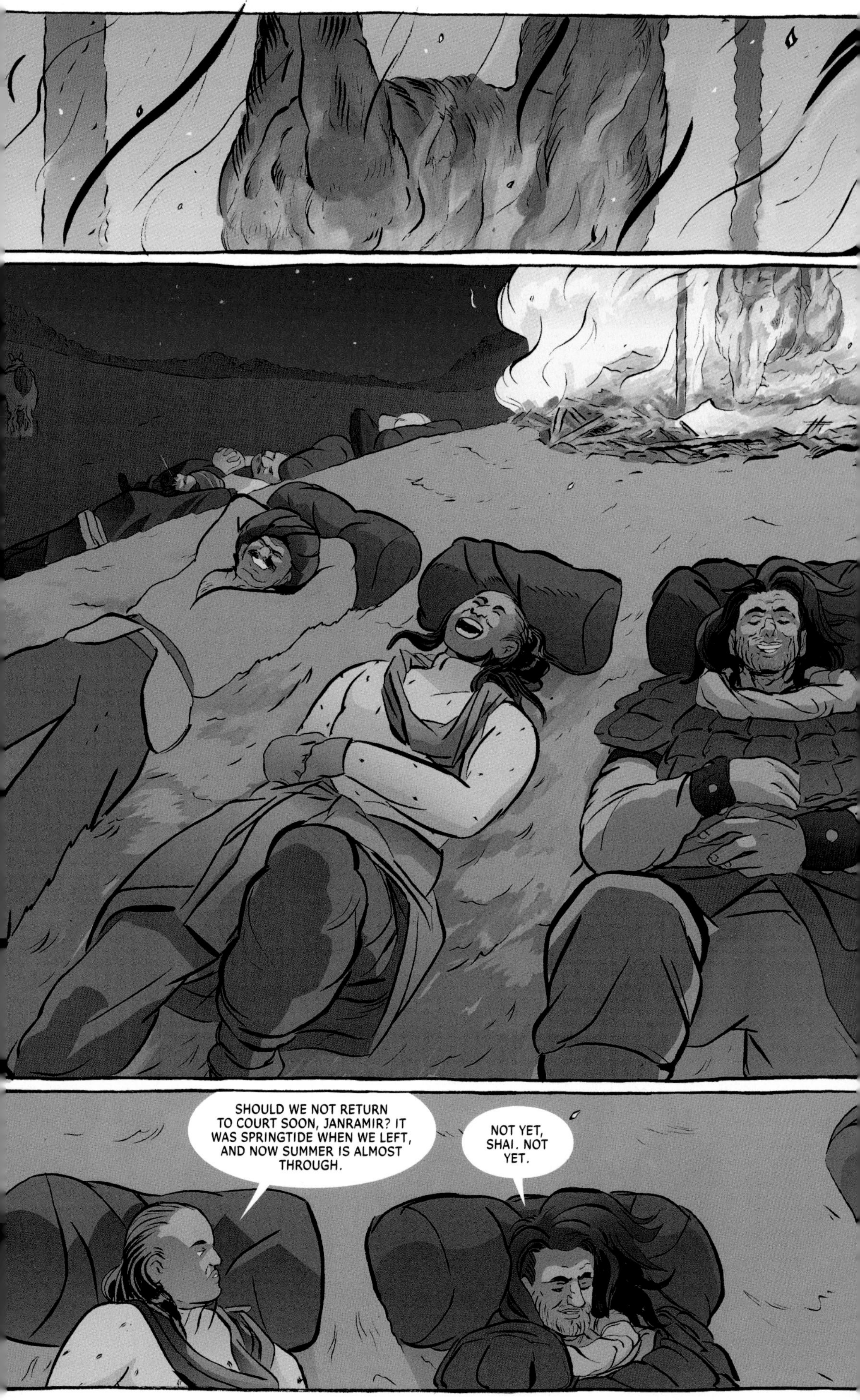
SHOULD WE NOT RETURN TO COURT SOON, JANRAMIR? IT WAS SPRINGTIDE WHEN WE LEFT, AND NOW SUMMER IS ALMOST THROUGH.
NOT YET, SHAI. NOT YET.

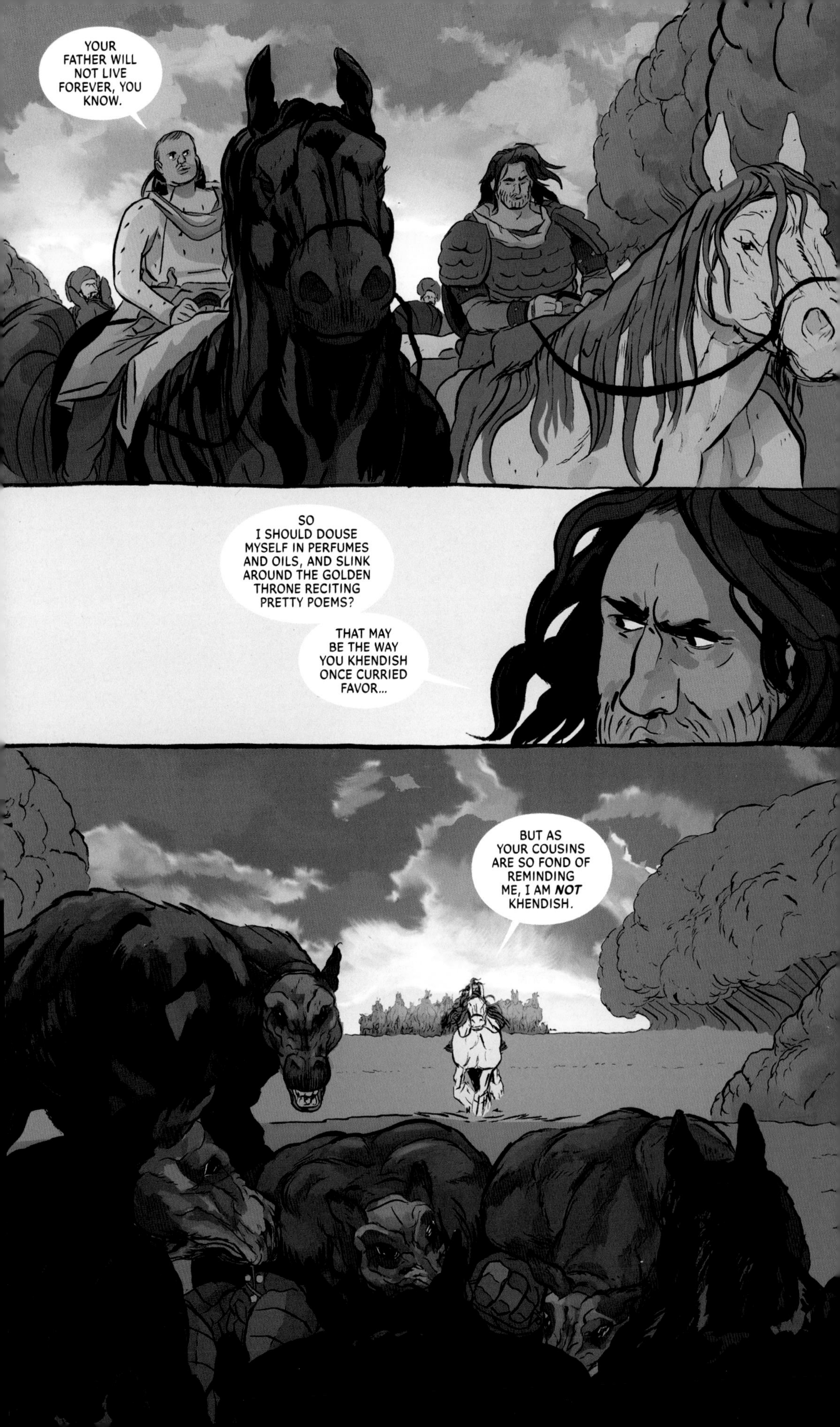
YOUR FATHER WILL NOT LIVE FOREVER, YOU KNOW.
SO I SHOULD DOUSE MYSELF IN PERFUMES AND OILS, AND SLINK AROUND THE GOLDEN THRONE RECITING PRETTY POEMS?
THAT MAY BE THE WAY YOU KHENDISH ONCE CURRIED FAVOR...
BUT AS YOUR COUSINS ARE SO FOND OF REMINDING ME, I AM *NOT* KHENDISH.

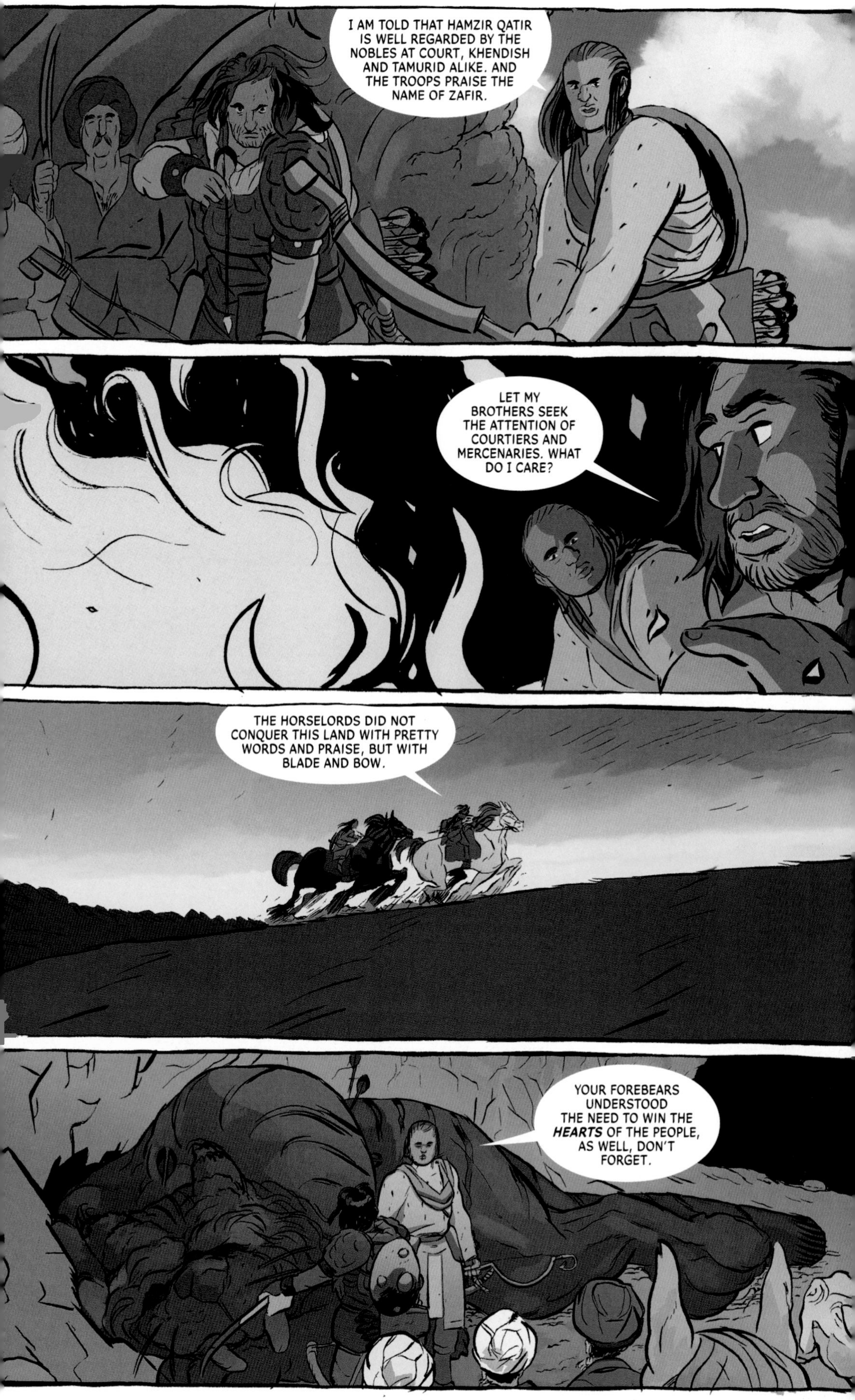
I AM TOLD THAT HAMZIR QATIR IS WELL REGARDED BY THE NOBLES AT COURT, KHENDISH AND TAMURID ALIKE. AND THE TROOPS PRAISE THE NAME OF ZAFIR.
LET MY BROTHERS SEEK THE ATTENTION OF COURTIERS AND MERCENARIES. WHAT DO I CARE?
THE HORSELORDS DID NOT CONQUER THIS LAND WITH PRETTY WORDS AND PRAISE, BUT WITH BLADE AND BOW.
YOUR FOREBEARS UNDERSTOOD THE NEED TO WIN THE ***HEARTS*** OF THE PEOPLE, AS WELL, DON'T FORGET.

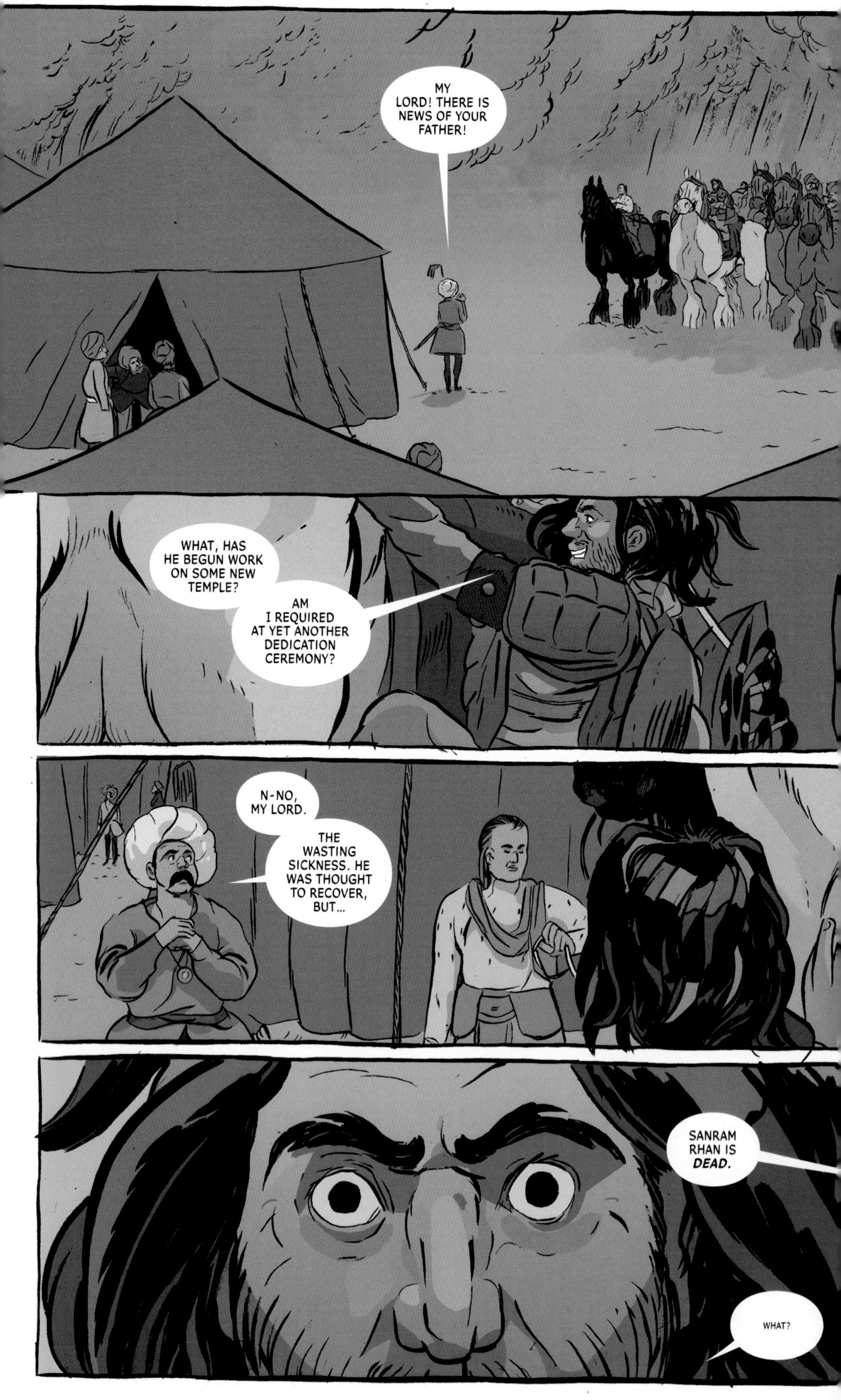
MY LORD! THERE IS NEWS OF YOUR FATHER!
WHAT, HAS HE BEGUN WORK ON SOME NEW TEMPLE?
AM I REQUIRED AT YET ANOTHER DEDICATION CEREMONY?
N-NO, MY LORD.
THE WASTING SICKNESS. HE WAS THOUGHT TO RECOVER, BUT...
SANRAM RHAN IS *DEAD.*
WHAT?

from the depths

I envy people of faith, for they live in a
world of answers. For a man of reason,
the world holds only questions.

—Pol Ravenstone's
private journal

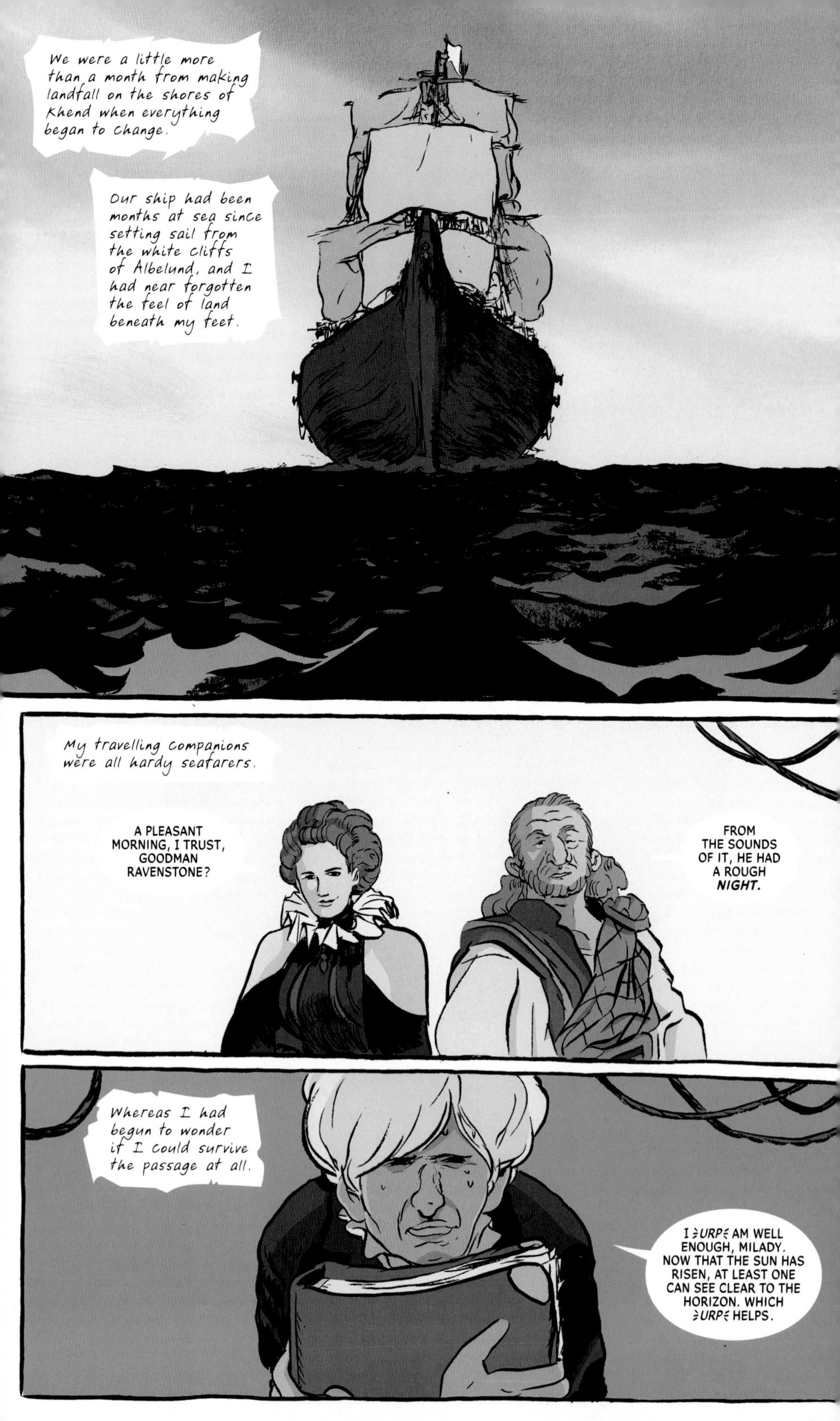
We were a little more than a month from making landfall on the shores of Khend when everything began to change.
Our ship had been months at sea since setting sail from the white cliffs of Albelund, and I had near forgotten the feel of land beneath my feet.
My travelling companions were all hardy seafarers.
A PLEASANT MORNING, I TRUST, GOODMAN RAVENSTONE?
FROM THE SOUNDS OF IT, HE HAD A ROUGH NIGHT.
Whereas I had begun to wonder if I could survive the passage at all.
I ≷URP≶ AM WELL ENOUGH, MILADY. NOW THAT THE SUN HAS RISEN, AT LEAST ONE CAN SEE CLEAR TO THE HORIZON. WHICH ≷URP≶ HELPS.

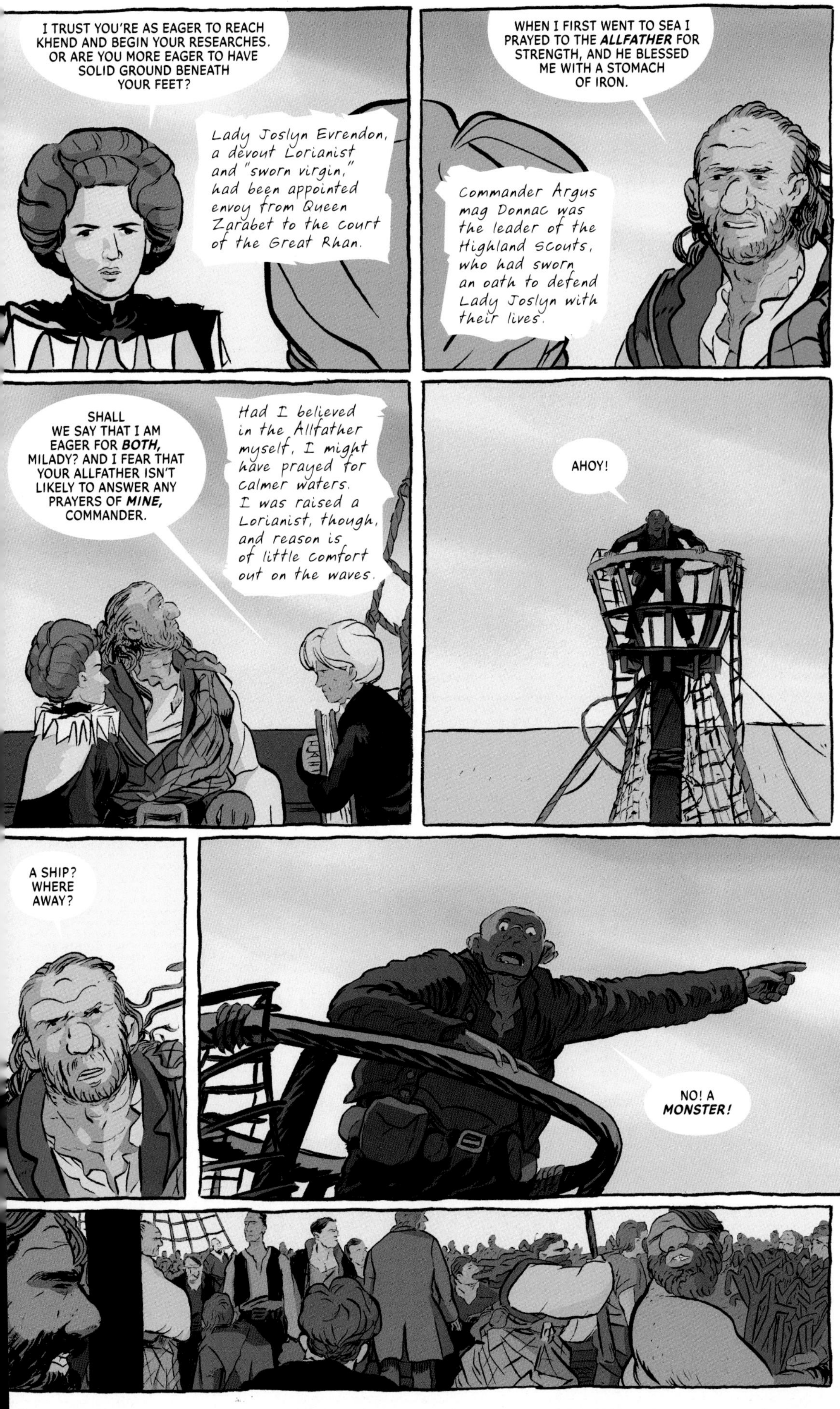
I TRUST YOU'RE AS EAGER TO REACH KHEND AND BEGIN YOUR RESEARCHES. OR ARE YOU MORE EAGER TO HAVE SOLID GROUND BENEATH YOUR FEET?
Lady Joslyn Evrendon, a devout Lorianist and "sworn virgin," had been appointed envoy from Queen Zarabet to the court of the Great Rhan.
WHEN I FIRST WENT TO SEA I PRAYED TO THE ALLFATHER FOR STRENGTH, AND HE BLESSED ME WITH A STOMACH OF IRON.
Commander Argus mag Donnac was the leader of the Highland Scouts, who had sworn an oath to defend Lady Joslyn with their lives.
SHALL WE SAY THAT I AM EAGER FOR BOTH, MILADY? AND I FEAR THAT YOUR ALLFATHER ISN'T LIKELY TO ANSWER ANY PRAYERS OF MINE, COMMANDER.
Had I believed in the Allfather myself, I might have prayed for calmer waters. I was raised a Lorianist, though, and reason is of little comfort out on the waves.
AHOY!
A SHIP? WHERE AWAY?
NO! A MONSTER!

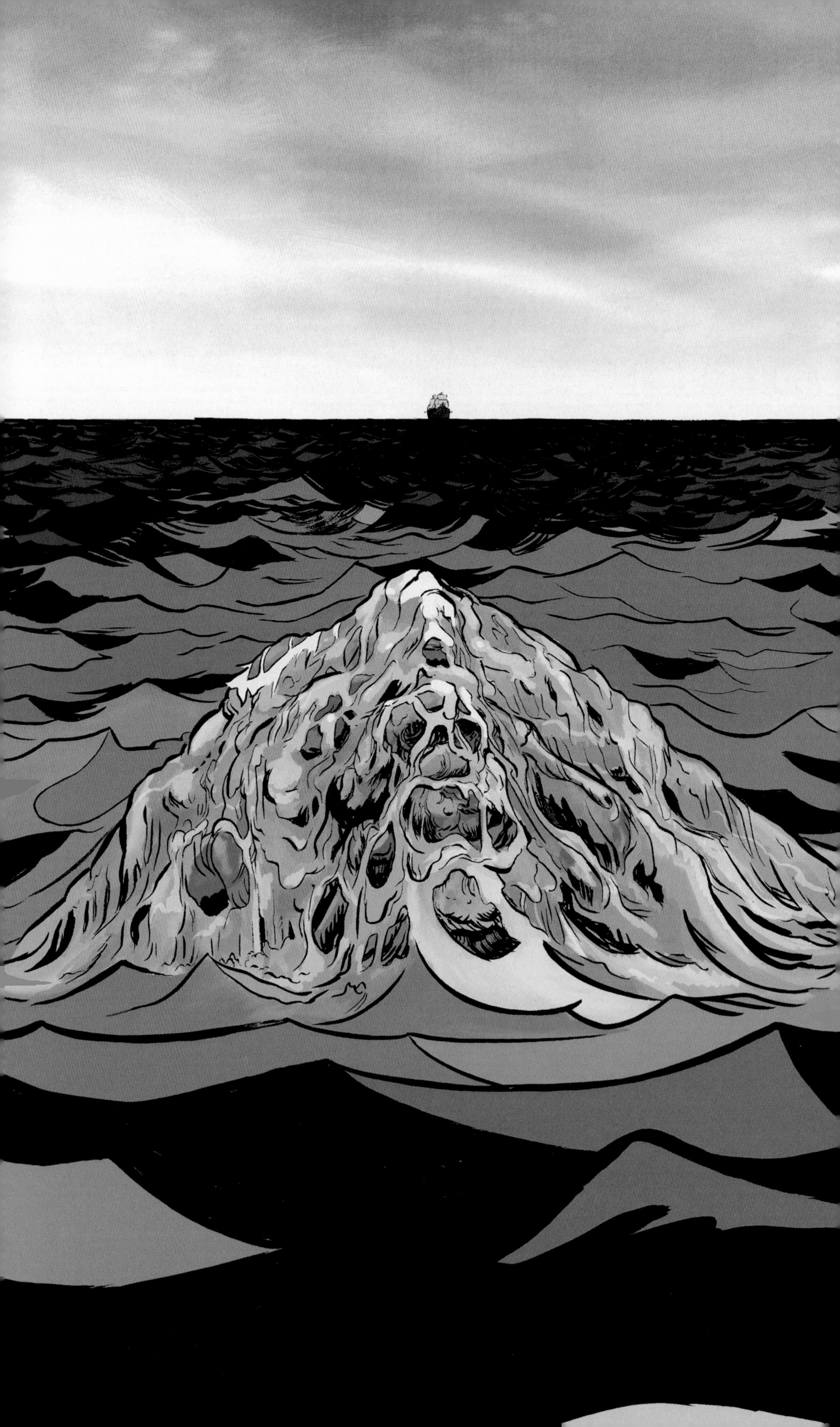

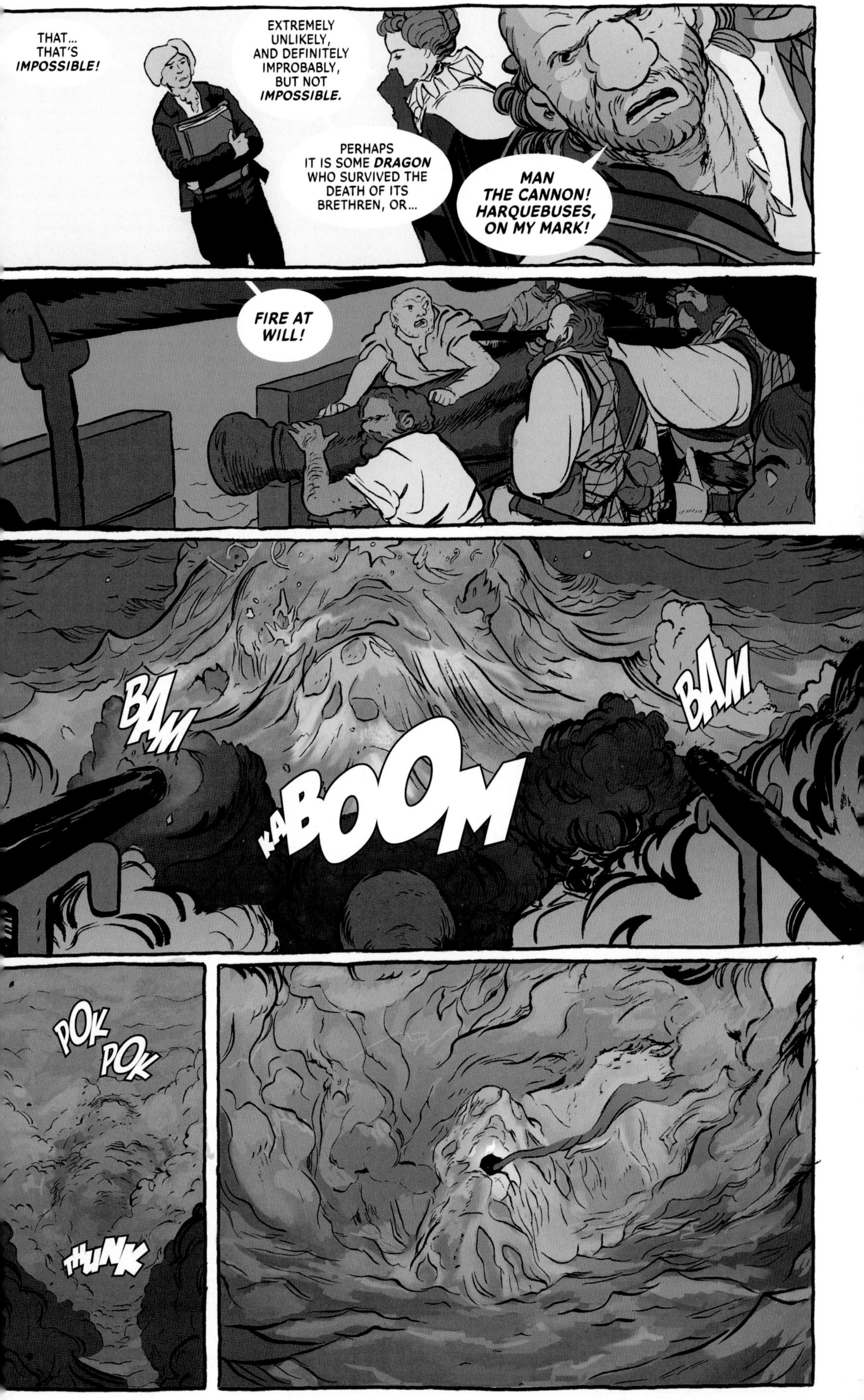
THAT... THAT'S *IMPOSSIBLE!*
EXTREMELY UNLIKELY, AND DEFINITELY IMPROBABLY, BUT NOT *IMPOSSIBLE.*
PERHAPS IT IS SOME *DRAGON* WHO SURVIVED THE DEATH OF ITS BRETHREN, OR...
MAN THE CANNON! HARQUEBUSES, ON MY MARK!
FIRE AT WILL!
BAM
KABOOM
BAM
POK
POK
THUNK

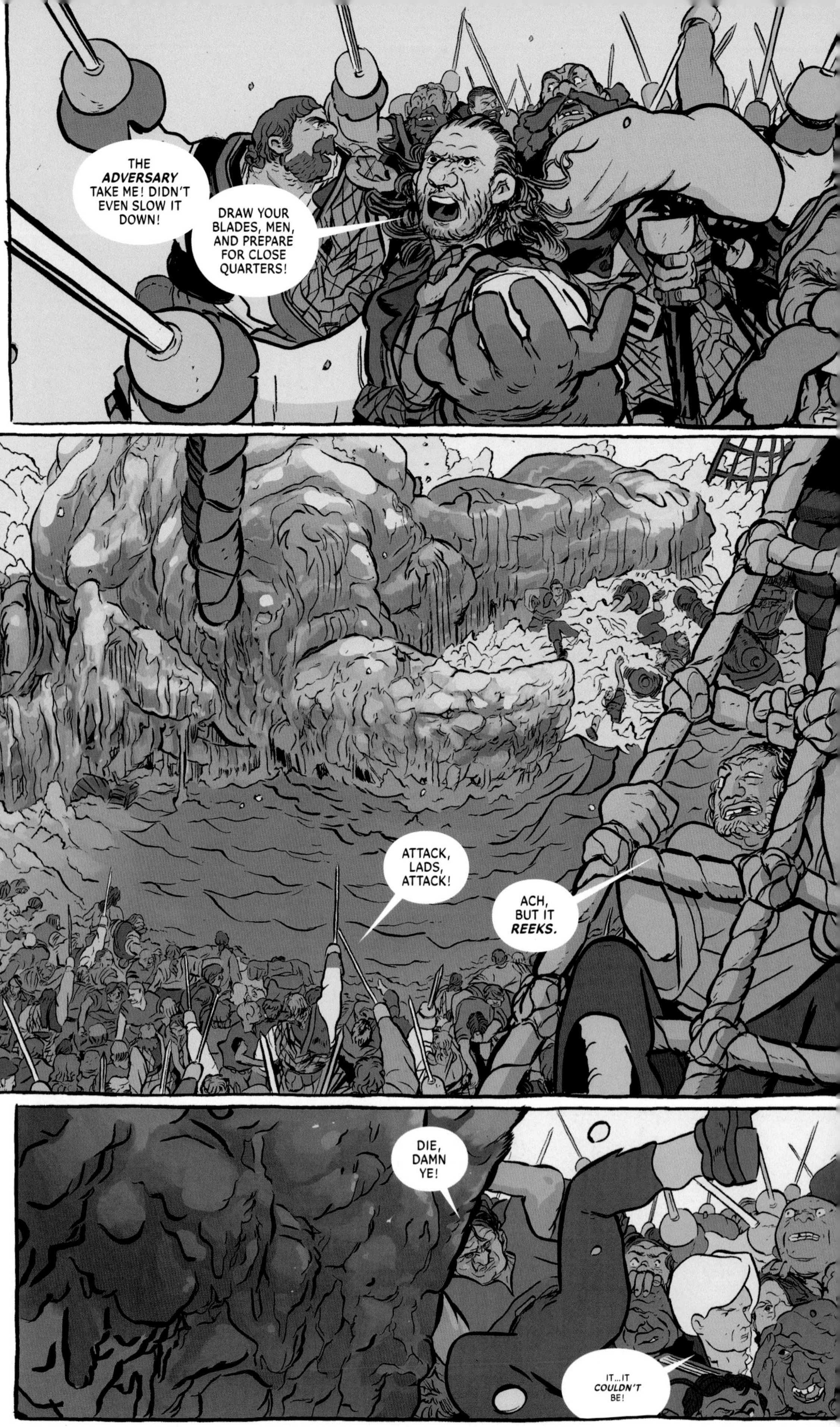
THE *ADVERSARY* TAKE ME! DIDN'T EVEN SLOW IT DOWN!
DRAW YOUR BLADES, MEN, AND PREPARE FOR CLOSE QUARTERS!
ATTACK, LADS, ATTACK!
ACH, BUT IT *REEKS.*
DIE, DAMN YE!
IT...IT *COULDN'T* BE!

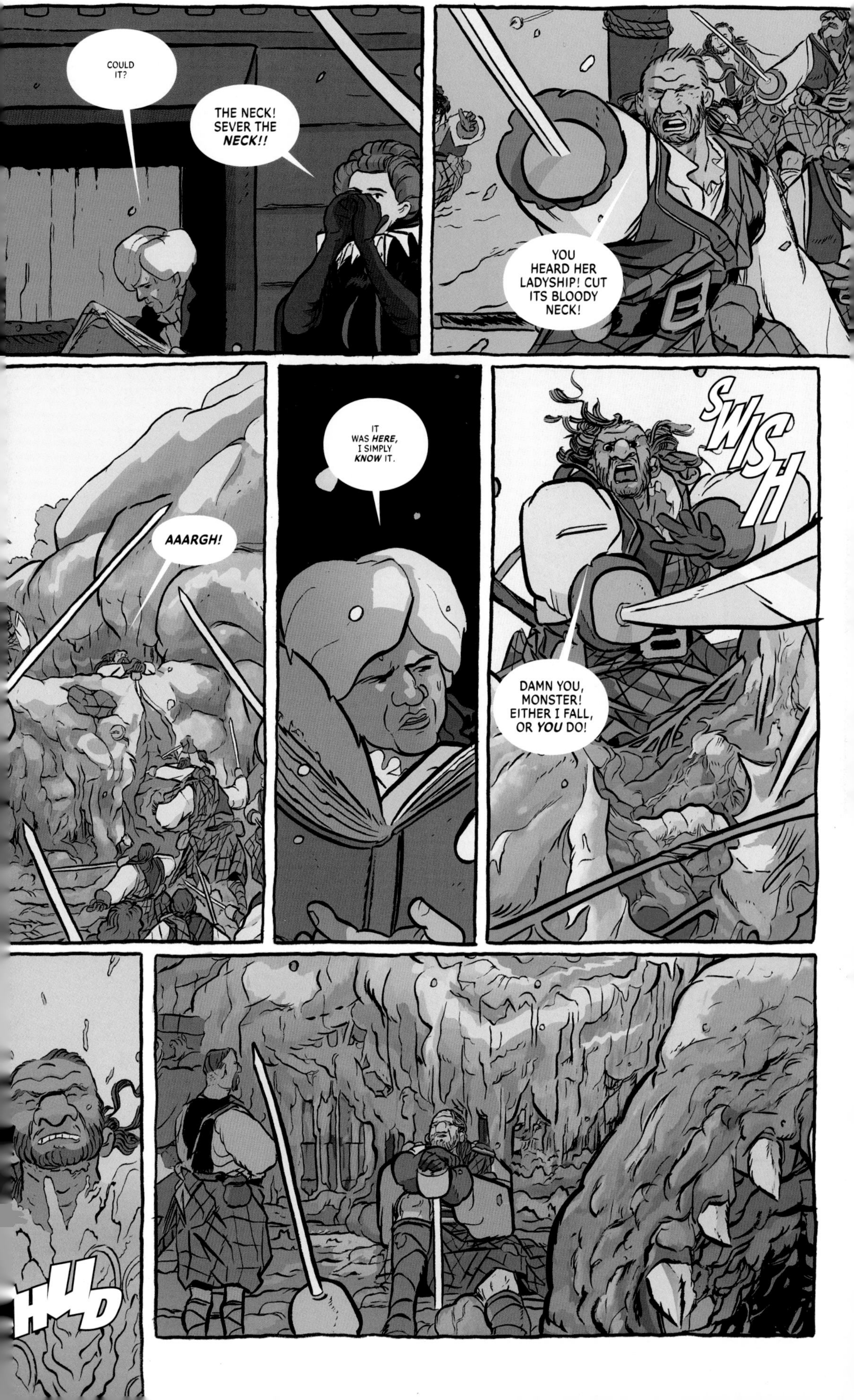
COULD IT?
THE NECK! SEVER THE *NECK!!*
YOU HEARD HER LADYSHIP! CUT ITS BLOODY NECK!
AAARGH!
IT WAS *HERE,* I SIMPLY *KNOW* IT.
SWISH
DAMN YOU, MONSTER! EITHER I FALL, OR *YOU* DO!
HUD

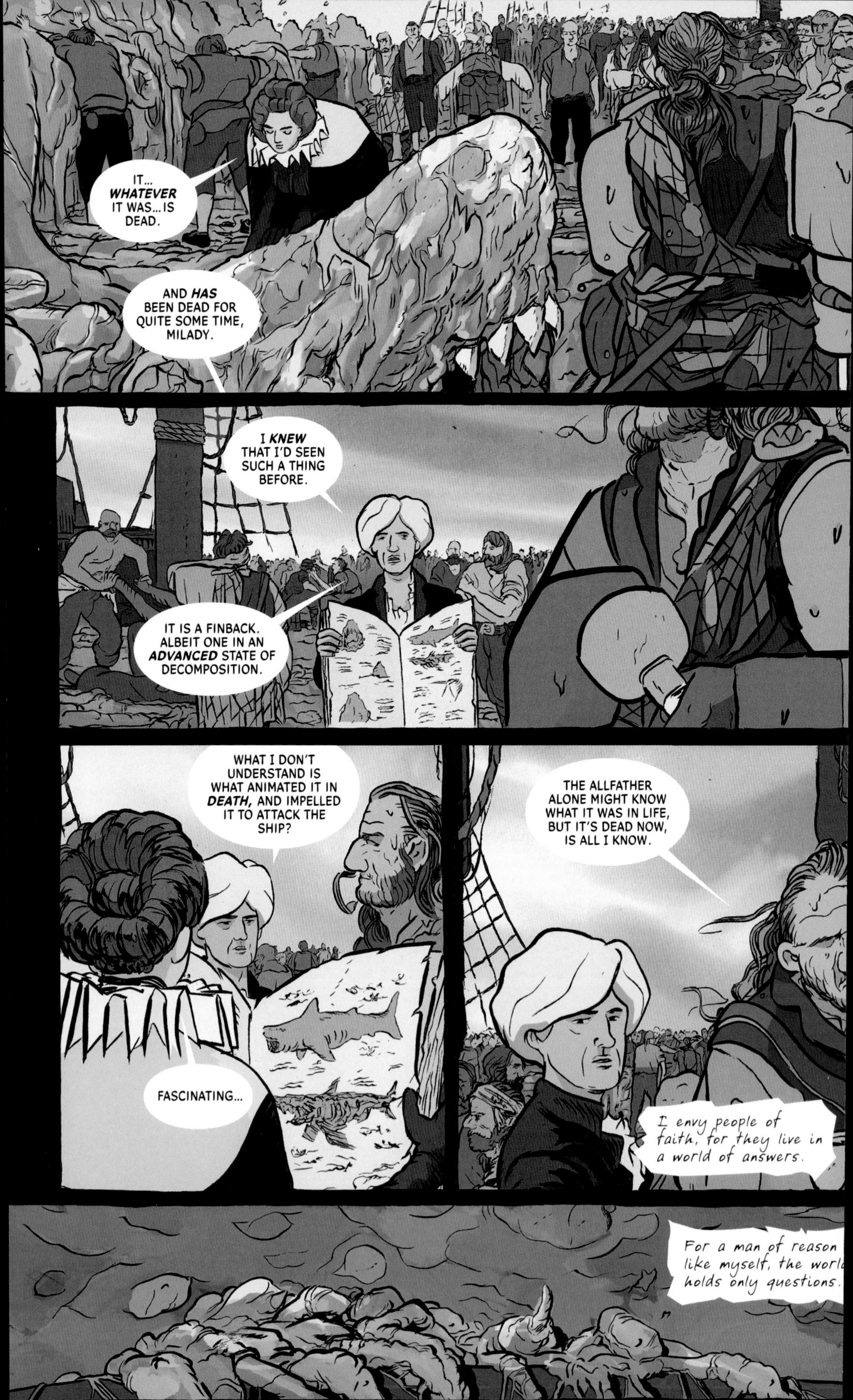
IT... *WHATEVER* IT WAS... IS DEAD.
AND *HAS* BEEN DEAD FOR QUITE SOME TIME, MILADY.
I *KNEW* THAT I'D SEEN SUCH A THING BEFORE.
IT IS A FINBACK. ALBEIT ONE IN AN *ADVANCED* STATE OF DECOMPOSITION.
WHAT I DON'T UNDERSTAND IS WHAT ANIMATED IT IN *DEATH,* AND IMPELLED IT TO ATTACK THE SHIP?
FASCINATING...
THE ALLFATHER ALONE MIGHT KNOW WHAT IT WAS IN LIFE, BUT IT'S DEAD NOW, IS ALL I KNOW.
I envy people of faith, for they live in a world of answers.
For a man of reason like myself, the world holds only questions.

ghost eaters

In life, the people often turn their backs to the Luminari.
We are the untouchable, who perform the unwholesome
acts that none others will do. Many shun us, fearing
contamination. The masks we wear do not simply hide
our faces, but save others the shame of looking upon us.
But in death, each soul is hungry for our help. The dead
feel no shame for what the light will expose, but instead
fear what the darkness holds.

—Sant Koel

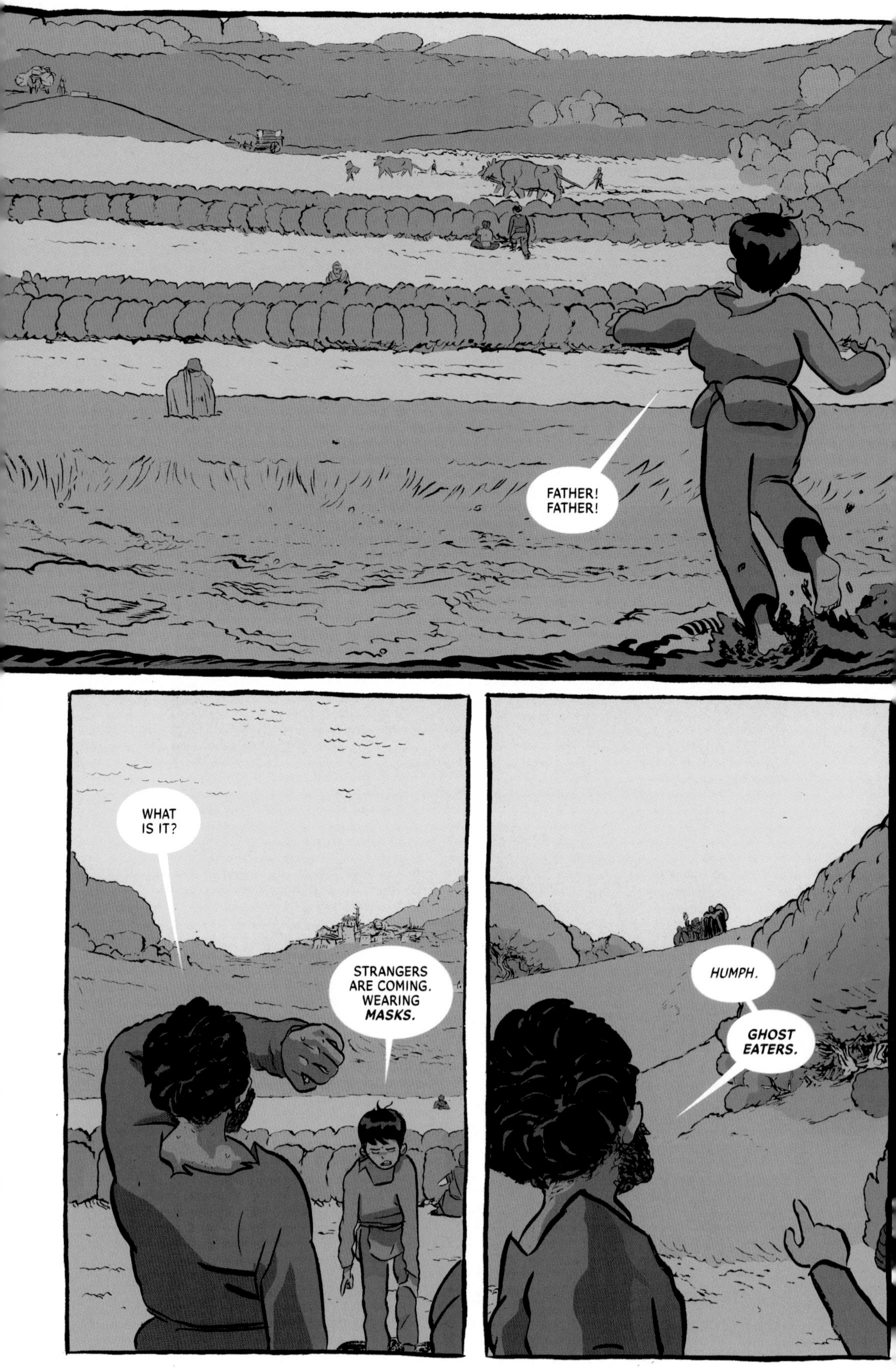
FATHER! FATHER!
WHAT IS IT?
STRANGERS ARE COMING. WEARING *MASKS.*
HUMPH.
GHOST EATERS.

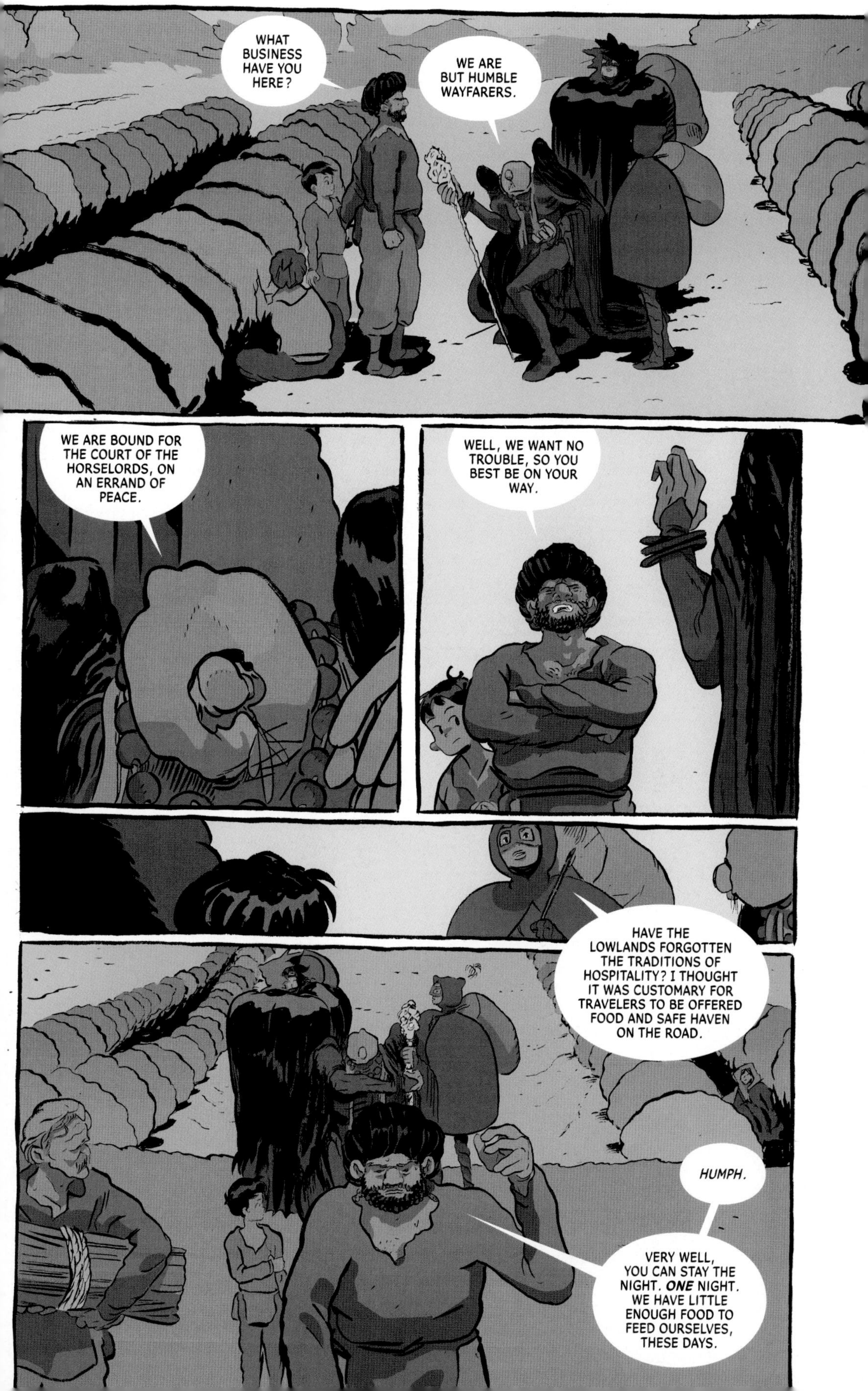
WHAT BUSINESS HAVE YOU HERE?
WE ARE BUT HUMBLE WAYFARERS.
WE ARE BOUND FOR THE COURT OF THE HORSELORDS, ON AN ERRAND OF PEACE.
WELL, WE WANT NO TROUBLE, SO YOU BEST BE ON YOUR WAY.
HAVE THE LOWLANDS FORGOTTEN THE TRADITIONS OF HOSPITALITY? I THOUGHT IT WAS CUSTOMARY FOR TRAVELERS TO BE OFFERED FOOD AND SAFE HAVEN ON THE ROAD.
HUMPH.
VERY WELL, YOU CAN STAY THE NIGHT. ONE NIGHT. WE HAVE LITTLE ENOUGH FOOD TO FEED OURSELVES, THESE DAYS.

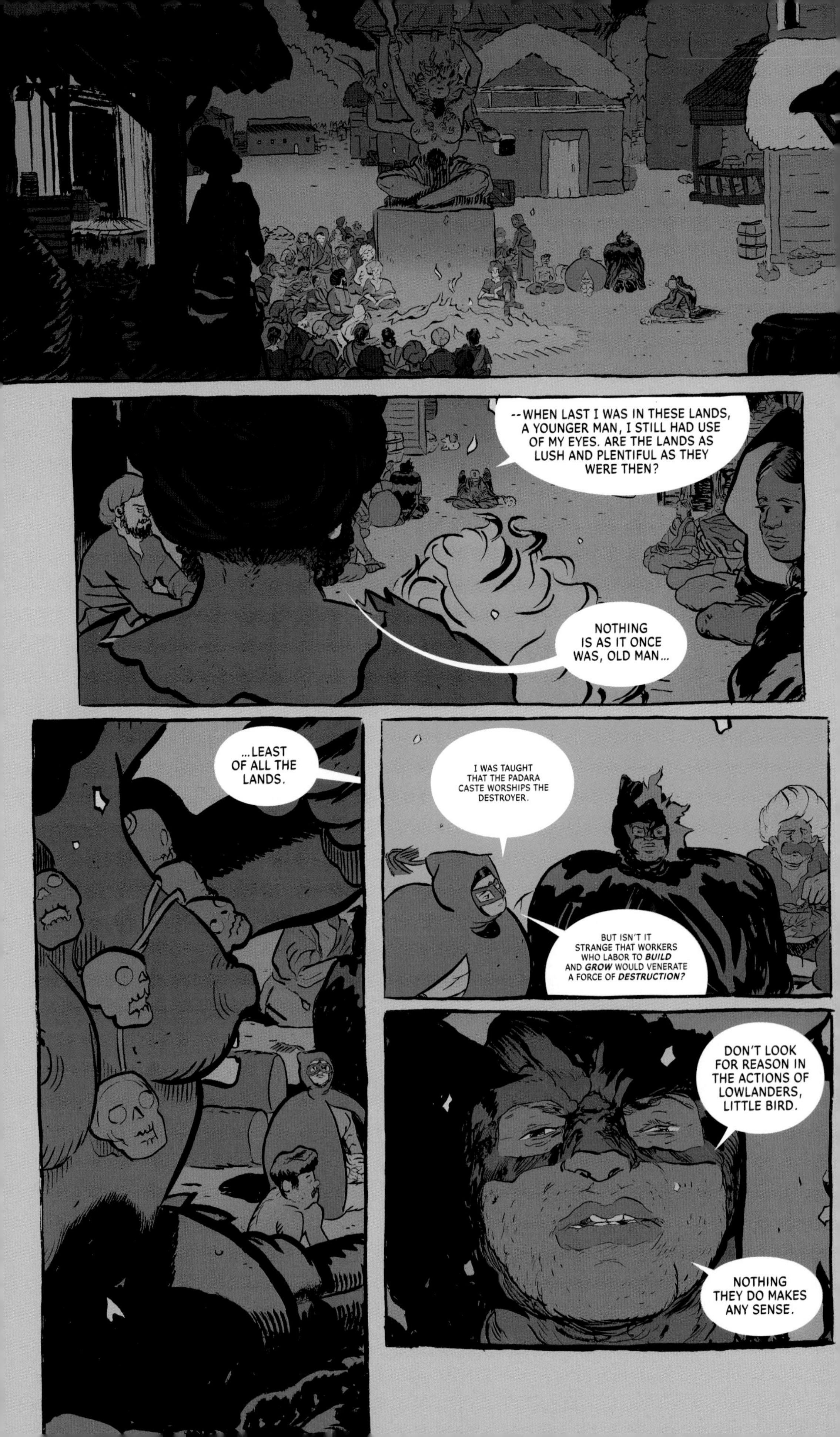
--WHEN LAST I WAS IN THESE LANDS, A YOUNGER MAN, I STILL HAD USE OF MY EYES. ARE THE LANDS AS LUSH AND PLENTIFUL AS THEY WERE THEN?
NOTHING IS AS IT ONCE WAS, OLD MAN...
...LEAST OF ALL THE LANDS.
I WAS TAUGHT THAT THE PADARA CASTE WORSHIPS THE DESTROYER.
BUT ISN'T IT STRANGE THAT WORKERS WHO LABOR TO *BUILD* AND *GROW* WOULD VENERATE A FORCE OF *DESTRUCTION?*
DON'T LOOK FOR REASON IN THE ACTIONS OF LOWLANDERS, LITTLE BIRD.
NOTHING THEY DO MAKES ANY SENSE.

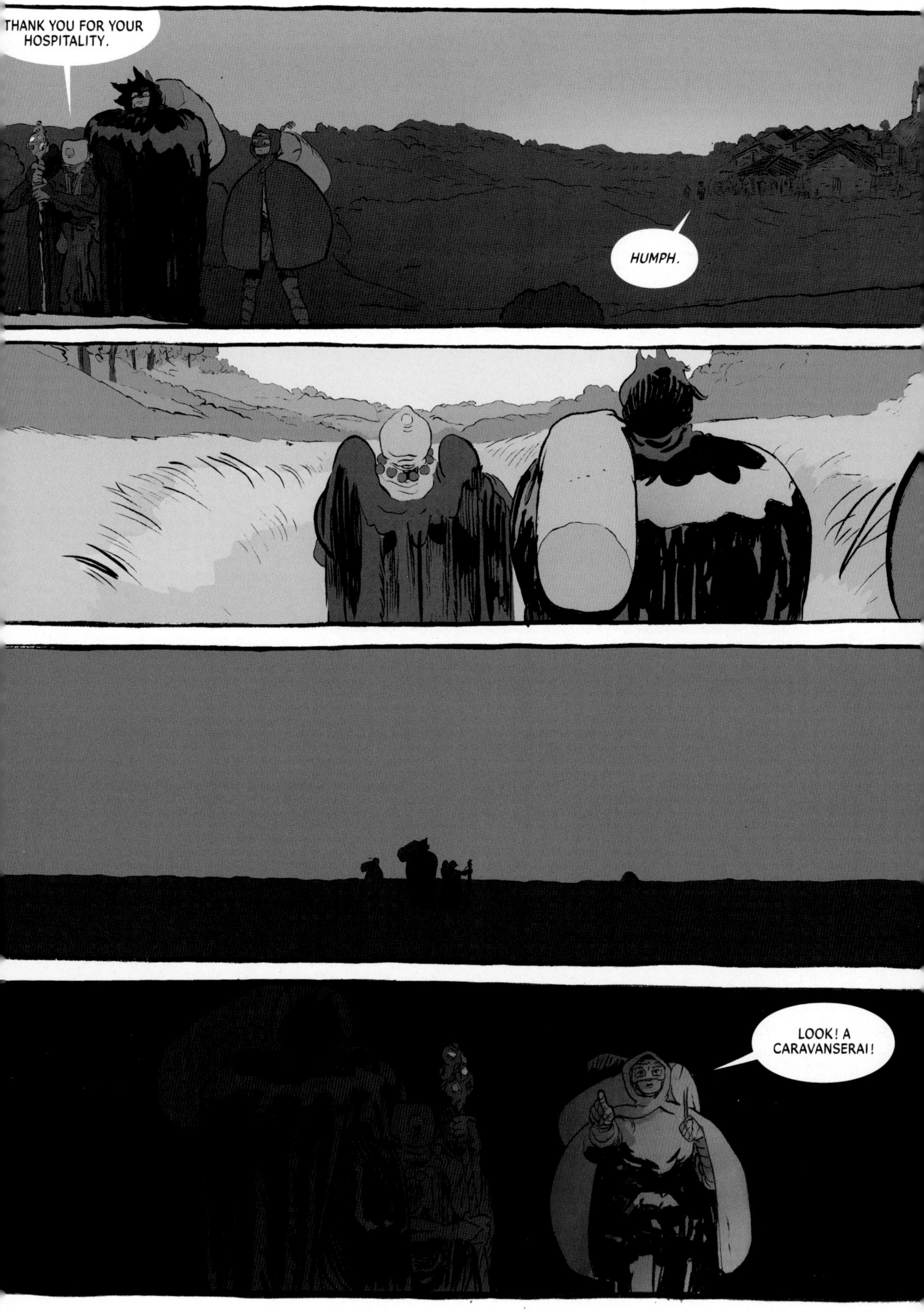
THANK YOU FOR YOUR HOSPITALITY.
HUMPH.
LOOK! A CARAVANSERAI!

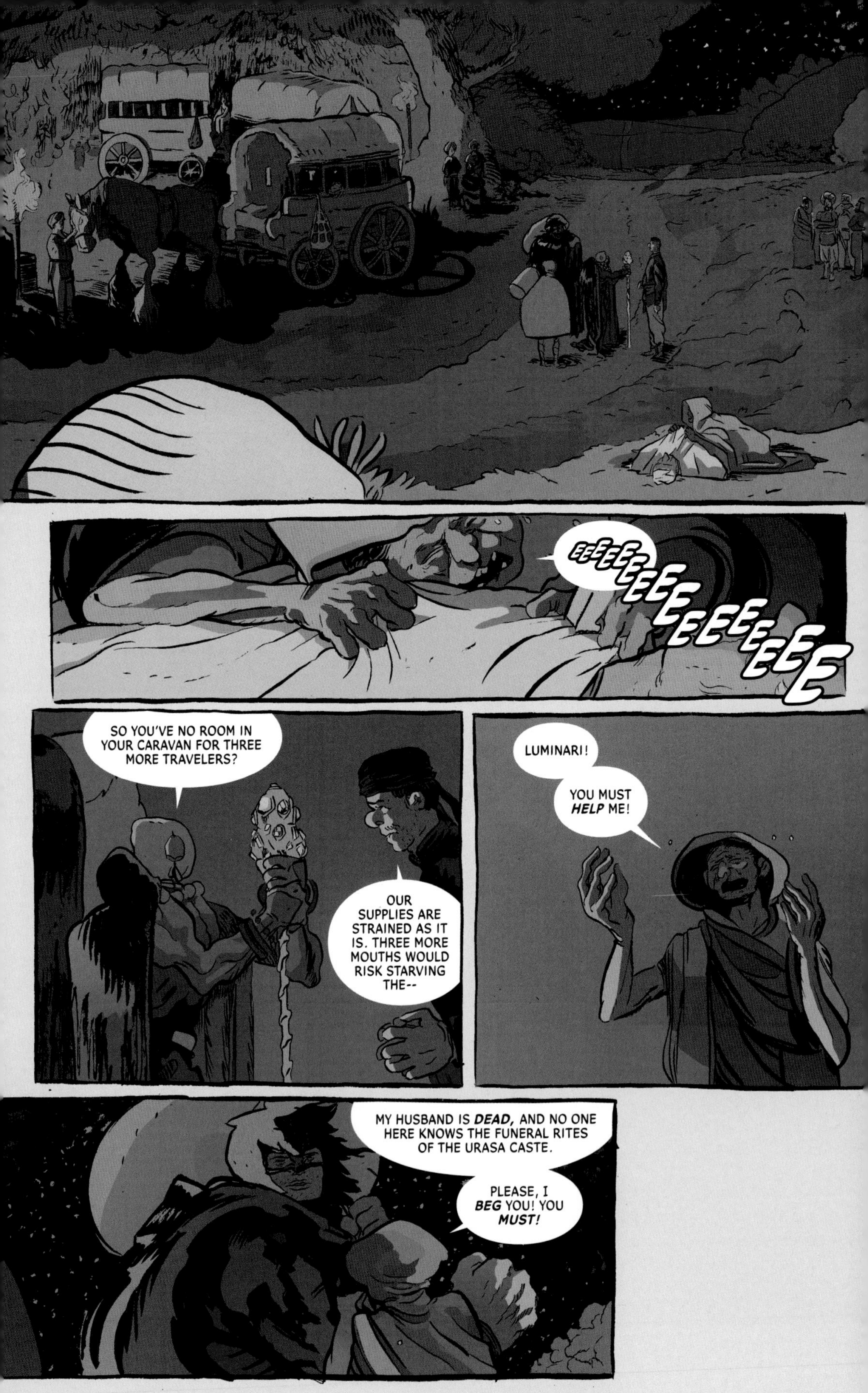
EEEEEEEEEEEEEEE
SO YOU'VE NO ROOM IN YOUR CARAVAN FOR THREE MORE TRAVELERS?
OUR SUPPLIES ARE STRAINED AS IT IS. THREE MORE MOUTHS WOULD RISK STARVING THE--
LUMINARI!
YOU MUST *HELP* ME!
MY HUSBAND IS *DEAD,* AND NO ONE HERE KNOWS THE FUNERAL RITES OF THE URASA CASTE.
PLEASE, I *BEG* YOU! YOU *MUST!*

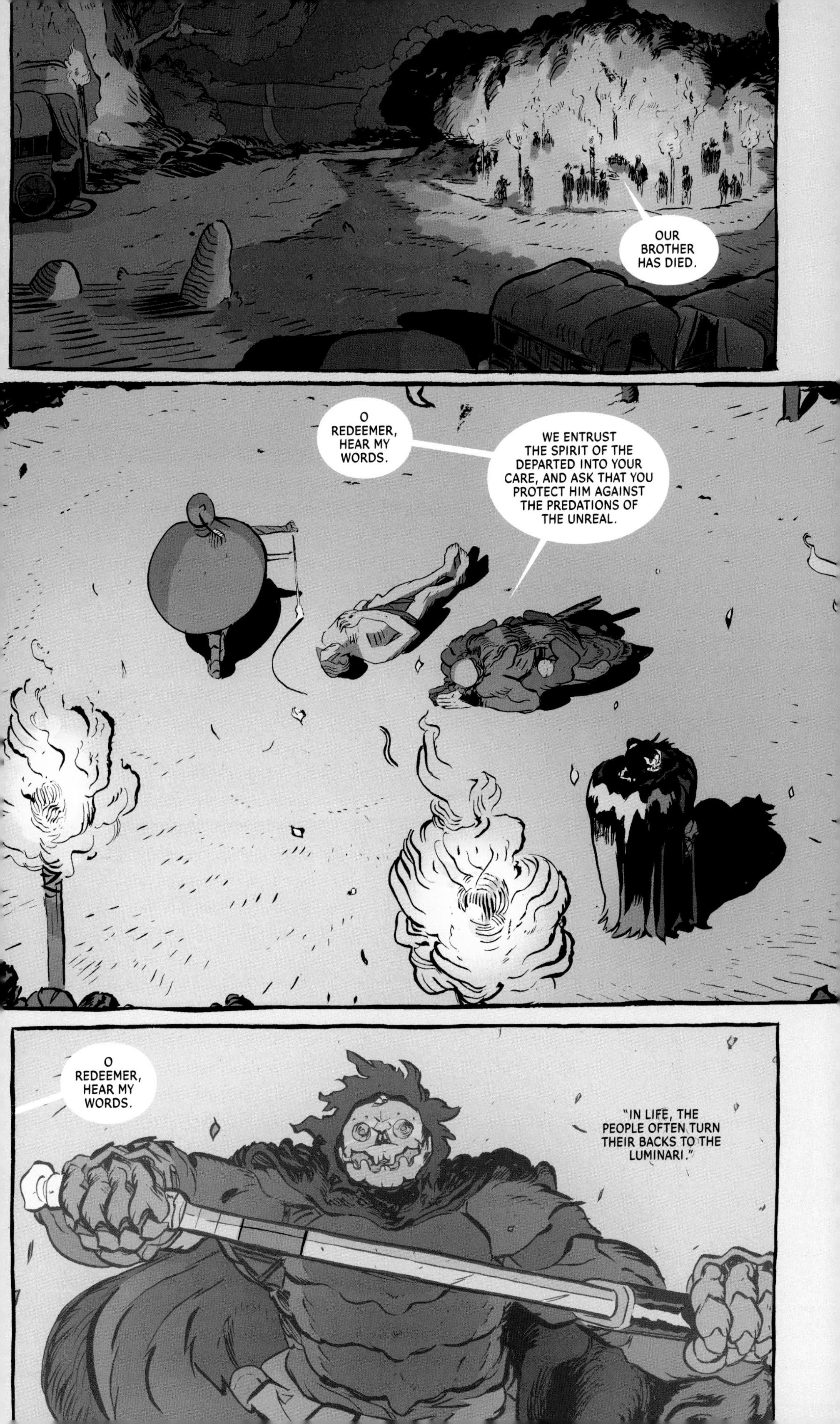
OUR BROTHER HAS DIED.
O REDEEMER, HEAR MY WORDS.
WE ENTRUST THE SPIRIT OF THE DEPARTED INTO YOUR CARE, AND ASK THAT YOU PROTECT HIM AGAINST THE PREDATIONS OF THE UNREAL.
O REDEEMER, HEAR MY WORDS.
"IN LIFE, THE PEOPLE OFTEN TURN THEIR BACKS TO THE LUMINARI."

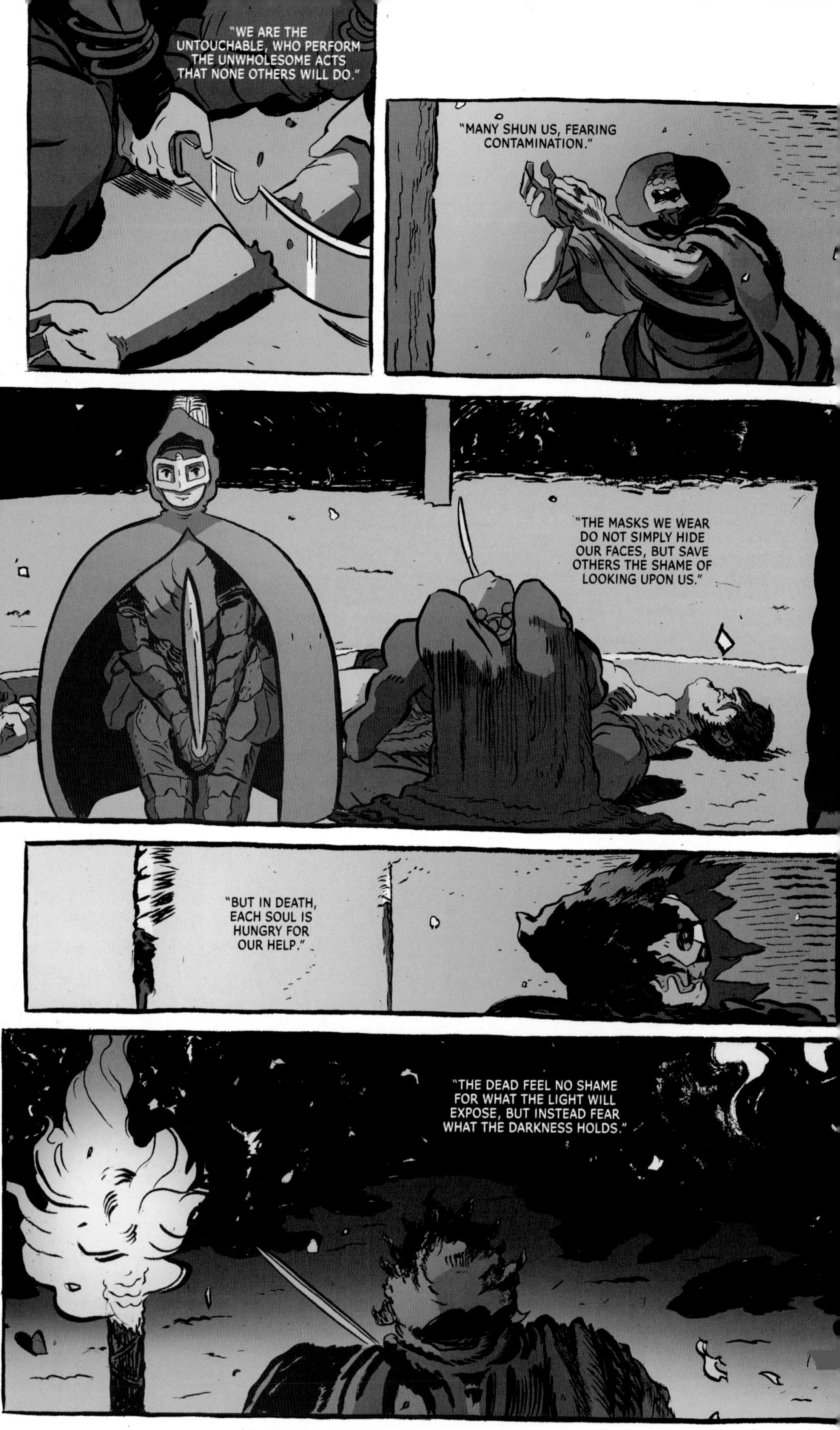
"WE ARE THE UNTOUCHABLE, WHO PERFORM THE UNWHOLESOME ACTS THAT NONE OTHERS WILL DO."
"MANY SHUN US, FEARING CONTAMINATION."
"THE MASKS WE WEAR DO NOT SIMPLY HIDE OUR FACES, BUT SAVE OTHERS THE SHAME OF LOOKING UPON US."
"BUT IN DEATH, EACH SOUL IS HUNGRY FOR OUR HELP."
"THE DEAD FEEL NO SHAME FOR WHAT THE LIGHT WILL EXPOSE, BUT INSTEAD FEAR WHAT THE DARKNESS HOLDS."

shadow of the unnamed

Baqhir came among the people as the Messenger of the Unnamed, and Baqhir's words are the echoes of the voice of the universe. The Tamurid hear the words of Baqhir, and put them into action. The Tamurid emperor is the shadow of the Unnamed, and his works and decrees are sacred.

—Ikandar, Conqueror and
Refuge of the World

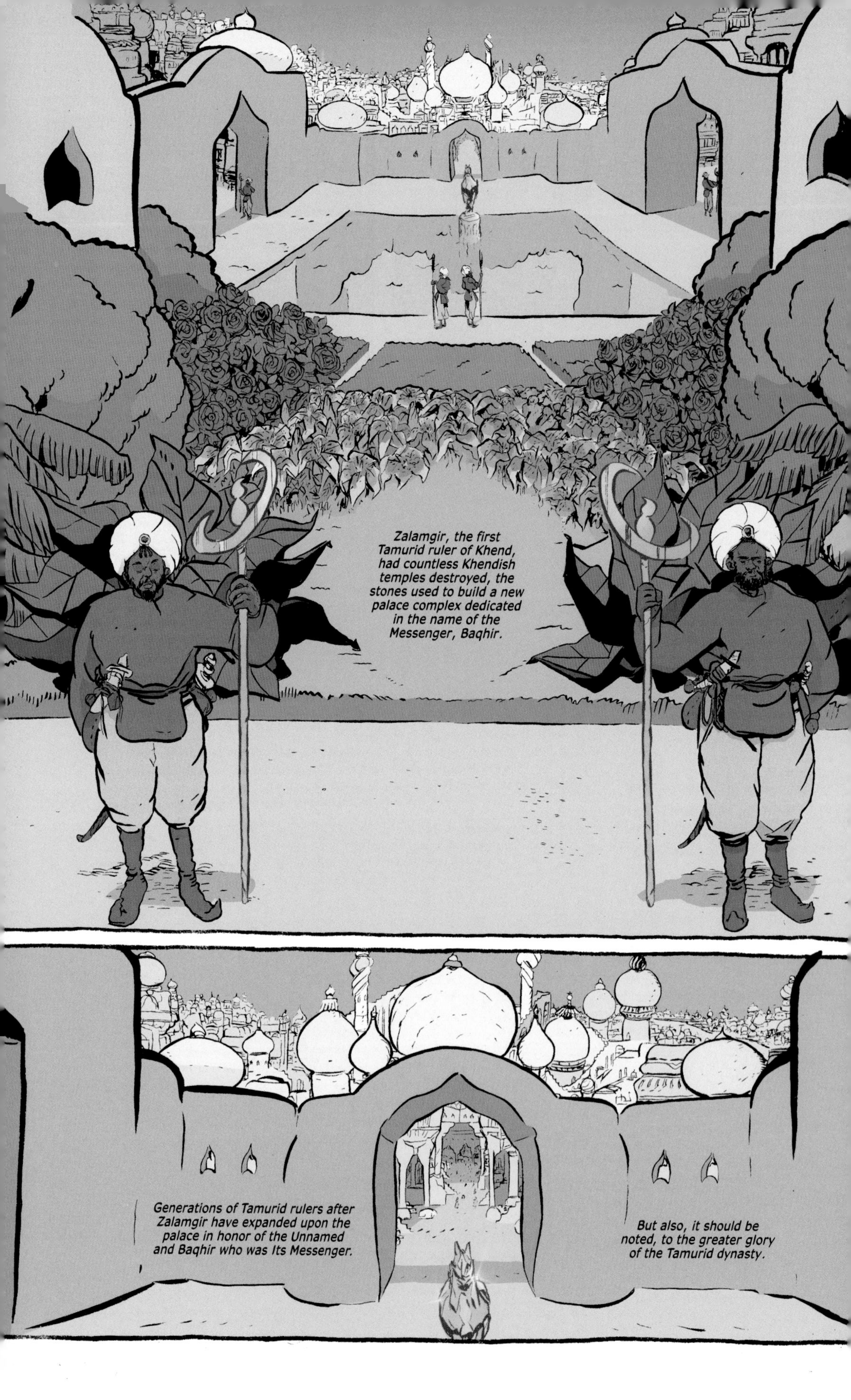
Zalamgir, the first Tamurid ruler of Khend, had countless Khendish temples destroyed, the stones used to build a new palace complex dedicated in the name of the Messenger, Baqhir.
Generations of Tamurid rulers after Zalamgir have expanded upon the palace in honor of the Unnamed and Baqhir who was Its Messenger.
But also, it should be noted, to the greater glory of the Tamurid dynasty.

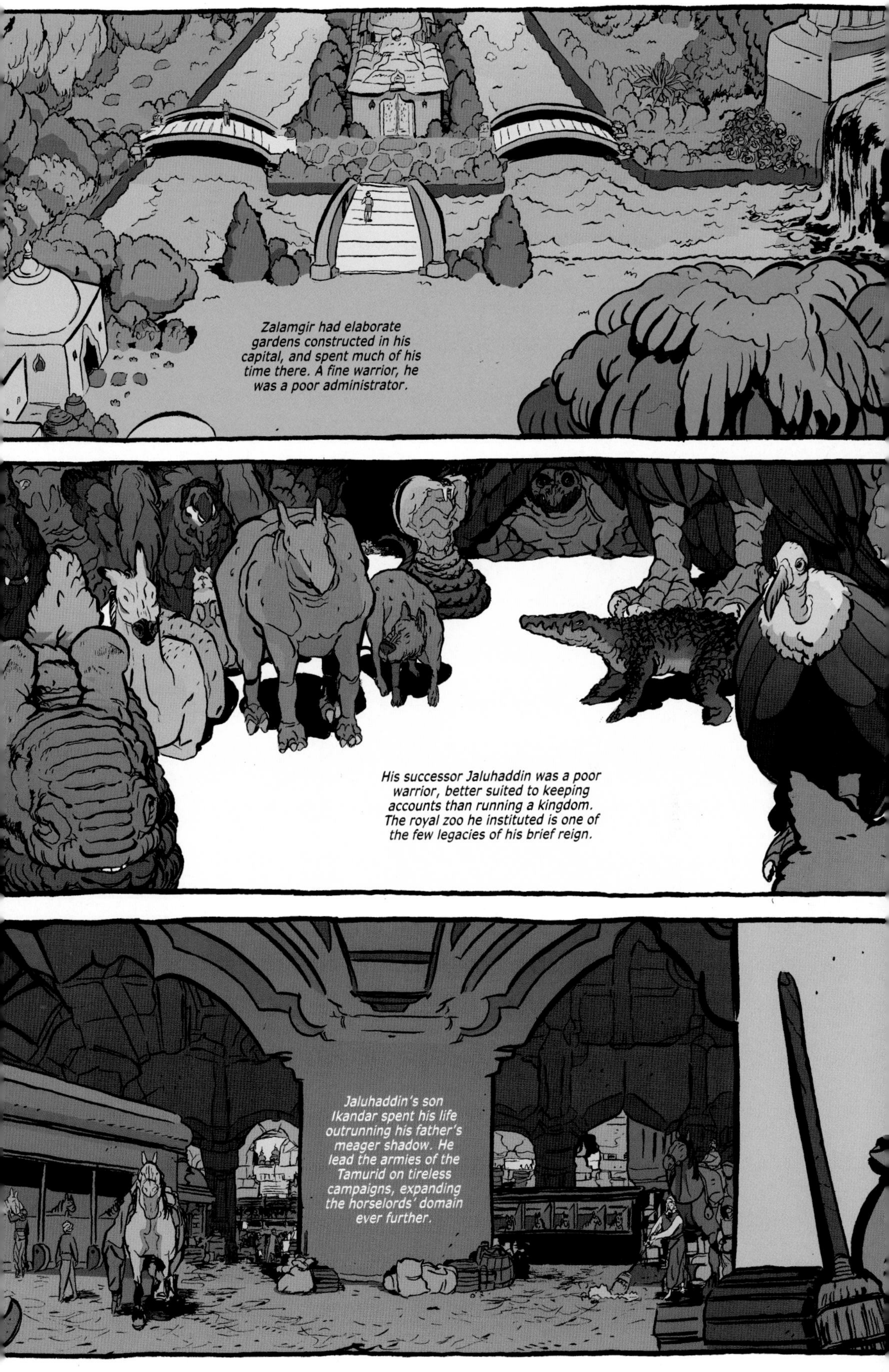
Zalamgir had elaborate gardens constructed in his capital, and spent much of his time there. A fine warrior, he was a poor administrator.
His successor Jaluhaddin was a poor warrior, better suited to keeping accounts than running a kingdom. The royal zoo he instituted is one of the few legacies of his brief reign.
Jaluhaddin's son Ikandar spent his life outrunning his father's meager shadow. He lead the armies of the Tamurid on tireless campaigns, expanding the horselords' domain ever further.

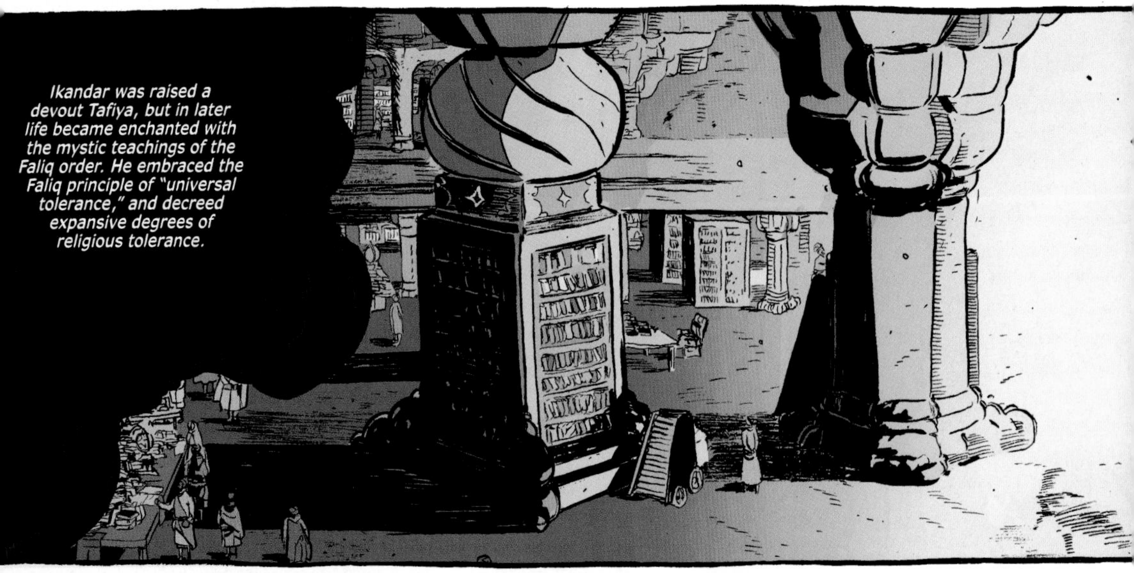
Ikandar was raised a devout Tafiya, but in later life became enchanted with the mystic teachings of the Faliq order. He embraced the Faliq principle of "universal tolerance," and decreed expansive degrees of religious tolerance.

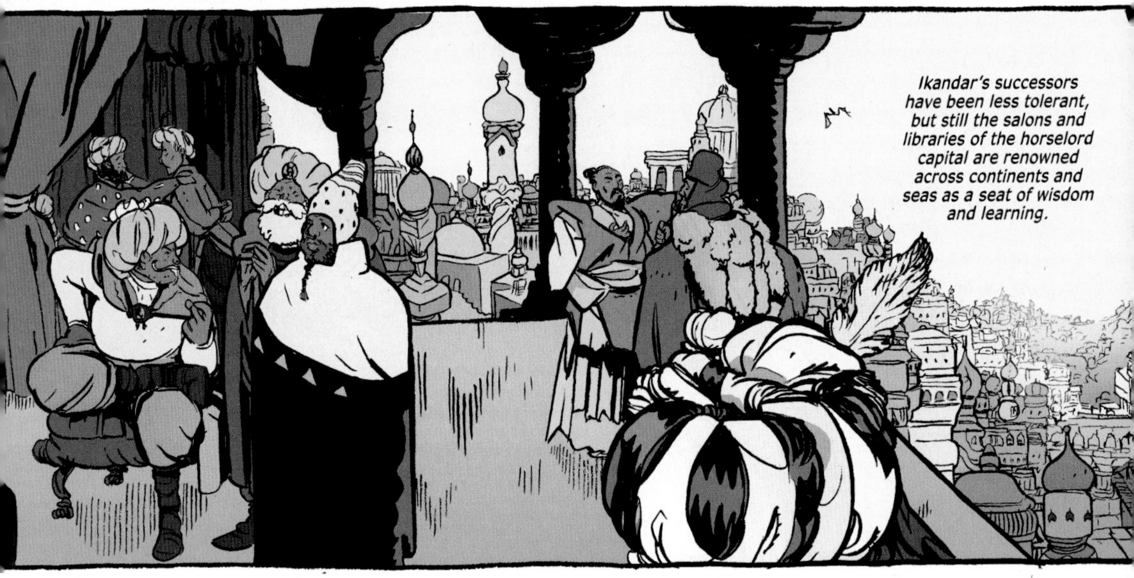
Ikandar's successors have been less tolerant, but still the salons and libraries of the horselord capital are renowned across continents and seas as a seat of wisdom and learning.

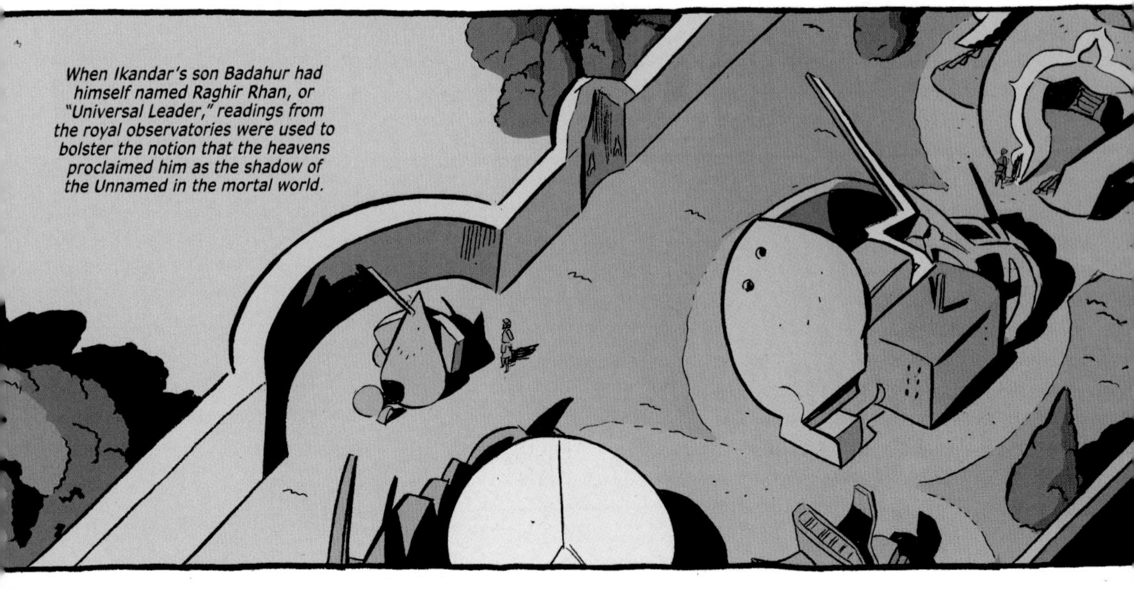
When Ikandar's son Badahur had himself named Raghir Rhan, or "Universal Leader," readings from the royal observatories were used to bolster the notion that the heavens proclaimed him as the shadow of the Unnamed in the mortal world.

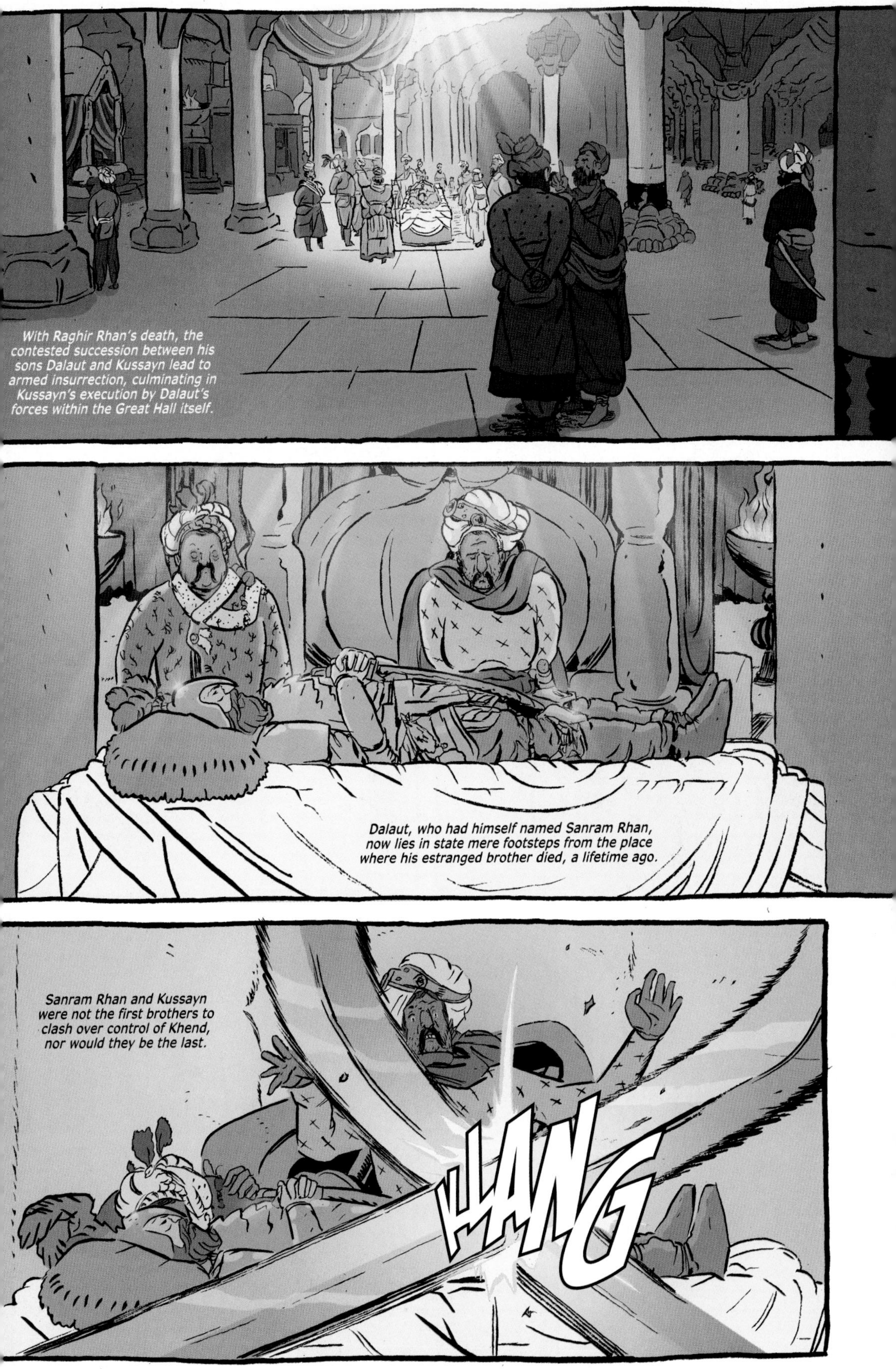

With Raghir Rhan's death, the contested succession between his sons Dalaut and Kussayn lead to armed insurrection, culminating in Kussayn's execution by Dalaut's forces within the Great Hall itself.
Dalaut, who had himself named Sanram Rhan, now lies in state mere footsteps from the place where his estranged brother died, a lifetime ago.
Sanram Rhan and Kussayn were not the first brothers to clash over control of Khend, nor would they be the last.
KLANG

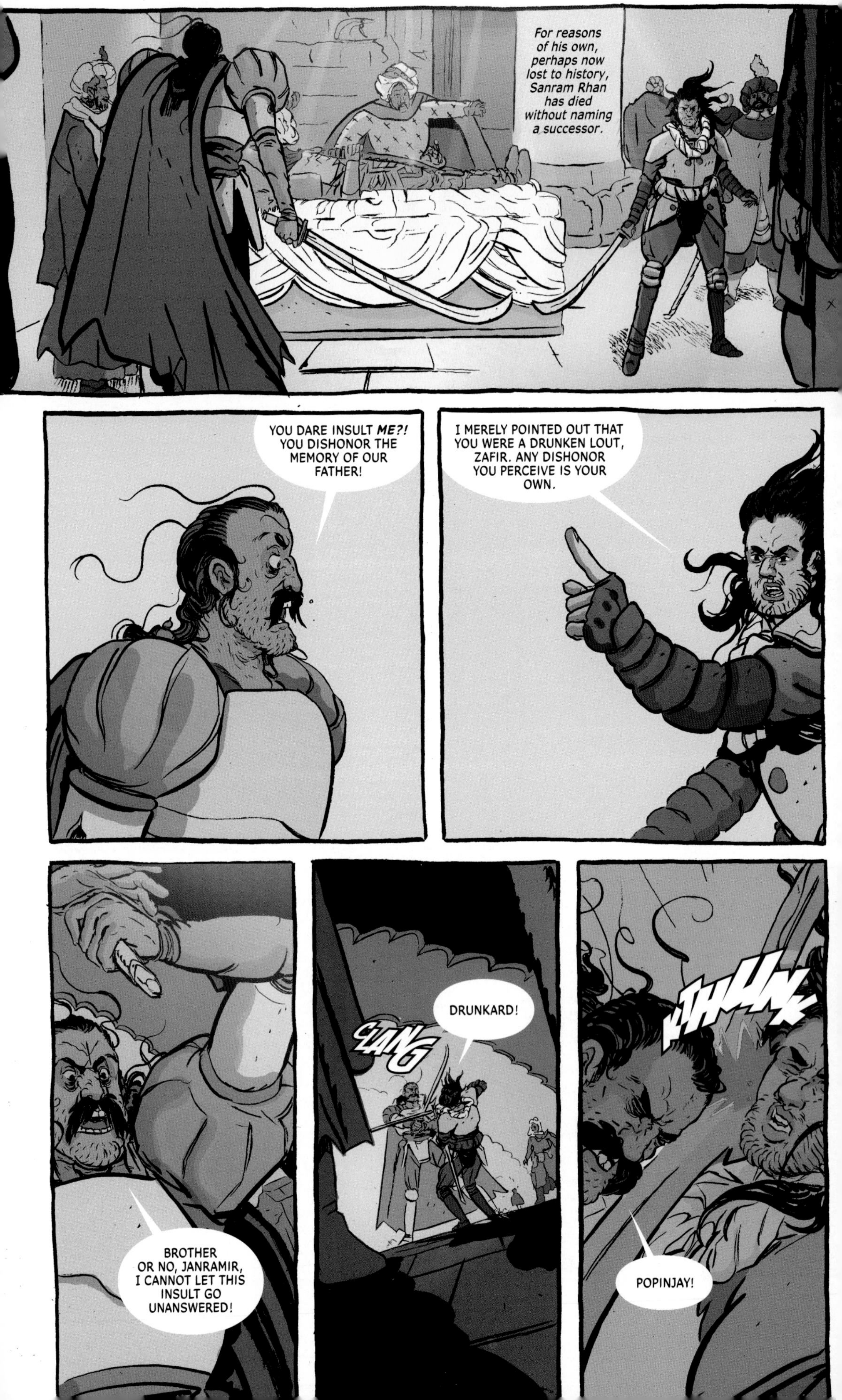
For reasons of his own, perhaps now lost to history, Sanram Rhan has died without naming a successor.
YOU DARE INSULT ME?! YOU DISHONOR THE MEMORY OF OUR FATHER!
I MERELY POINTED OUT THAT YOU WERE A DRUNKEN LOUT, ZAFIR. ANY DISHONOR YOU PERCEIVE IS YOUR OWN.
BROTHER OR NO, JANRAMIR, I CANNOT LET THIS INSULT GO UNANSWERED!
CLANG
DRUNKARD!
KTHUNK
POPINJAY!

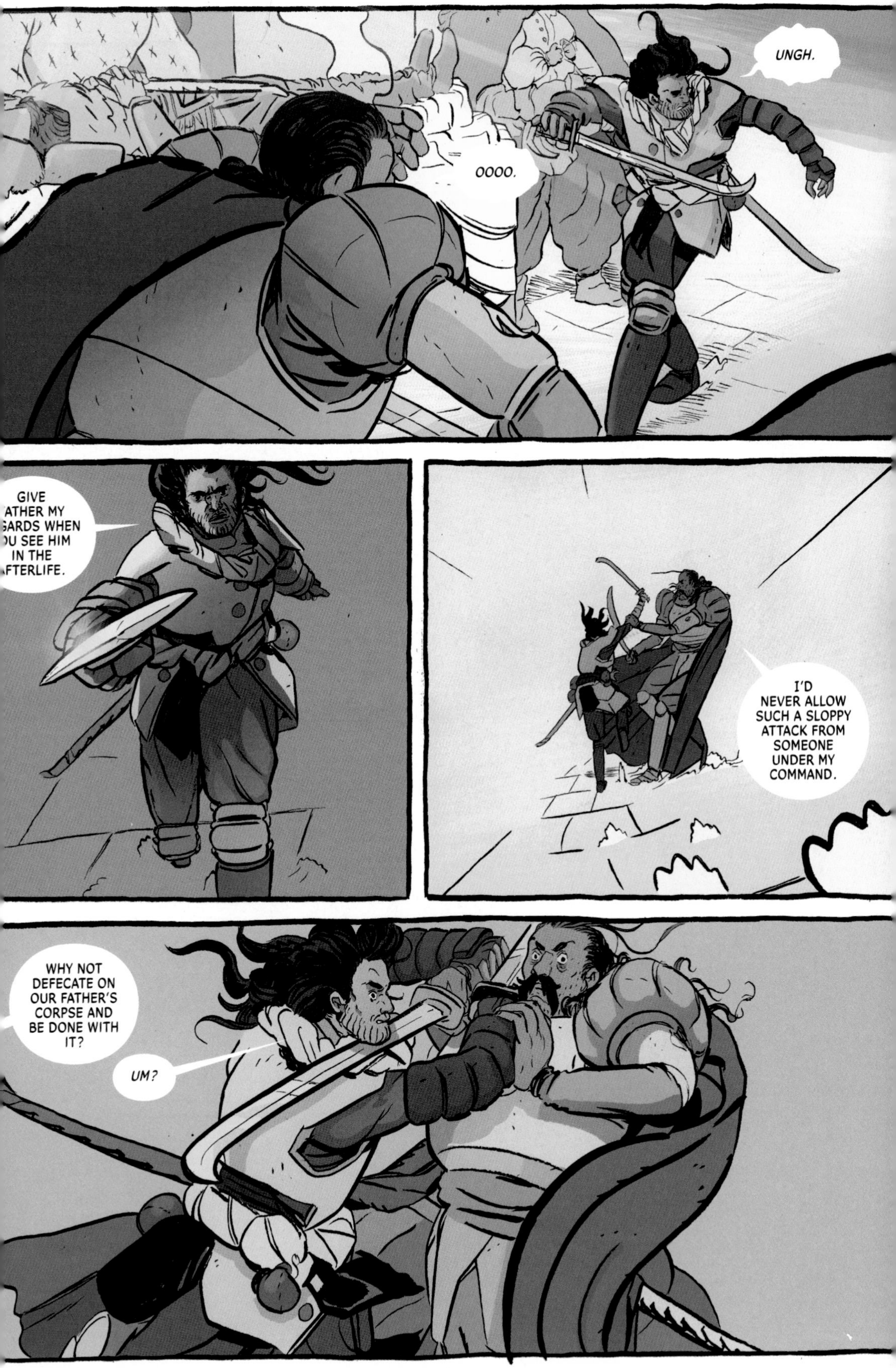

UNGH.
OOOO.
GIVE
ATHER MY
GARDS WHEN
OU SEE HIM
IN THE
FTERLIFE.
I'D NEVER ALLOW SUCH A SLOPPY ATTACK FROM SOMEONE UNDER MY COMMAND.
WHY NOT DEFECATE ON OUR FATHER'S CORPSE AND BE DONE WITH IT?
UM?

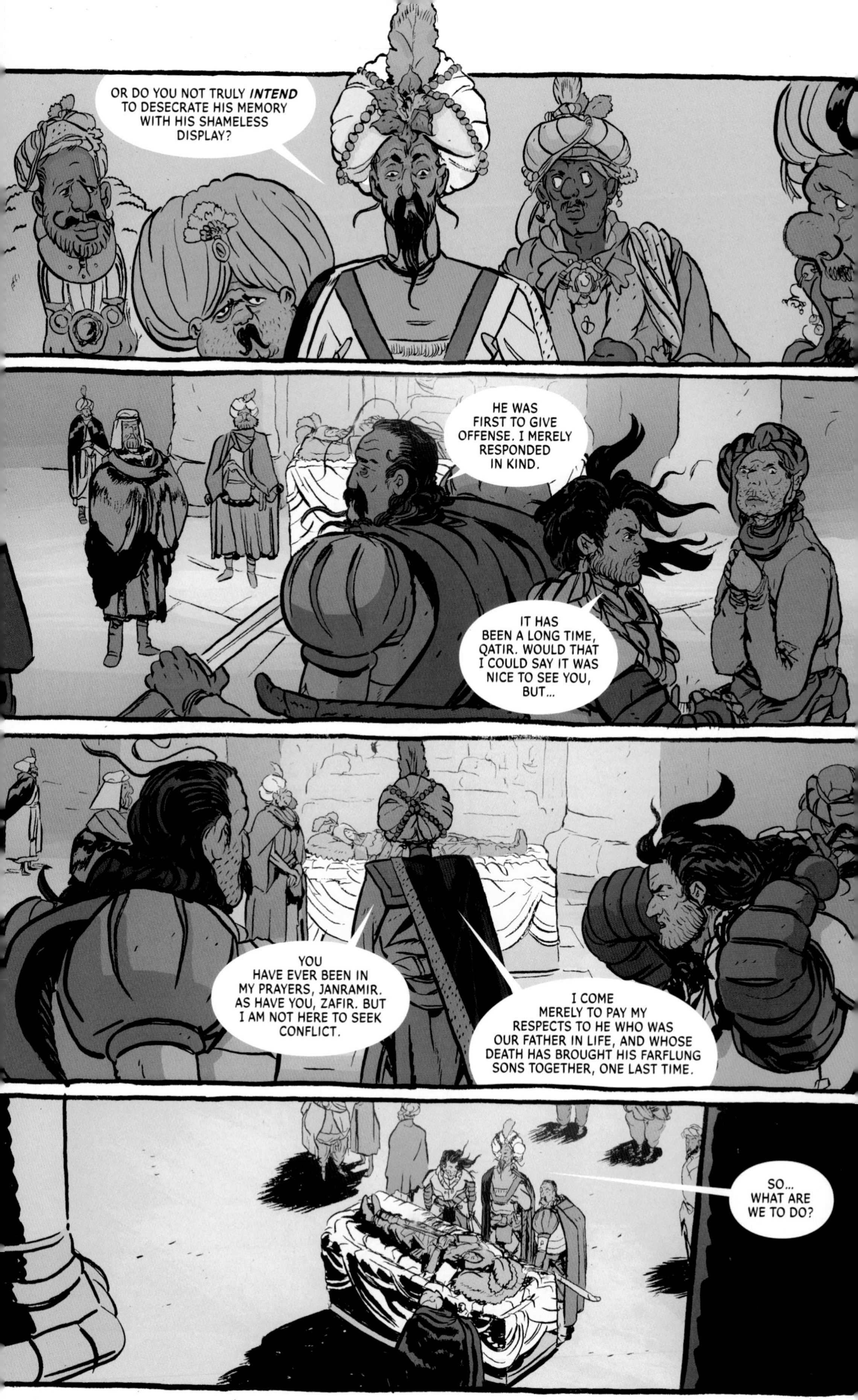
OR DO YOU NOT TRULY *INTEND* TO DESECRATE HIS MEMORY WITH HIS SHAMELESS DISPLAY?
HE WAS FIRST TO GIVE OFFENSE. I MERELY RESPONDED IN KIND.
IT HAS BEEN A LONG TIME, QATIR. WOULD THAT I COULD SAY IT WAS NICE TO SEE YOU, BUT...
YOU HAVE EVER BEEN IN MY PRAYERS, JANRAMIR. AS HAVE YOU, ZAFIR. BUT I AM NOT HERE TO SEEK CONFLICT.
I COME MERELY TO PAY MY RESPECTS TO HE WHO WAS OUR FATHER IN LIFE, AND WHOSE DEATH HAS BROUGHT HIS FARFLUNG SONS TOGETHER, ONE LAST TIME.
SO... WHAT ARE WE TO DO?

Land of a thousand gods

There are realities beyond the
realm of senses, and the world
is larger than any of us imagine.

—Pol Ravenstone's
private journal

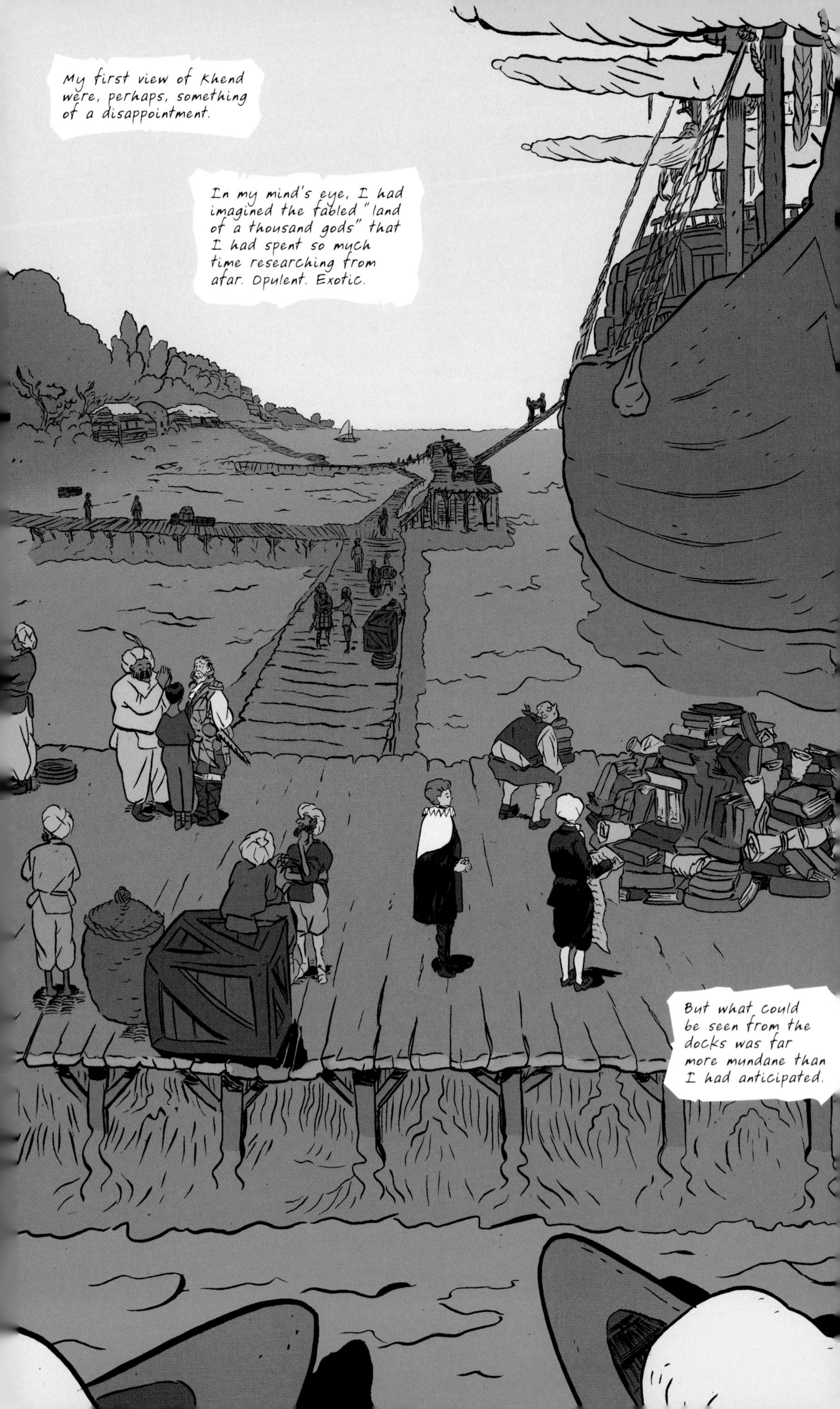
My first view of Khend were, perhaps, something of a disappointment.
In my mind's eye, I had imagined the fabled "land of a thousand gods" that I had spent so much time researching from afar. Opulent. Exotic.
But what could be seen from the docks was far more mundane than I had anticipated.

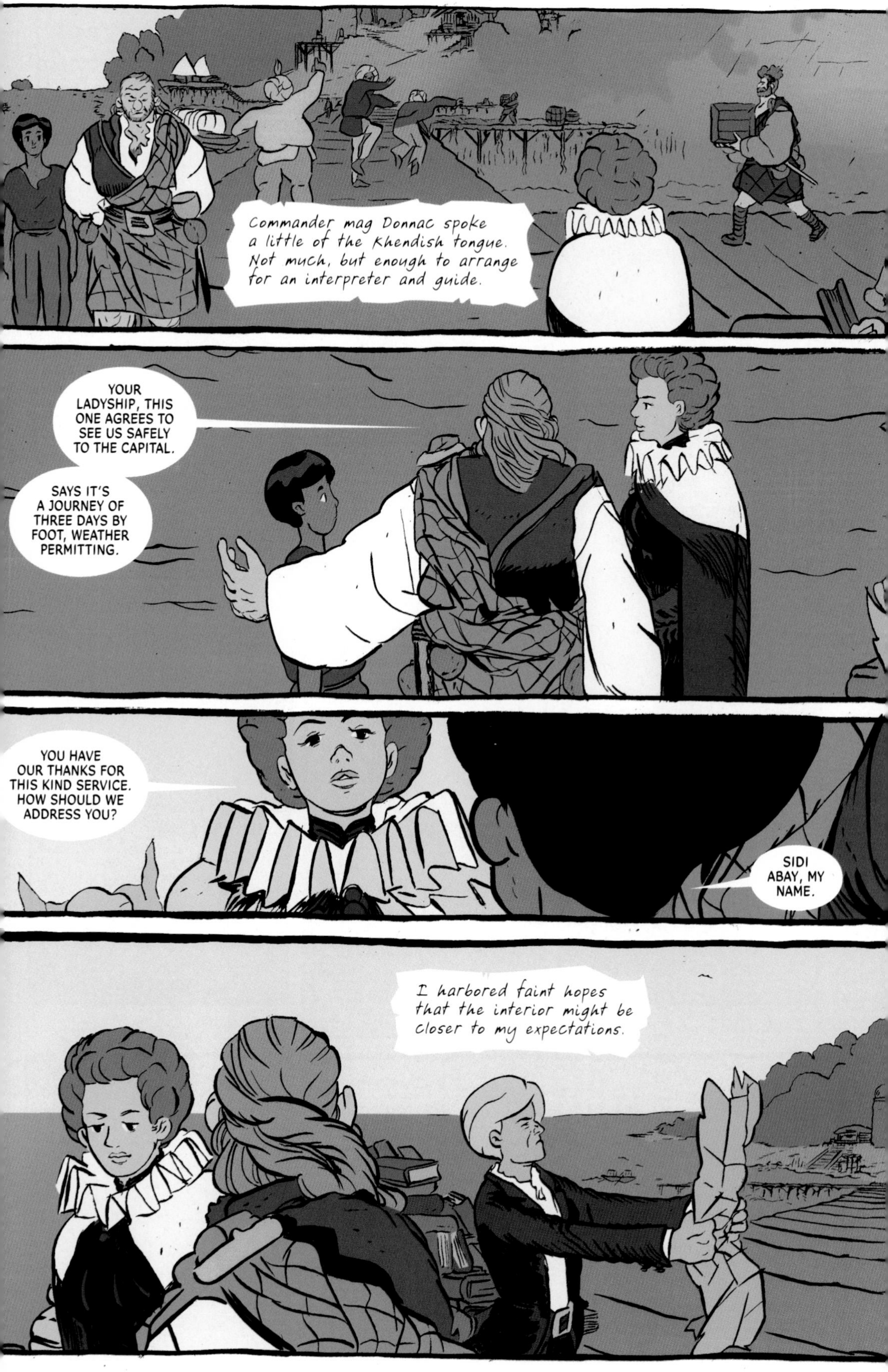
Commander mag Donnac spoke a little of the Khendish tongue. Not much, but enough to arrange for an interpreter and guide.
YOUR LADYSHIP, THIS ONE AGREES TO SEE US SAFELY TO THE CAPITAL.
SAYS IT'S A JOURNEY OF THREE DAYS BY FOOT, WEATHER PERMITTING.
YOU HAVE OUR THANKS FOR THIS KIND SERVICE. HOW SHOULD WE ADDRESS YOU?
SIDI ABAY, MY NAME.
I harbored faint hopes that the interior might be closer to my expectations.

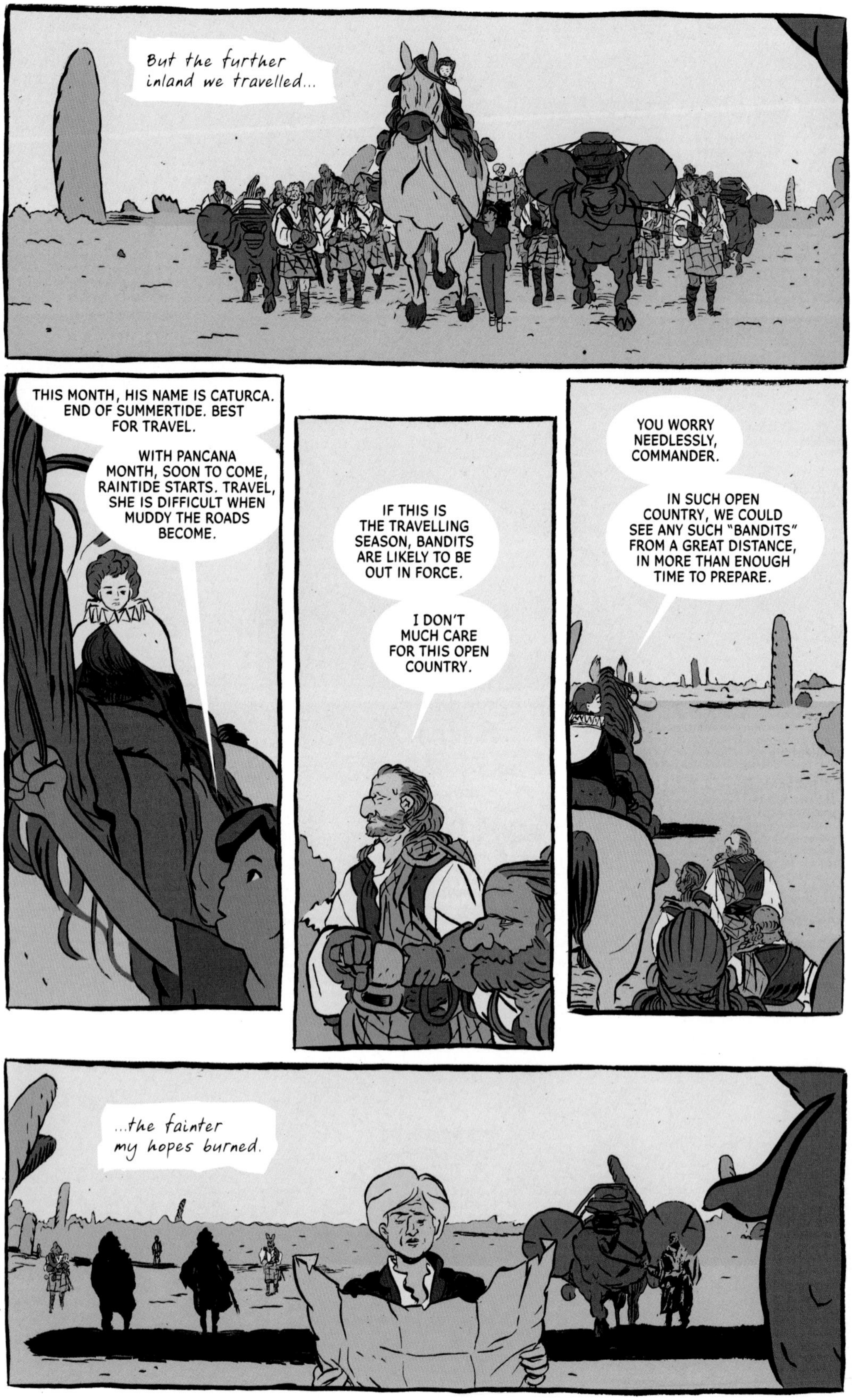
But the further inland we travelled...
THIS MONTH, HIS NAME IS CATURCA. END OF SUMMERTIDE. BEST FOR TRAVEL.
WITH PANCANA MONTH, SOON TO COME, RAINTIDE STARTS. TRAVEL, SHE IS DIFFICULT WHEN MUDDY THE ROADS BECOME.
IF THIS IS THE TRAVELLING SEASON, BANDITS ARE LIKELY TO BE OUT IN FORCE.
I DON'T MUCH CARE FOR THIS OPEN COUNTRY.
YOU WORRY NEEDLESSLY, COMMANDER.
IN SUCH OPEN COUNTRY, WE COULD SEE ANY SUCH "BANDITS" FROM A GREAT DISTANCE, IN MORE THAN ENOUGH TIME TO PREPARE.
...the fainter my hopes burned.

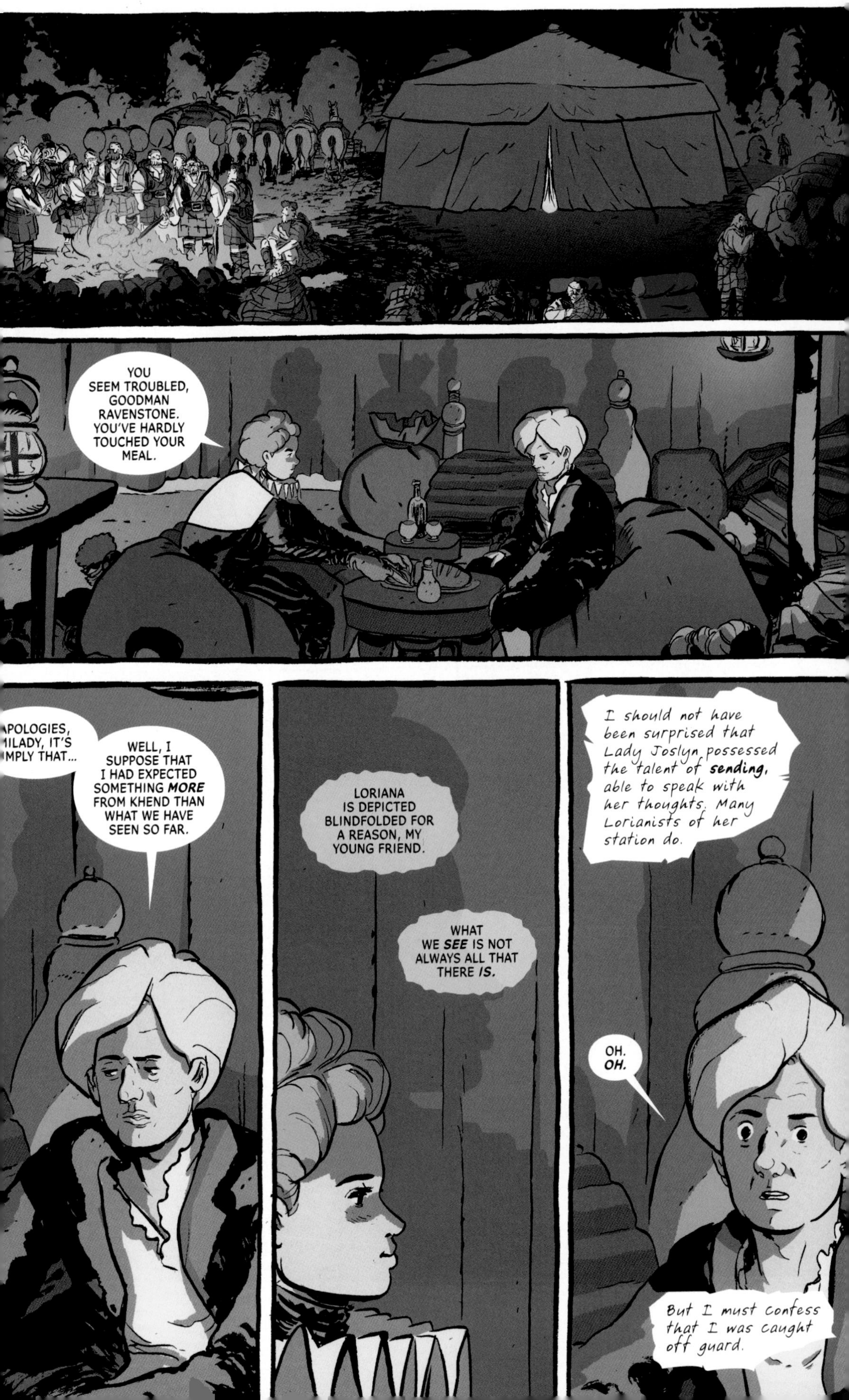
YOU SEEM TROUBLED, GOODMAN RAVENSTONE. YOU'VE HARDLY TOUCHED YOUR MEAL.
POLOGIES, ILADY, IT'S MPLY THAT...
WELL, I SUPPOSE THAT I HAD EXPECTED SOMETHING MORE FROM KHEND THAN WHAT WE HAVE SEEN SO FAR.
LORIANA IS DEPICTED BLINDFOLDED FOR A REASON, MY YOUNG FRIEND.
WHAT WE SEE IS NOT ALWAYS ALL THAT THERE IS.
I should not have been surprised that Lady Joslyn possessed the talent of sending, able to speak with her thoughts. Many Lorianists of her station do.
OH. OH.
But I must confess that I was caught off guard.

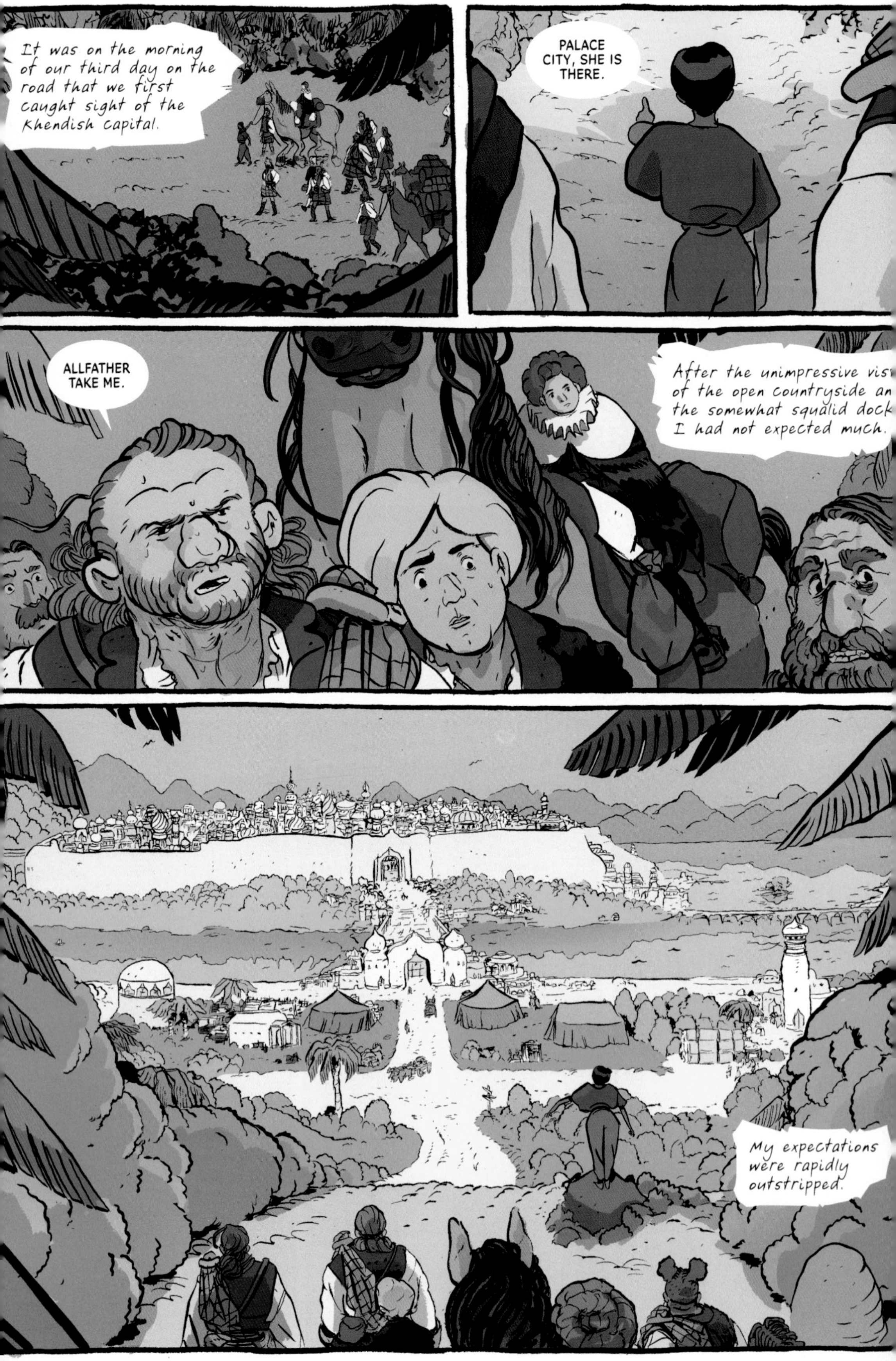
It was on the morning of our third day on the road that we first caught sight of the Khendish capital.
PALACE CITY, SHE IS THERE.
ALLFATHER TAKE ME.
After the unimpressive vis of the open countryside an the somewhat squalid dock I had not expected much.
My expectations were rapidly outstripped.

AND THERE ARE INTELLIGENCES THERE, IN THE VOID BETWEEN WORLDS.

DAEMONS THAT HUNGER.

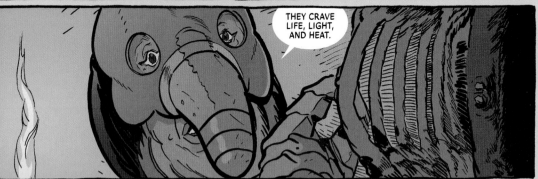

THEY CRAVE LIFE, LIGHT, AND HEAT.

AND LIKE A MOTH TO A FLAME, THEY ARE DRAWN TO *OUR* WORLD.

BUT WHILE THE MOTH IS *CONSUMED* BY THE FLAME, THE LIGHT OF LIFE IS CONSUMED BY THE DAEMON'S TOUCH.

EXTINGUISHING IT *FOREVER.*

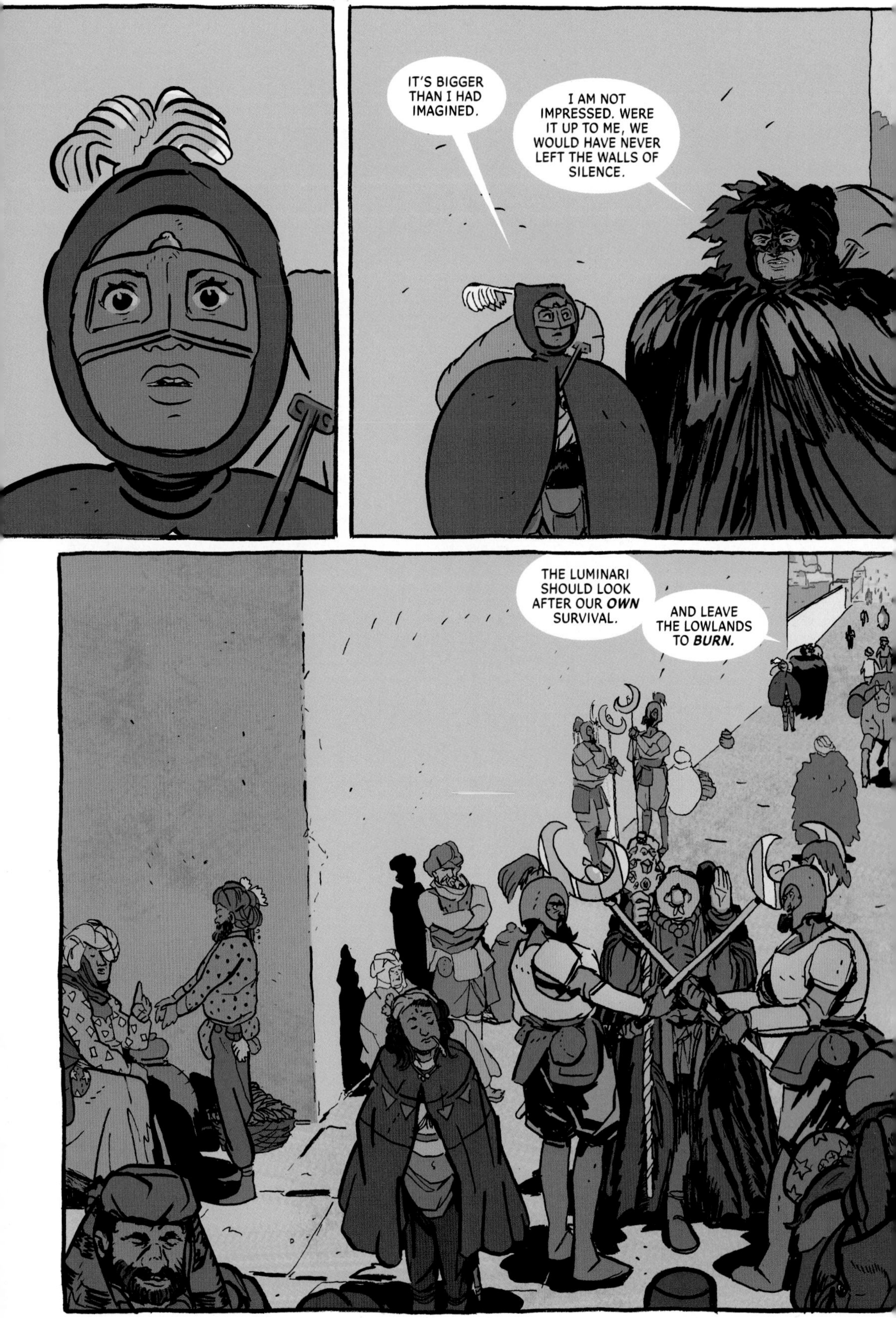
IT'S BIGGER THAN I HAD IMAGINED.
I AM NOT IMPRESSED. WERE IT UP TO ME, WE WOULD HAVE NEVER LEFT THE WALLS OF SILENCE.
THE LUMINARI SHOULD LOOK AFTER OUR *OWN* SURVIVAL.
AND LEAVE THE LOWLANDS TO ***BURN.***

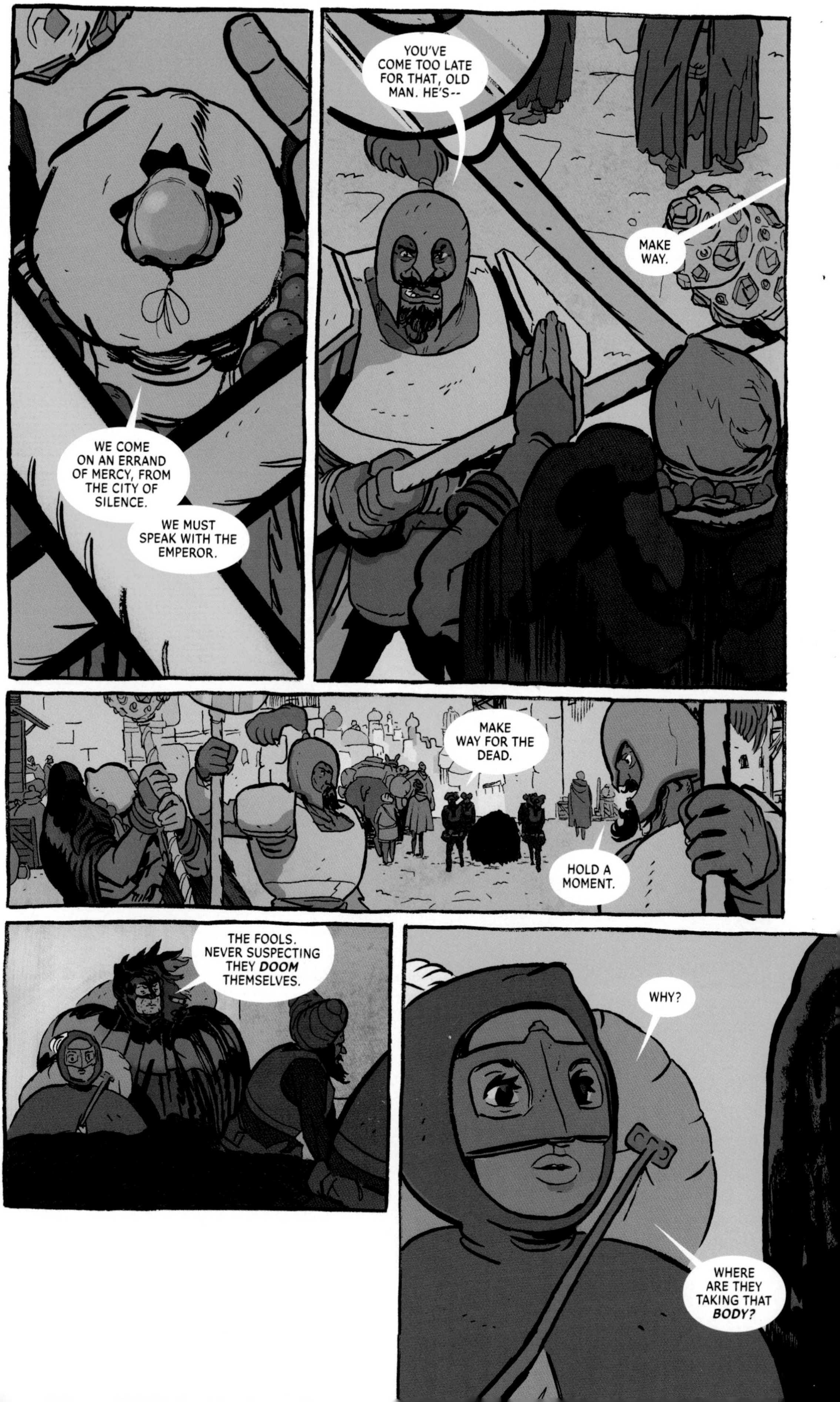
WE COME ON AN ERRAND OF MERCY, FROM THE CITY OF SILENCE.
WE MUST SPEAK WITH THE EMPEROR.
YOU'VE COME TOO LATE FOR THAT, OLD MAN. HE'S--
MAKE WAY.
MAKE WAY FOR THE DEAD.
HOLD A MOMENT.
THE FOOLS. NEVER SUSPECTING THEY *DOOM* THEMSELVES.
WHY?
WHERE ARE THEY TAKING THAT *BODY?*

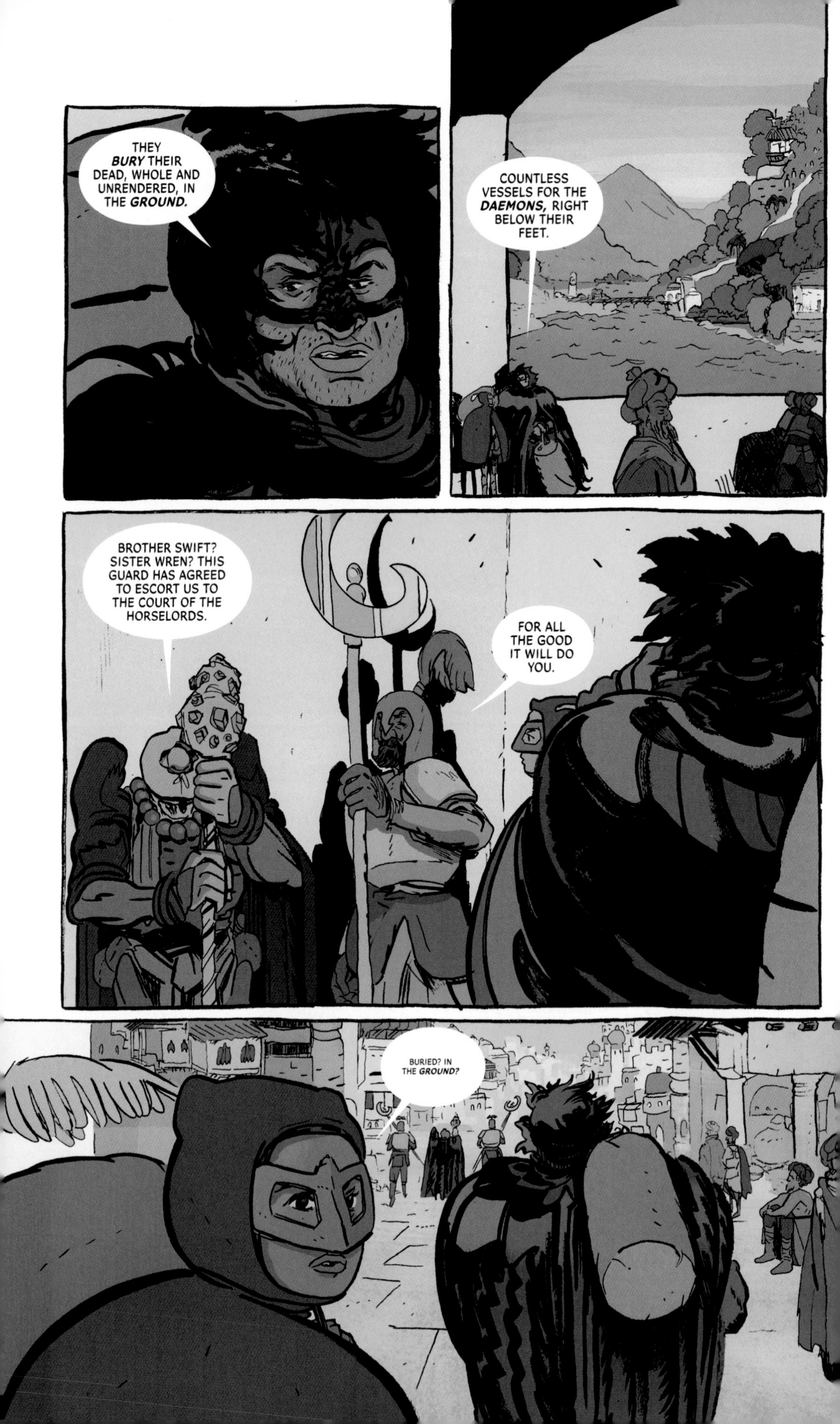
THEY *BURY* THEIR DEAD, WHOLE AND UNRENDERED, IN THE *GROUND.*
COUNTLESS VESSELS FOR THE *DAEMONS,* RIGHT BELOW THEIR FEET.
BROTHER SWIFT? SISTER WREN? THIS GUARD HAS AGREED TO ESCORT US TO THE COURT OF THE HORSELORDS.
FOR ALL THE GOOD IT WILL DO YOU.
BURIED? IN THE *GROUND?*

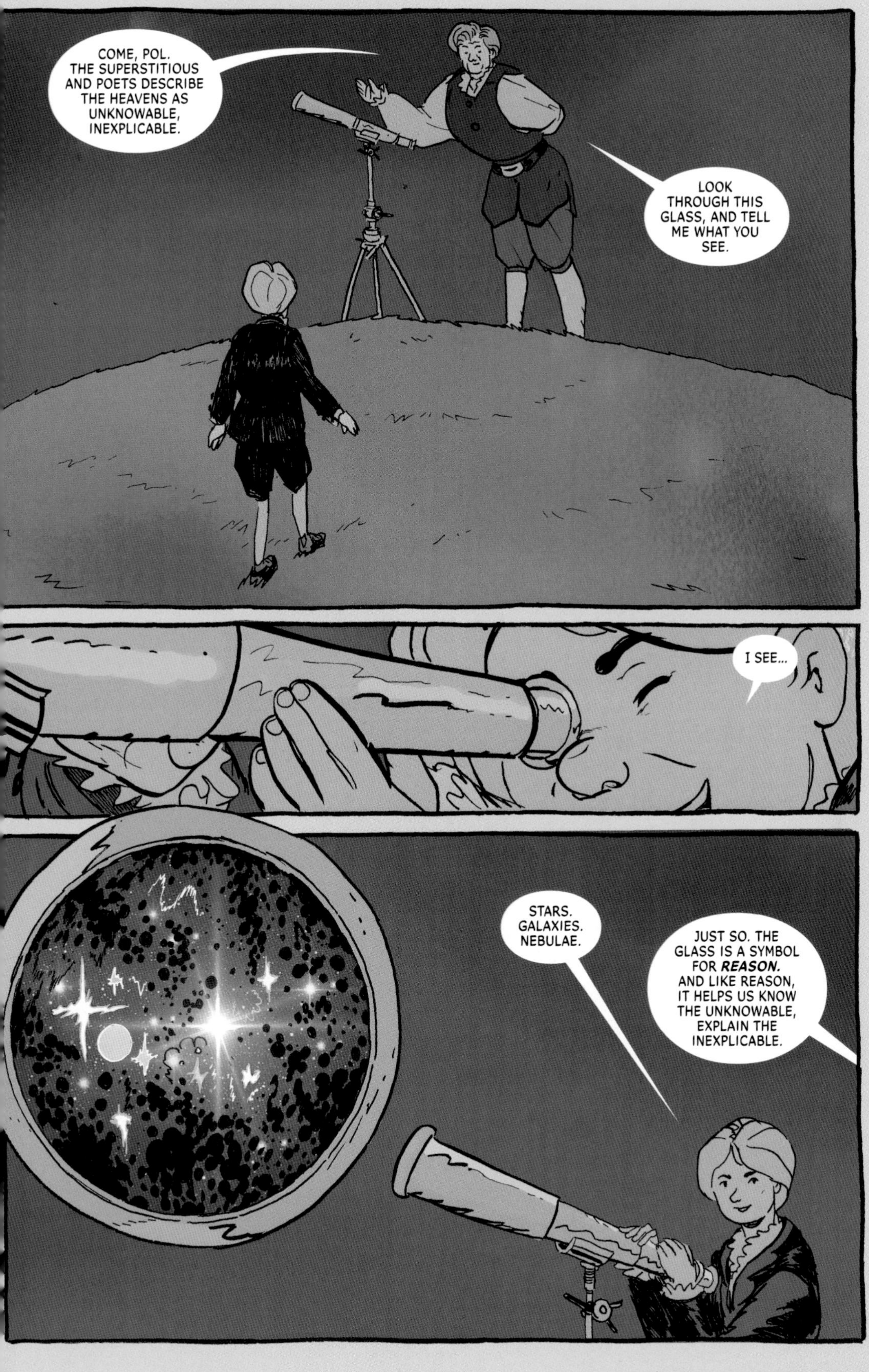
COME, POL. THE SUPERSTITIOUS AND POETS DESCRIBE THE HEAVENS AS UNKNOWABLE, INEXPLICABLE.
LOOK THROUGH THIS GLASS, AND TELL ME WHAT YOU SEE.
I SEE...
STARS. GALAXIES. NEBULAE.
JUST SO. THE GLASS IS A SYMBOL FOR ***REASON.*** AND LIKE REASON, IT HELPS US KNOW THE UNKNOWABLE, EXPLAIN THE INEXPLICABLE.

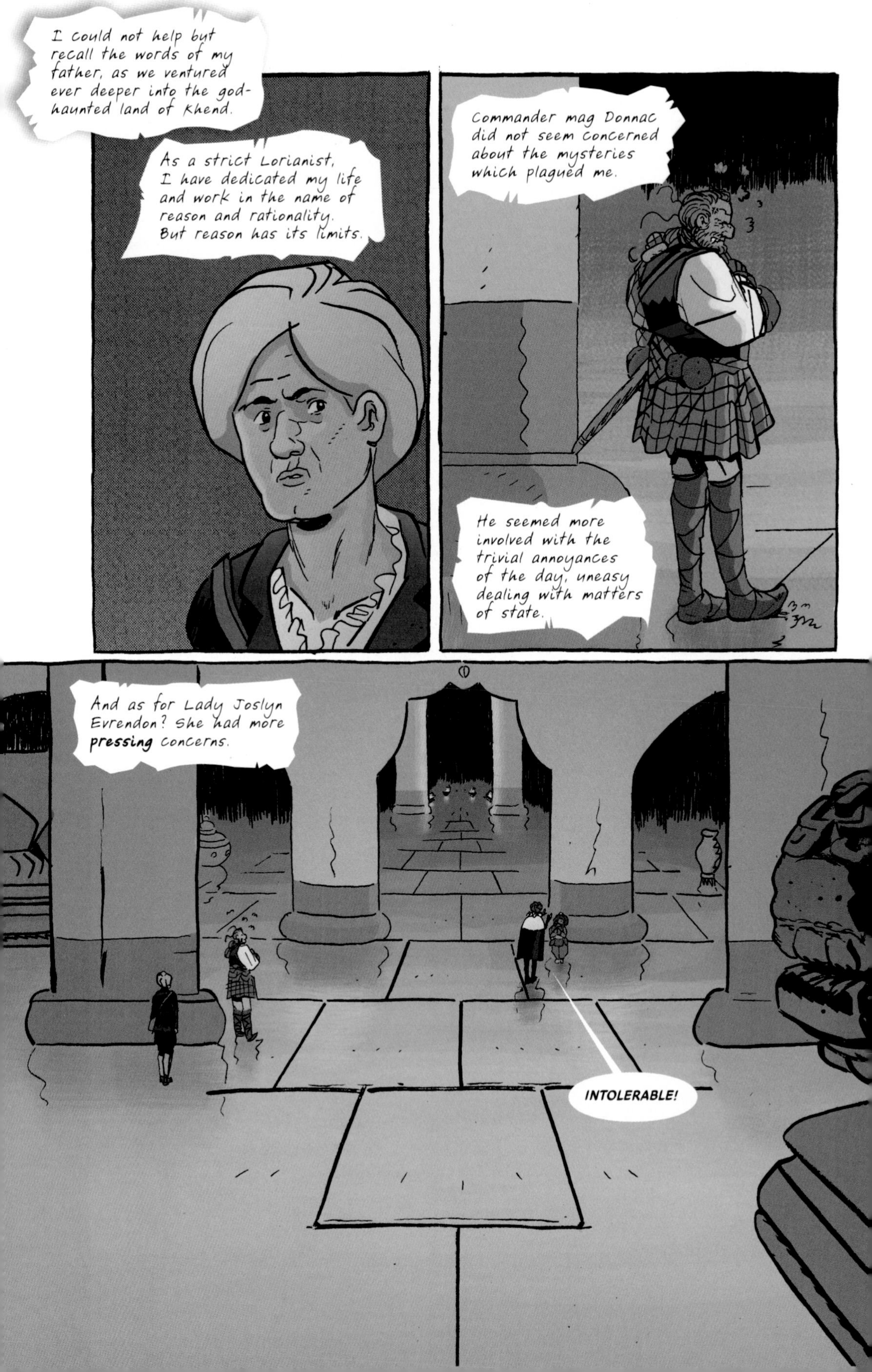
I could not help but recall the words of my father, as we ventured ever deeper into the god-haunted land of Khend.
As a strict Lorianist, I have dedicated my life and work in the name of reason and rationality. But reason has its limits.
Commander mag Donnac did not seem concerned about the mysteries which plagued me.
He seemed more involved with the trivial annoyances of the day, uneasy dealing with matters of state.
And as for Lady Joslyn Evrendon? She had more **pressing** concerns.
INTOLERABLE!

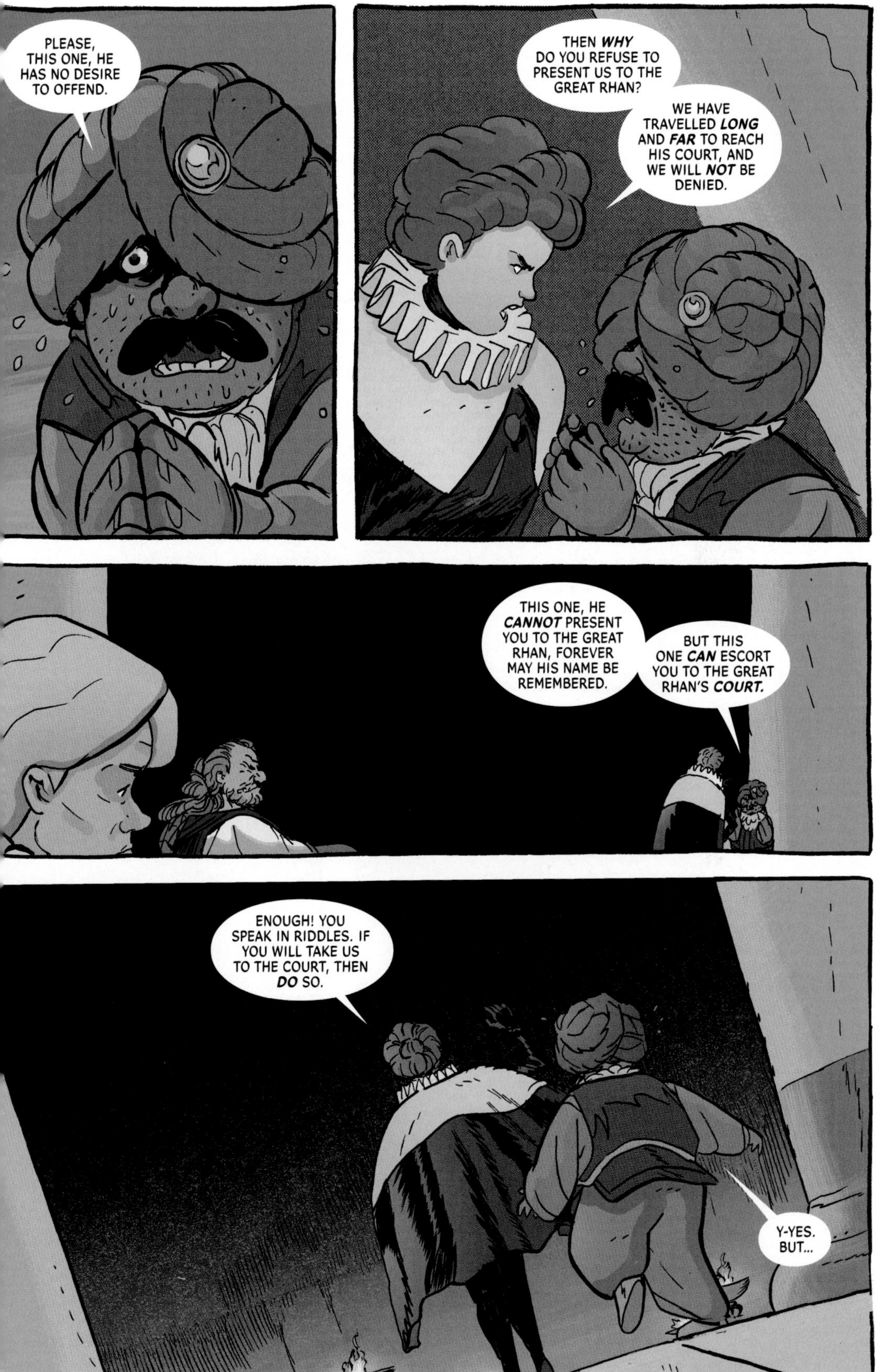
PLEASE, THIS ONE, HE HAS NO DESIRE TO OFFEND.
THEN *WHY* DO YOU REFUSE TO PRESENT US TO THE GREAT RHAN?
WE HAVE TRAVELLED *LONG* AND *FAR* TO REACH HIS COURT, AND WE WILL *NOT* BE DENIED.
THIS ONE, HE *CANNOT* PRESENT YOU TO THE GREAT RHAN, FOREVER MAY HIS NAME BE REMEMBERED.
BUT THIS ONE *CAN* ESCORT YOU TO THE GREAT RHAN'S *COURT.*
ENOUGH! YOU SPEAK IN RIDDLES. IF YOU WILL TAKE US TO THE COURT, THEN *DO* SO.
Y-YES. BUT...

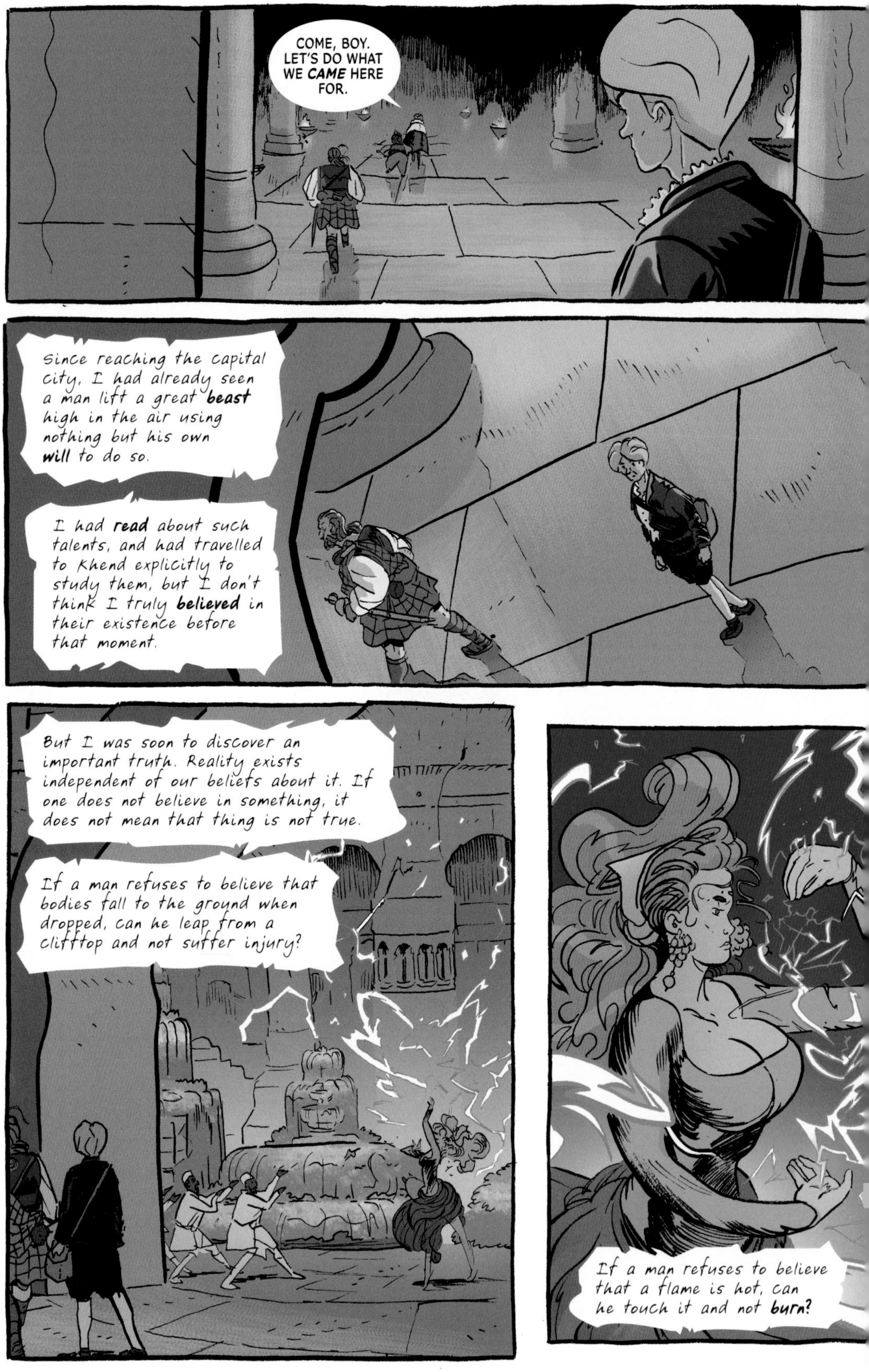
COME, BOY. LET'S DO WHAT WE CAME HERE FOR.
Since reaching the capital city, I had already seen a man lift a great beast high in the air using nothing but his own will to do so.
I had read about such talents, and had travelled to Khend explicitly to study them, but I don't think I truly believed in their existence before that moment.
But I was soon to discover an important truth. Reality exists independent of our beliefs about it. If one does not believe in something, it does not mean that thing is not true.
If a man refuses to believe that bodies fall to the ground when dropped, can he leap from a clifftop and not suffer injury?
If a man refuses to believe that a flame is hot, can he touch it and not burn?

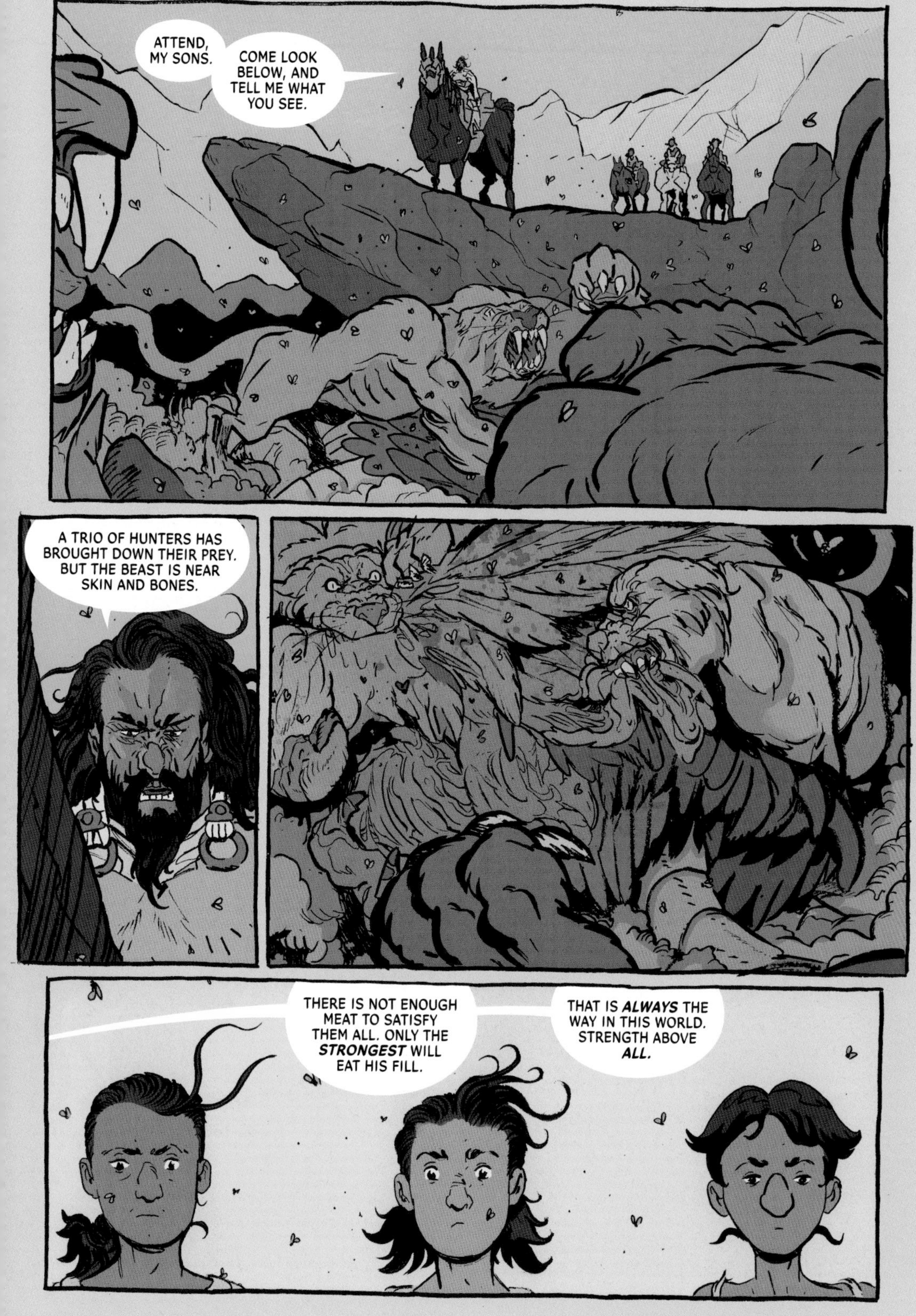
ATTEND, MY SONS.
COME LOOK BELOW, AND TELL ME WHAT YOU SEE.
A TRIO OF HUNTERS HAS BROUGHT DOWN THEIR PREY. BUT THE BEAST IS NEAR SKIN AND BONES.
THERE IS NOT ENOUGH MEAT TO SATISFY THEM ALL. ONLY THE ***STRONGEST*** WILL EAT HIS FILL.
THAT IS ***ALWAYS*** THE WAY IN THIS WORLD. STRENGTH ABOVE ***ALL.***

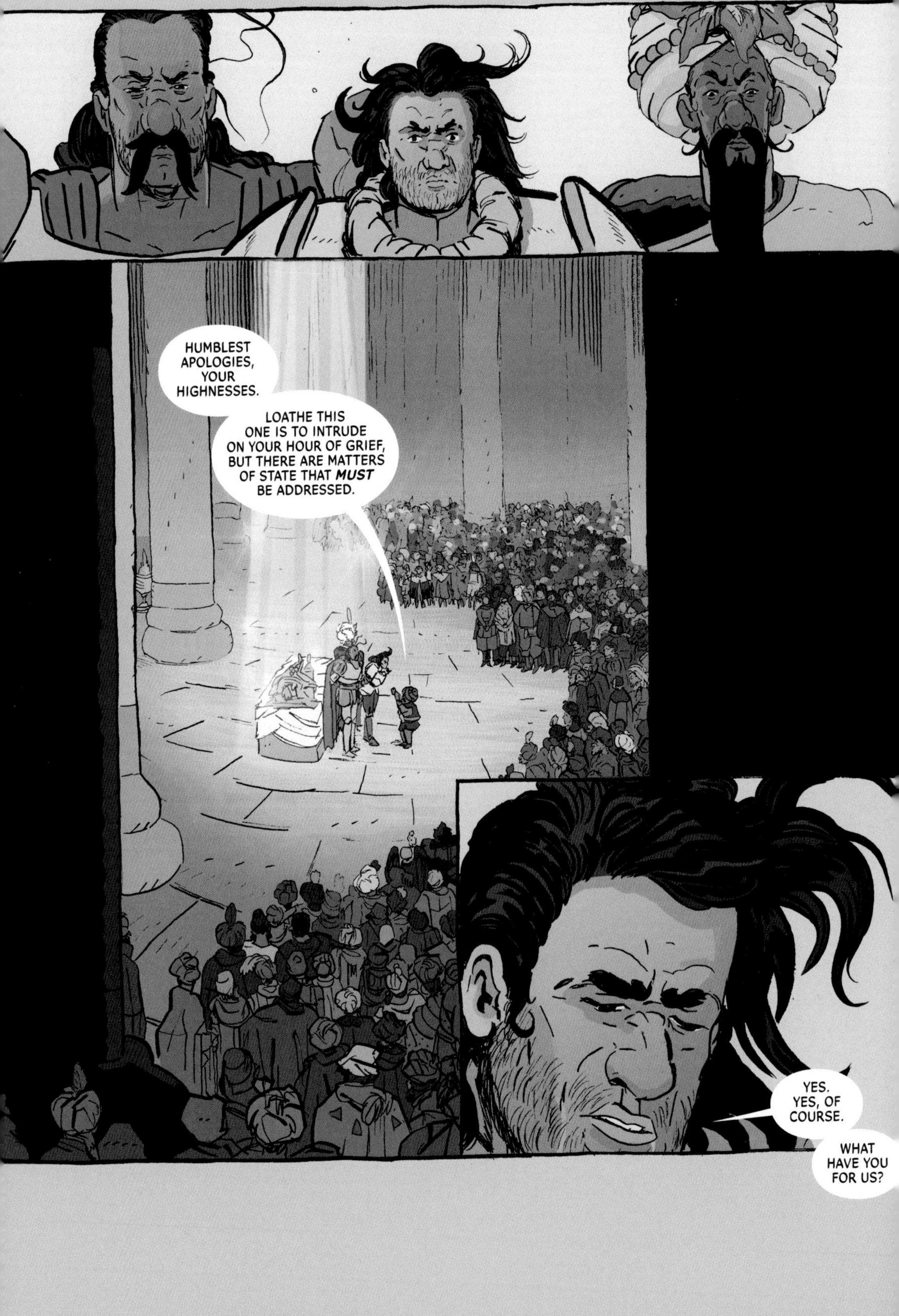
HUMBLEST APOLOGIES, YOUR HIGHNESSES.
LOATHE THIS ONE IS TO INTRUDE ON YOUR HOUR OF GRIEF, BUT THERE ARE MATTERS OF STATE THAT *MUST* BE ADDRESSED.
YES. YES, OF COURSE.
WHAT HAVE YOU FOR US?

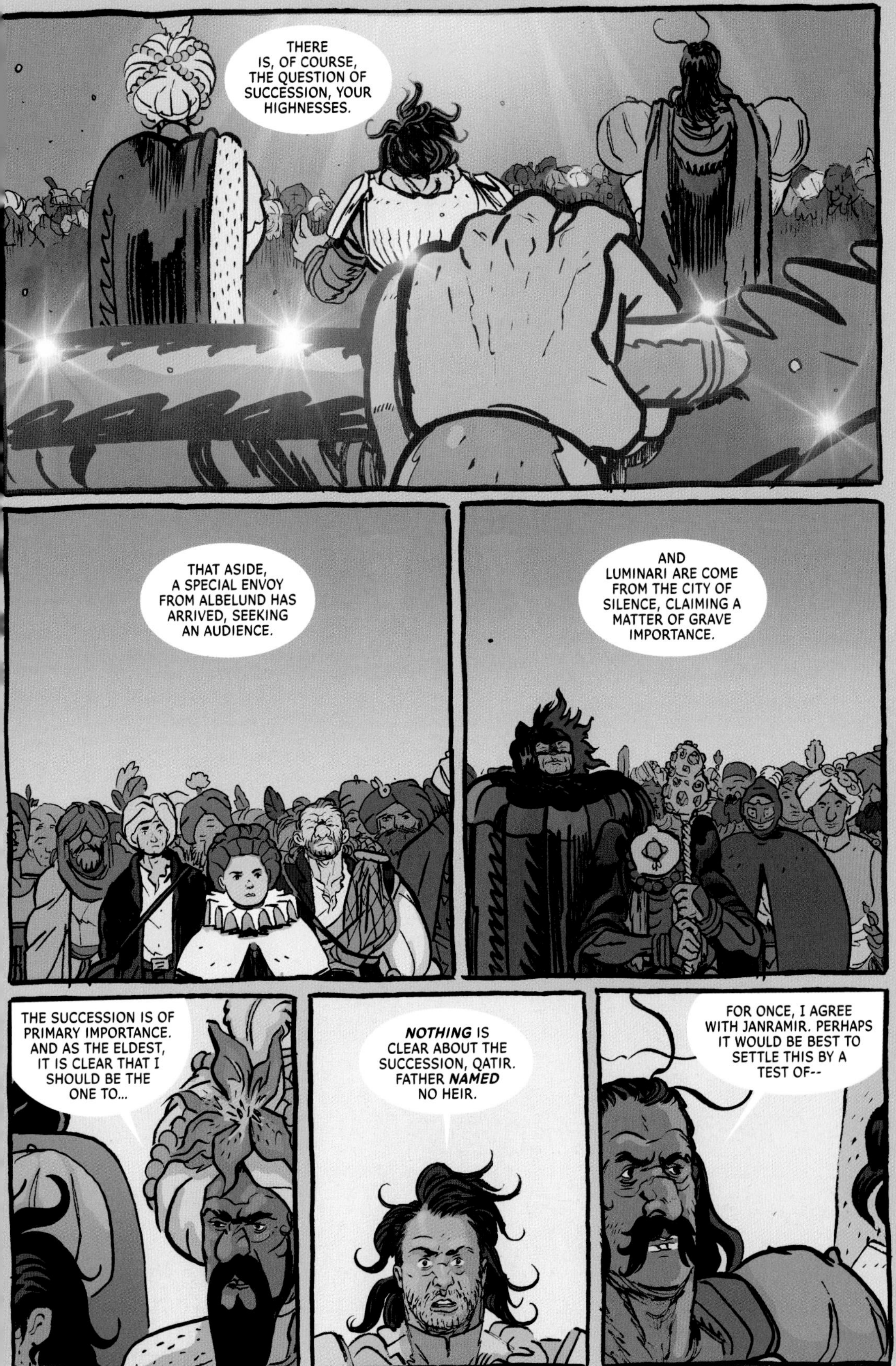
THERE IS, OF COURSE, THE QUESTION OF SUCCESSION, YOUR HIGHNESSES.
THAT ASIDE, A SPECIAL ENVOY FROM ALBELUND HAS ARRIVED, SEEKING AN AUDIENCE.
AND LUMINARI ARE COME FROM THE CITY OF SILENCE, CLAIMING A MATTER OF GRAVE IMPORTANCE.
THE SUCCESSION IS OF PRIMARY IMPORTANCE. AND AS THE ELDEST, IT IS CLEAR THAT I SHOULD BE THE ONE TO...
NOTHING IS CLEAR ABOUT THE SUCCESSION, QATIR. FATHER *NAMED* NO HEIR.
FOR ONCE, I AGREE WITH JANRAMIR. PERHAPS IT WOULD BE BEST TO SETTLE THIS BY A TEST OF--

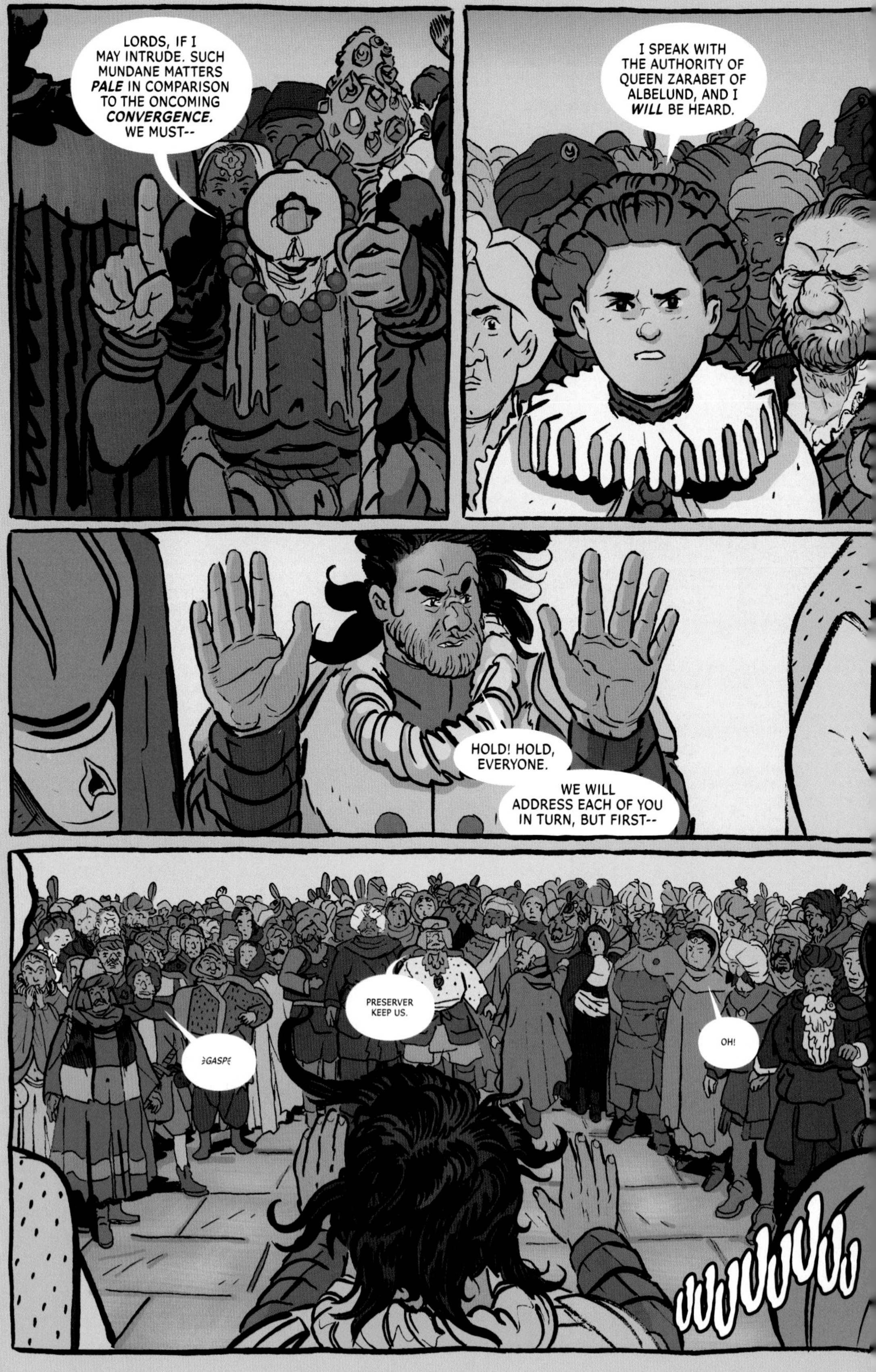

LORDS, IF I MAY INTRUDE. SUCH MUNDANE MATTERS ***PALE*** IN COMPARISON TO THE ONCOMING ***CONVERGENCE.*** WE MUST--
I SPEAK WITH THE AUTHORITY OF QUEEN ZARABET OF ALBELUND, AND I ***WILL*** BE HEARD.
HOLD! HOLD, EVERYONE.
WE WILL ADDRESS EACH OF YOU IN TURN, BUT FIRST--
GASP
PRESERVER KEEP US.
OH!

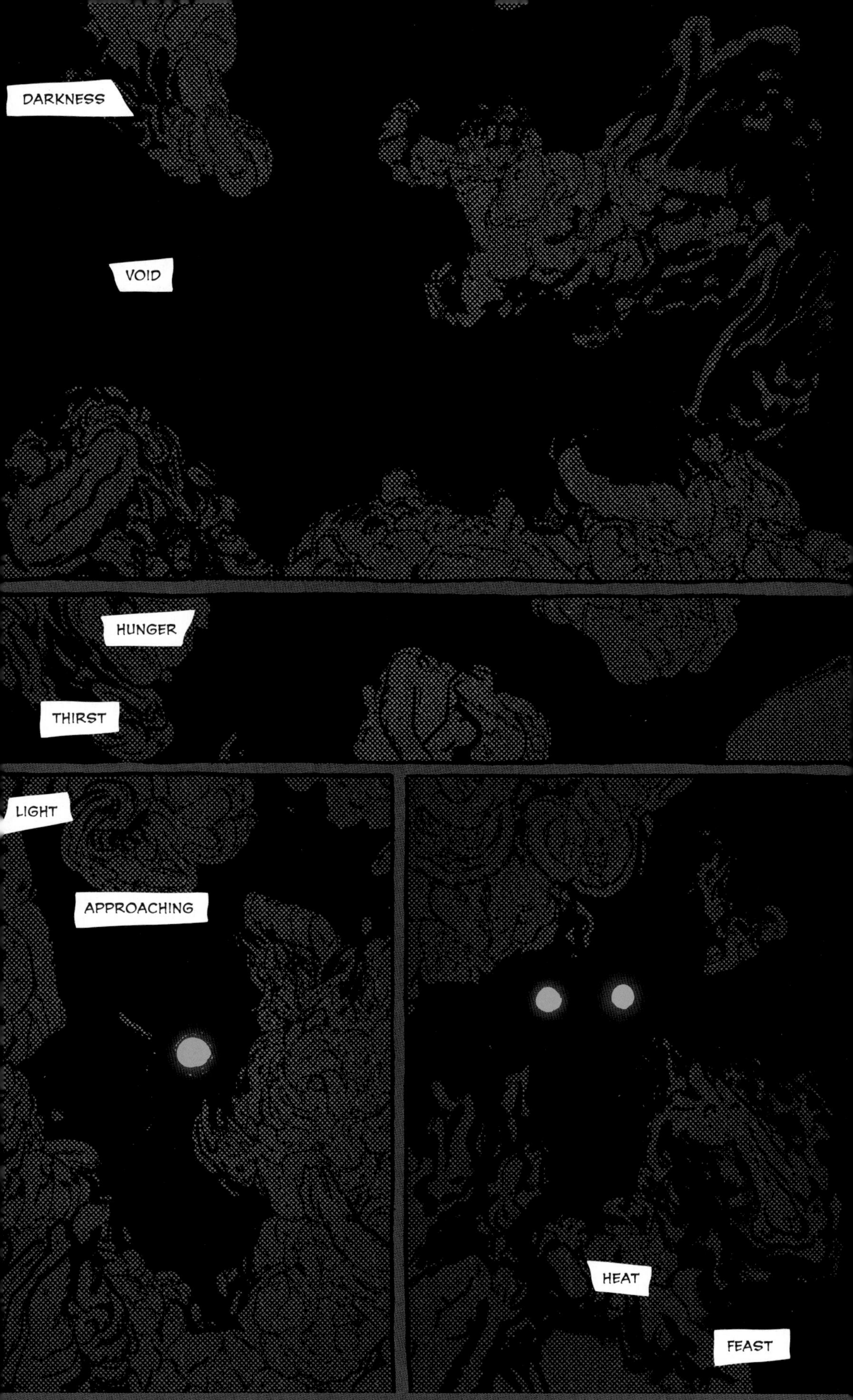
DARKNESS
VOID
HUNGER
THIRST
LIGHT
APPROACHING
HEAT
FEAST

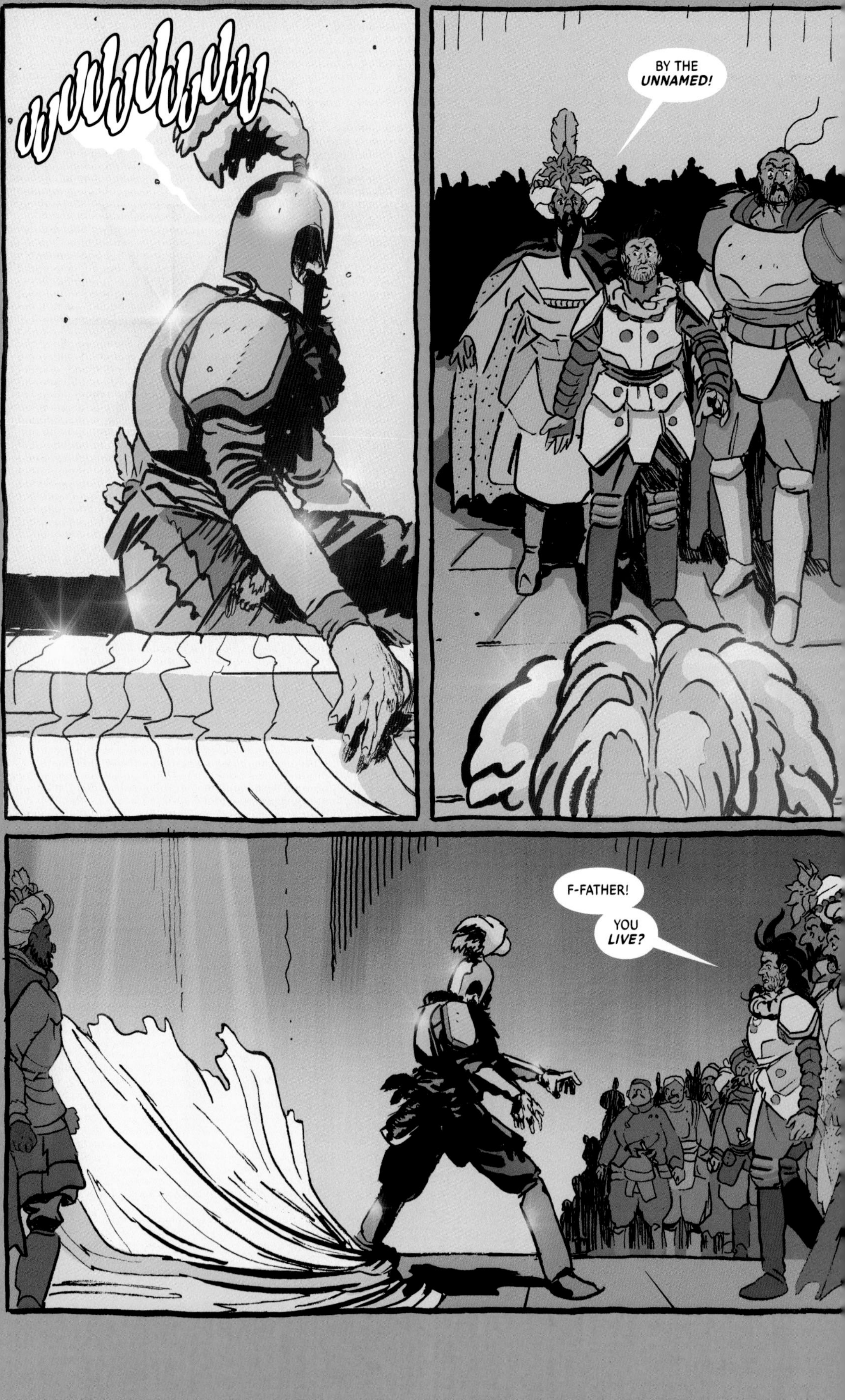

wwhhhhhhhhh
BY THE UNNAMED!
F-FATHER!
YOU LIVE?

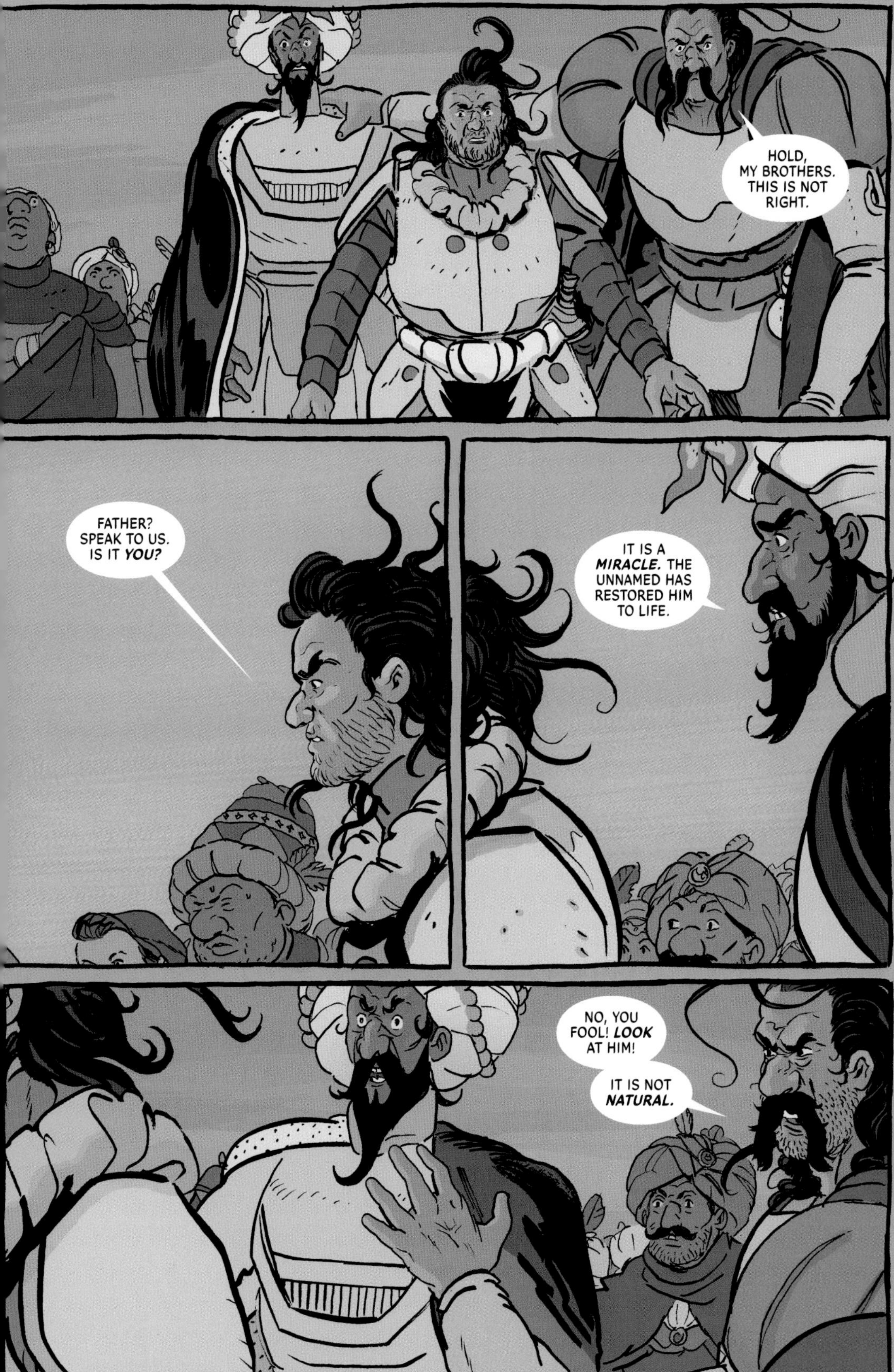
HOLD, MY BROTHERS. THIS IS NOT RIGHT.
FATHER? SPEAK TO US. IS IT *YOU?*
IT IS A *MIRACLE.* THE UNNAMED HAS RESTORED HIM TO LIFE.
NO, YOU FOOL! *LOOK* AT HIM!
IT IS NOT *NATURAL.*

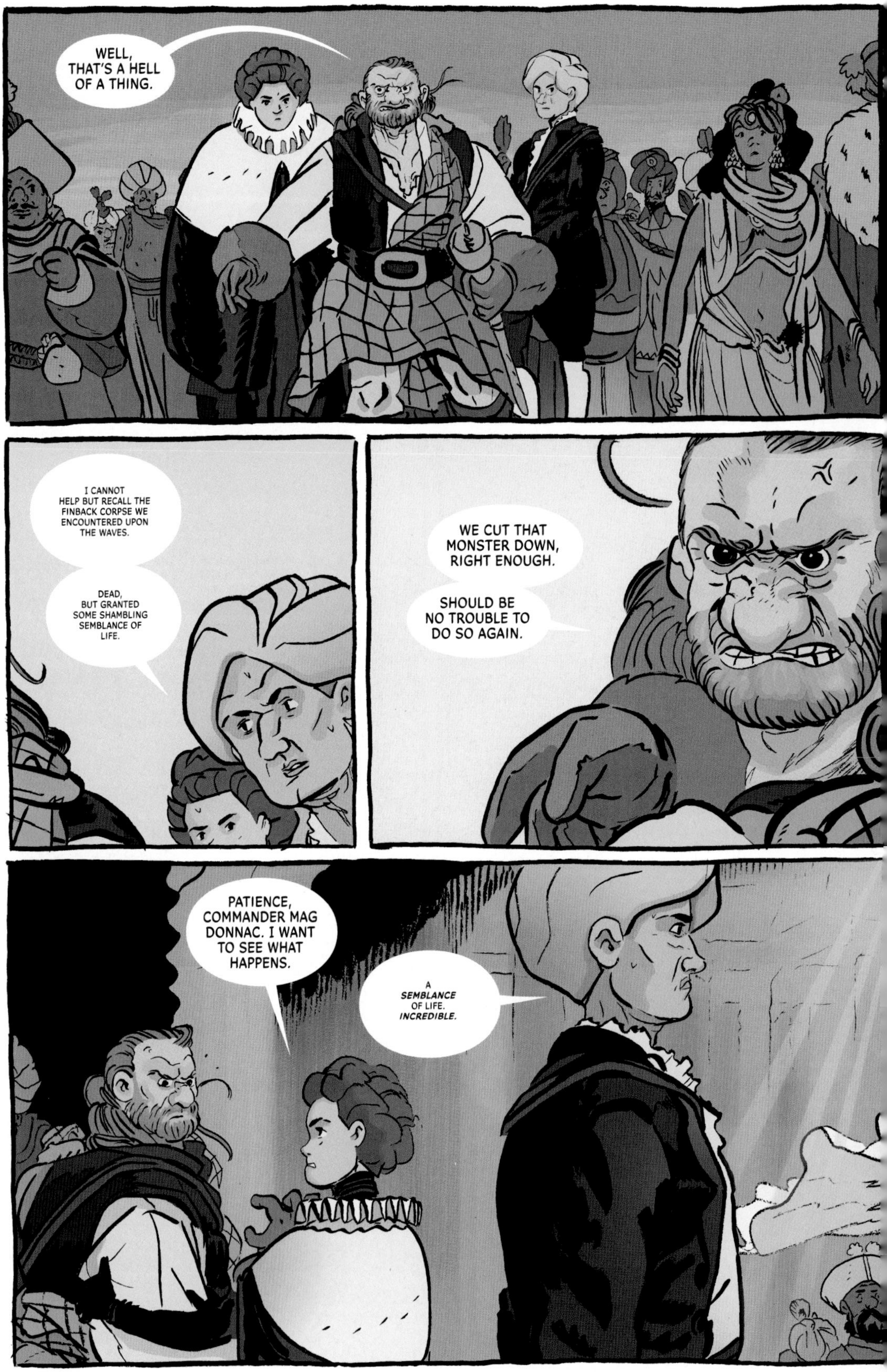
WELL, THAT'S A HELL OF A THING.
I CANNOT HELP BUT RECALL THE FINBACK CORPSE WE ENCOUNTERED UPON THE WAVES.
DEAD, BUT GRANTED SOME SHAMBLING SEMBLANCE OF LIFE.
WE CUT THAT MONSTER DOWN, RIGHT ENOUGH.
SHOULD BE NO TROUBLE TO DO SO AGAIN.
PATIENCE, COMMANDER MAG DONNAC. I WANT TO SEE WHAT HAPPENS.
A *SEMBLANCE* OF LIFE. *INCREDIBLE.*

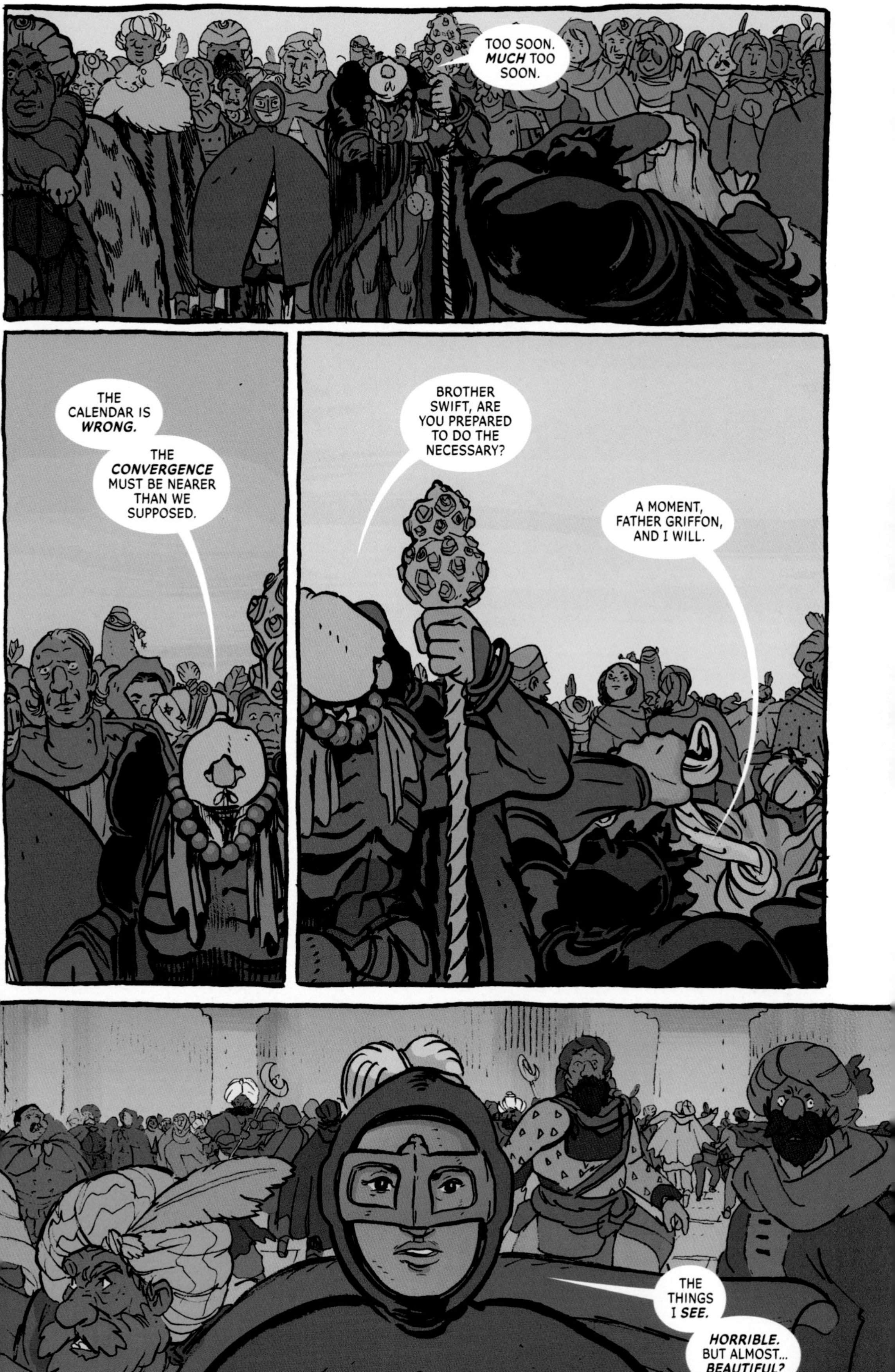

TOO SOON. *MUCH* TOO SOON.
THE CALENDAR IS *WRONG.*
THE *CONVERGENCE* MUST BE NEARER THAN WE SUPPOSED.
BROTHER SWIFT, ARE YOU PREPARED TO DO THE NECESSARY?
A MOMENT, FATHER GRIFFON, AND I WILL.
THE THINGS I *SEE.*
HORRIBLE. BUT ALMOST... *BEAUTIFUL?*

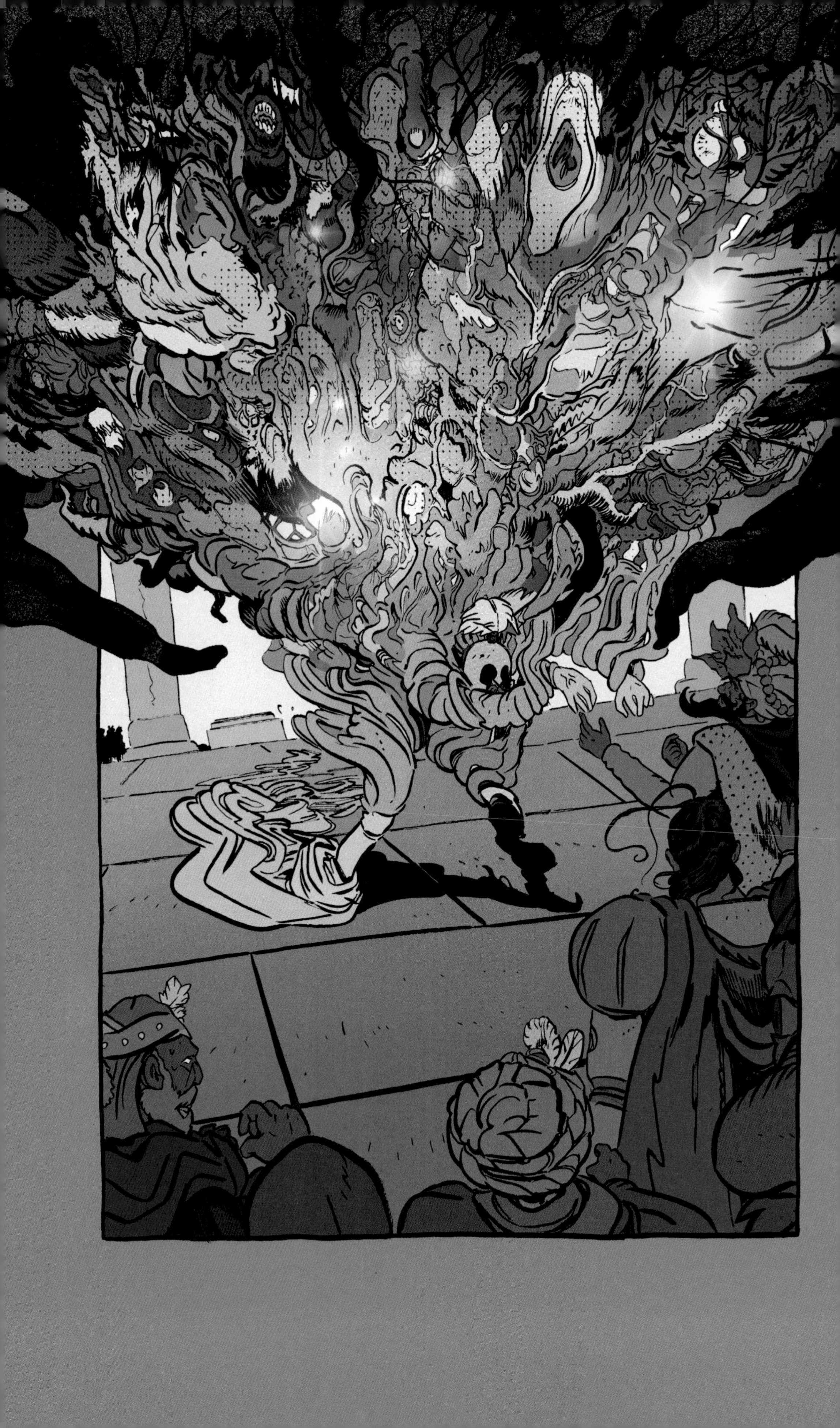

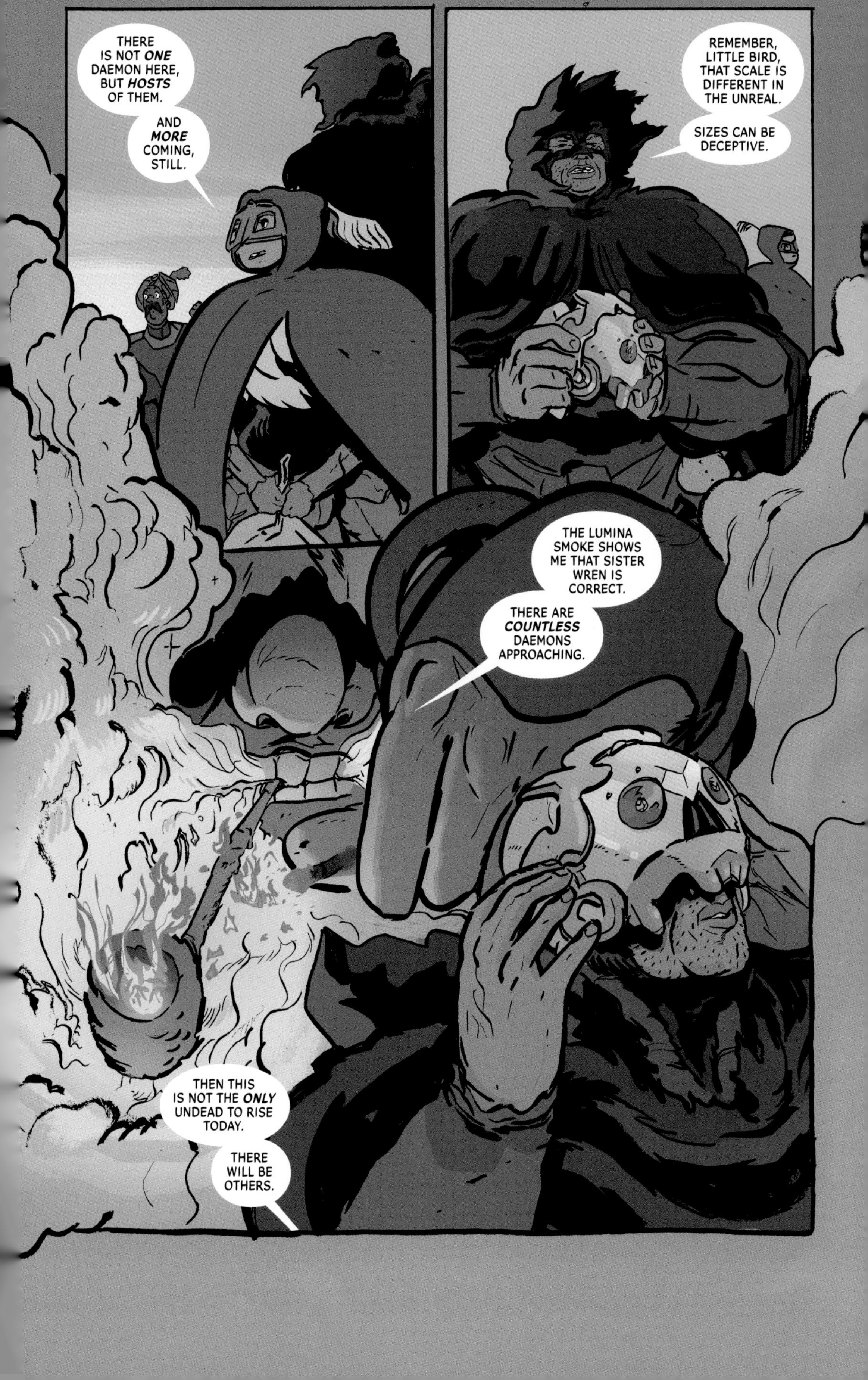
THERE IS NOT *ONE* DAEMON HERE, BUT *HOSTS* OF THEM.
AND *MORE* COMING, STILL.
REMEMBER, LITTLE BIRD, THAT SCALE IS DIFFERENT IN THE UNREAL.
SIZES CAN BE DECEPTIVE.
THE LUMINA SMOKE SHOWS ME THAT SISTER WREN IS CORRECT.
THERE ARE *COUNTLESS* DAEMONS APPROACHING.
THEN THIS IS NOT THE *ONLY* UNDEAD TO RISE TODAY.
THERE WILL BE OTHERS.

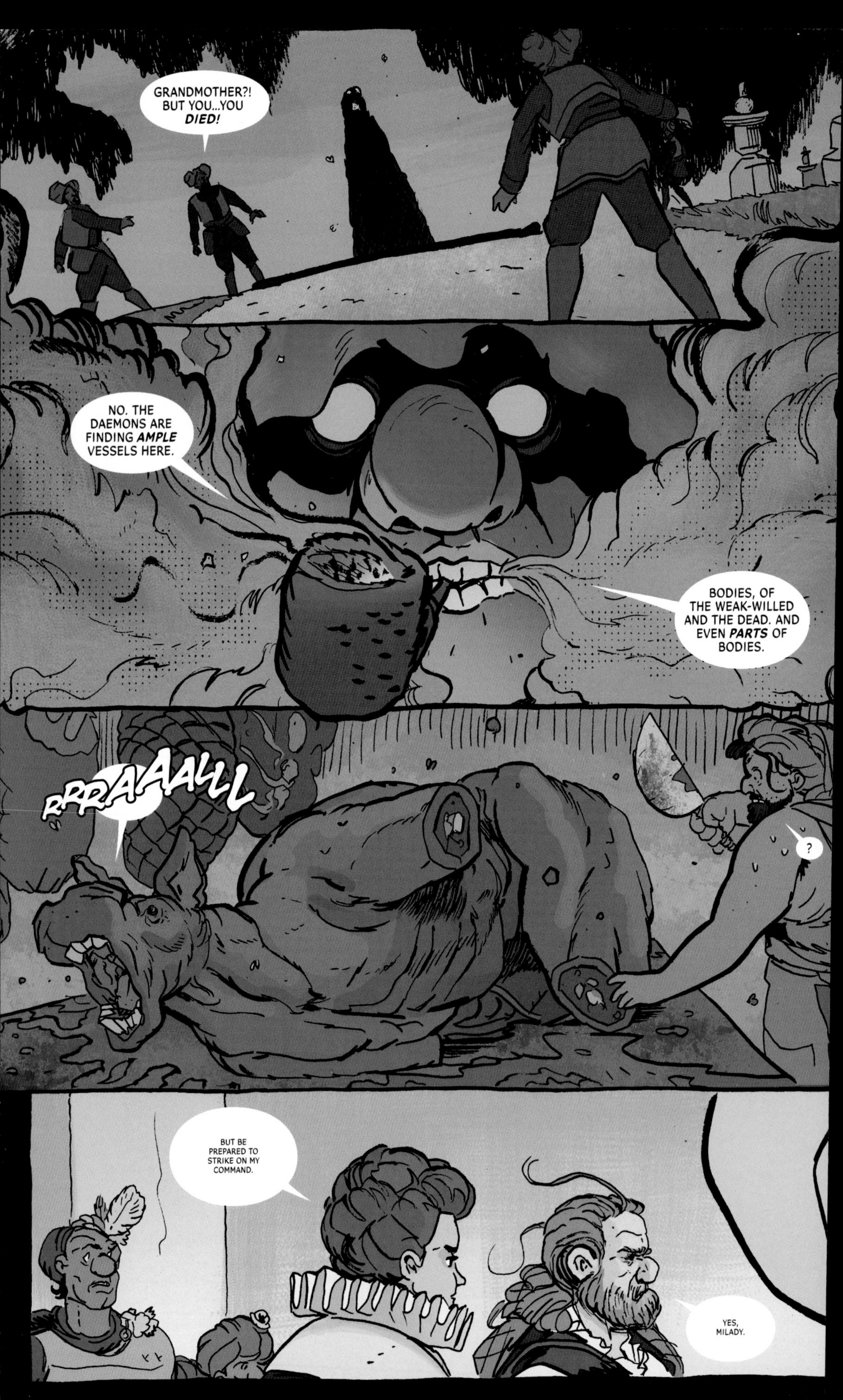
GRANDMOTHER?! BUT YOU...YOU *DIED!*
NO. THE DAEMONS ARE FINDING *AMPLE* VESSELS HERE.
BODIES, OF THE WEAK-WILLED AND THE DEAD. AND EVEN *PARTS* OF BODIES.
RRRAAAALLL
?
BUT BE PREPARED TO STRIKE ON MY COMMAND.
YES, MILADY.

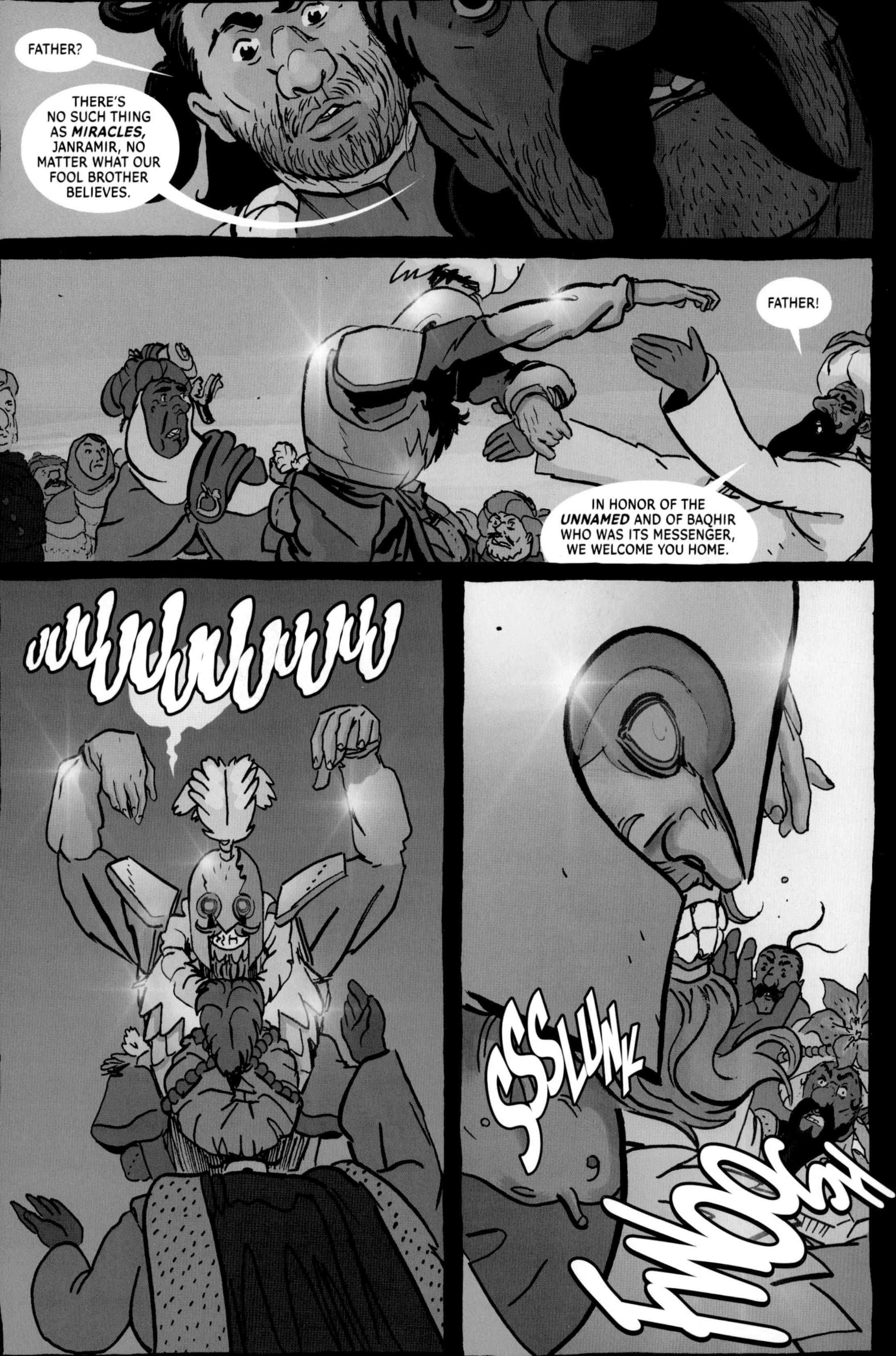
FATHER?
THERE'S NO SUCH THING AS *MIRACLES,* JANRAMIR, NO MATTER WHAT OUR FOOL BROTHER BELIEVES.
FATHER!
IN HONOR OF THE *UNNAMED* AND OF BAQHIR WHO WAS ITS MESSENGER, WE WELCOME YOU HOME.
SSSLUNK
WHOOSH

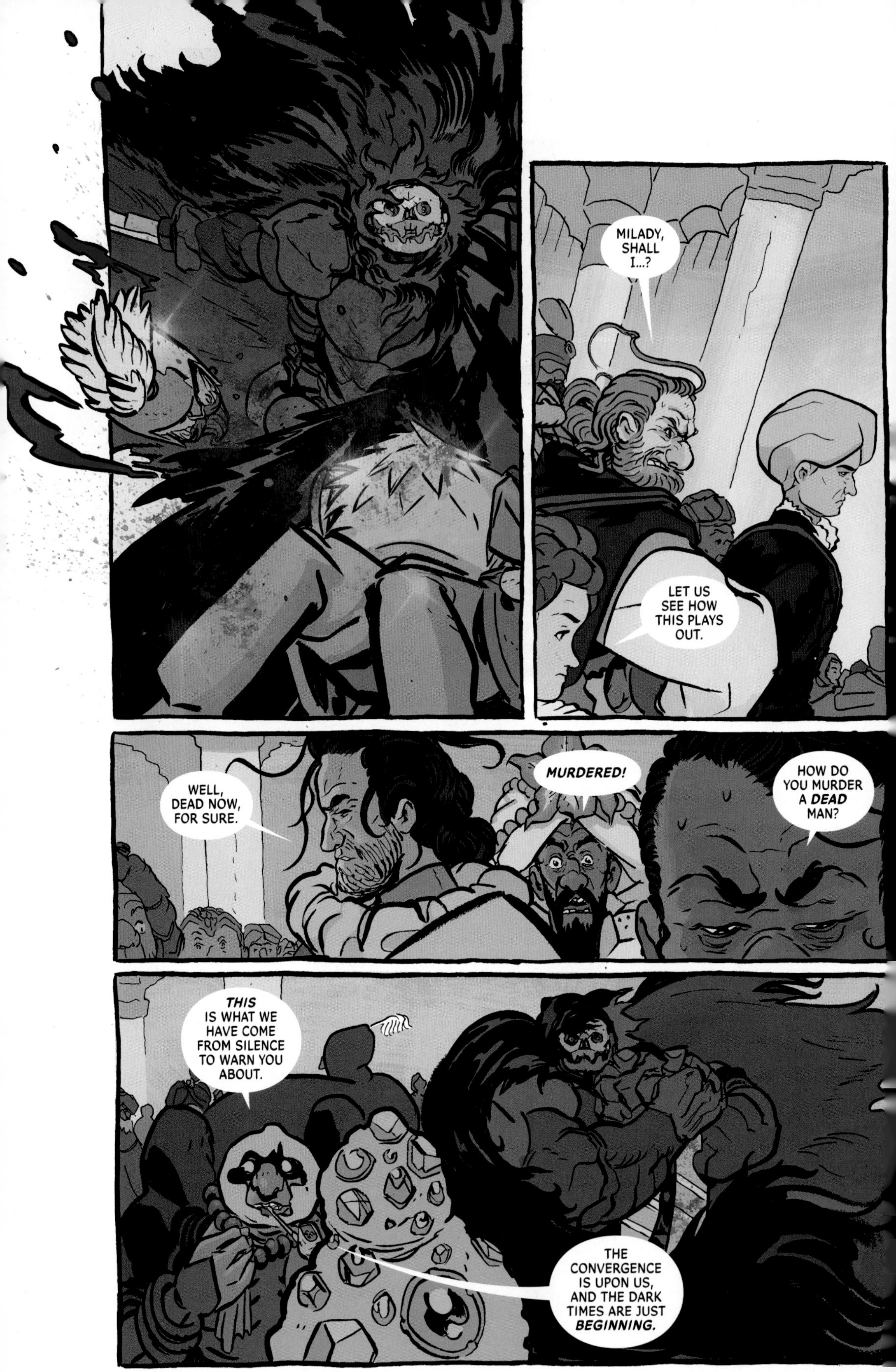
MILADY, SHALL I...?
LET US SEE HOW THIS PLAYS OUT.
WELL, DEAD NOW, FOR SURE.
MURDERED!
HOW DO YOU MURDER A DEAD MAN?
THIS IS WHAT WE HAVE COME FROM SILENCE TO WARN YOU ABOUT.
THE CONVERGENCE IS UPON US, AND THE DARK TIMES ARE JUST BEGINNING.

last days

The branches of the World Tree
are without number, but they are
nothing compared to the countless
dangers that lurk in the Unreal.

—Sant Koel

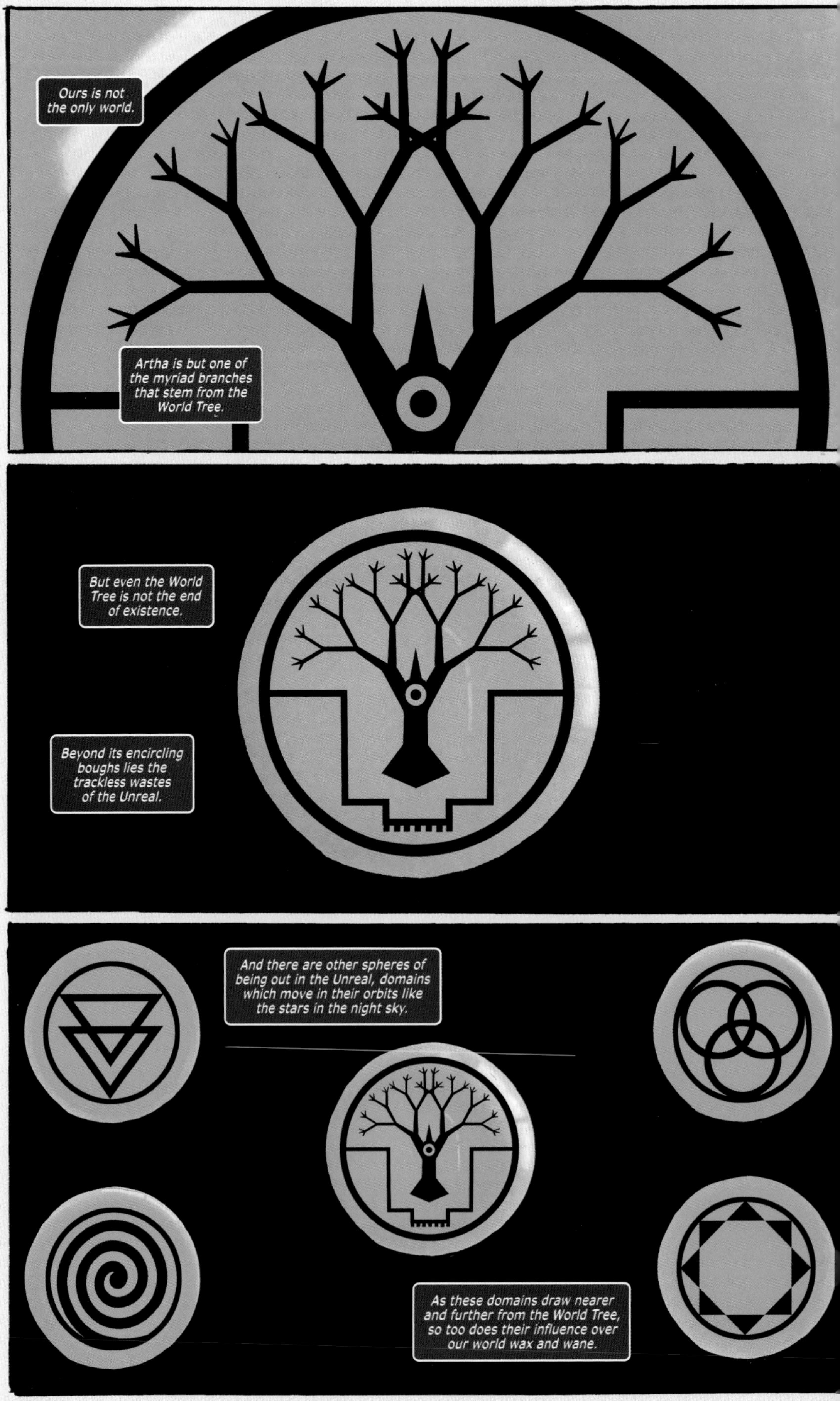

Ours is not the only world.
Artha is but one of the myriad branches that stem from the World Tree.
But even the World Tree is not the end of existence.
Beyond its encircling boughs lies the trackless wastes of the Unreal.
And there are other spheres of being out in the Unreal, domains which move in their orbits like the stars in the night sky.
As these domains draw nearer and further from the World Tree, so too does their influence over our world wax and wane.

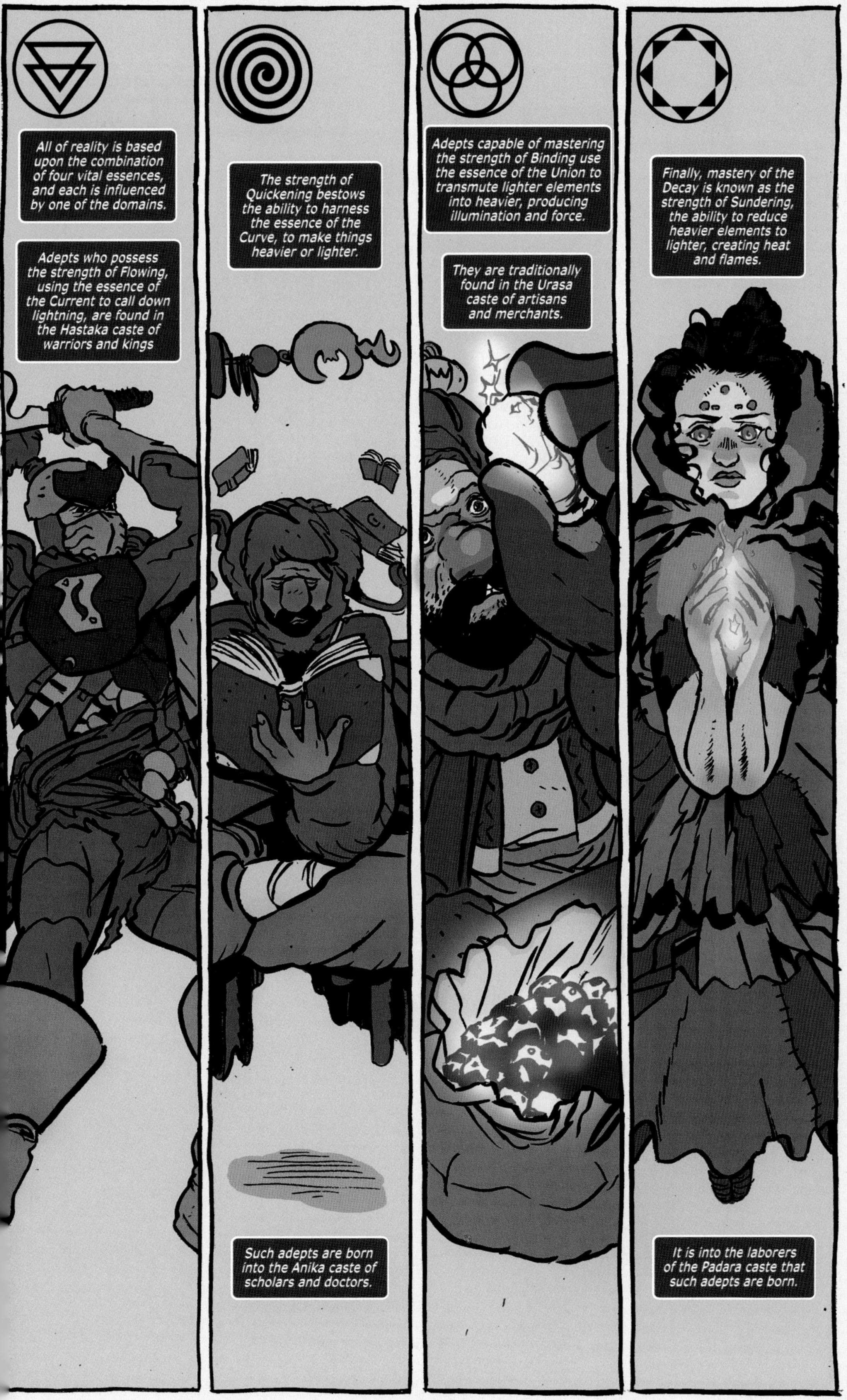
All of reality is based upon the combination of four vital essences, and each is influenced by one of the domains.
Adepts who possess the strength of Flowing, using the essence of the Current to call down lightning, are found in the Hastaka caste of warriors and kings
The strength of Quickening bestows the ability to harness the essence of the Curve, to make things heavier or lighter.
Such adepts are born into the Anika caste of scholars and doctors.
Adepts capable of mastering the strength of Binding use the essence of the Union to transmute lighter elements into heavier, producing illumination and force.
They are traditionally found in the Urasa caste of artisans and merchants.
Finally, mastery of the Decay is known as the strength of Sundering, the ability to reduce heavier elements to lighter, creating heat and flames.
It is into the laborers of the Padara caste that such adepts are born.

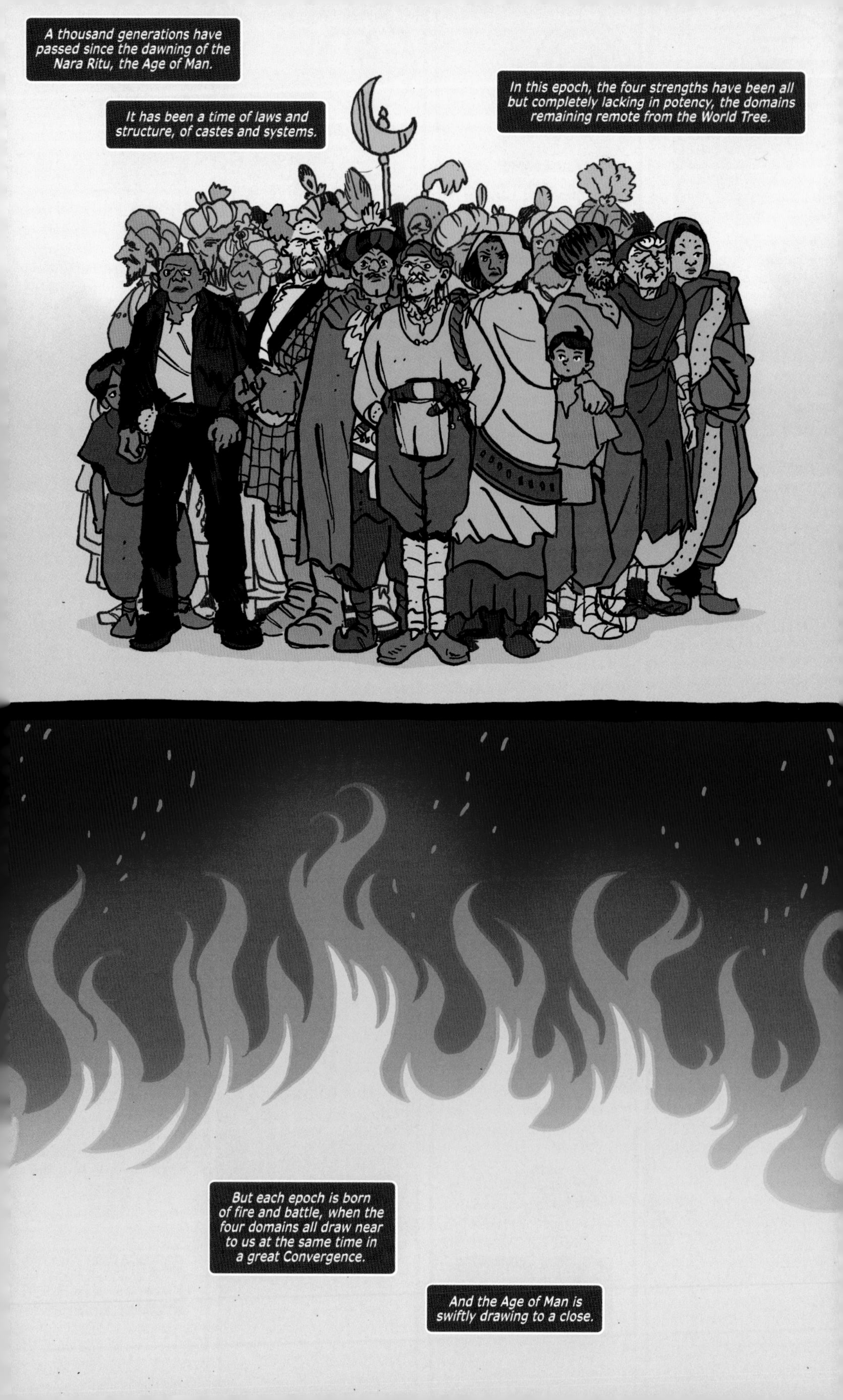
A thousand generations have passed since the dawning of the Nara Ritu, the Age of Man.
It has been a time of laws and structure, of castes and systems.
In this epoch, the four strengths have been all but completely lacking in potency, the domains remaining remote from the World Tree.
But each epoch is born of fire and battle, when the four domains all draw near to us at the same time in a great Convergence.
And the Age of Man is swiftly drawing to a close.

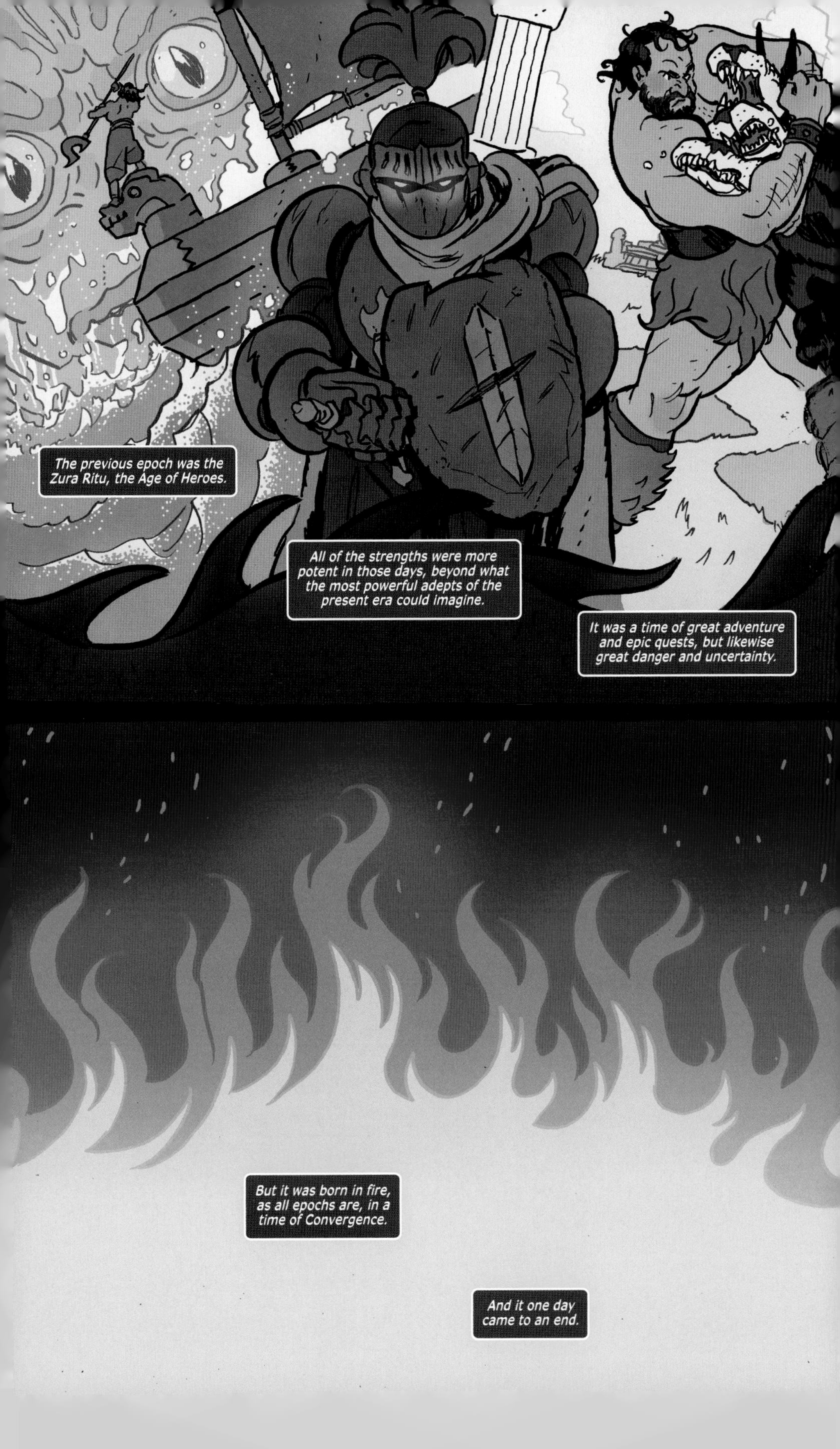
The previous epoch was the Zura Ritu, the Age of Heroes.
All of the strengths were more potent in those days, beyond what the most powerful adepts of the present era could imagine.
It was a time of great adventure and epic quests, but likewise great danger and uncertainty.
But it was born in fire, as all epochs are, in a time of Convergence.
And it one day came to an end.

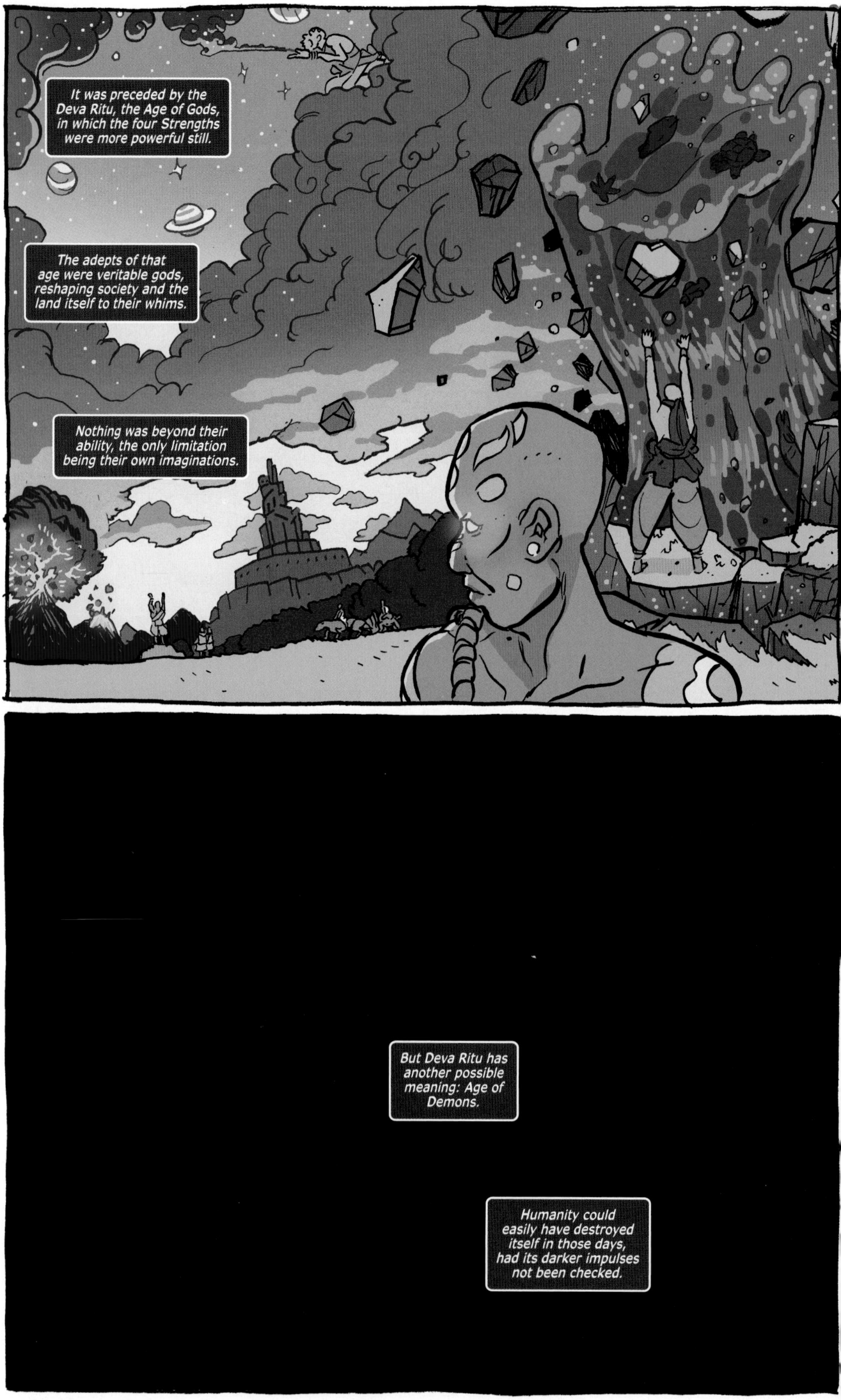
It was preceded by the Deva Ritu, the Age of Gods, in which the four Strengths were more powerful still.
The adepts of that age were veritable gods, reshaping society and the land itself to their whims.
Nothing was beyond their ability, the only limitation being their own imaginations.
But Deva Ritu has another possible meaning: Age of Demons.
Humanity could easily have destroyed itself in those days, had its darker impulses not been checked.

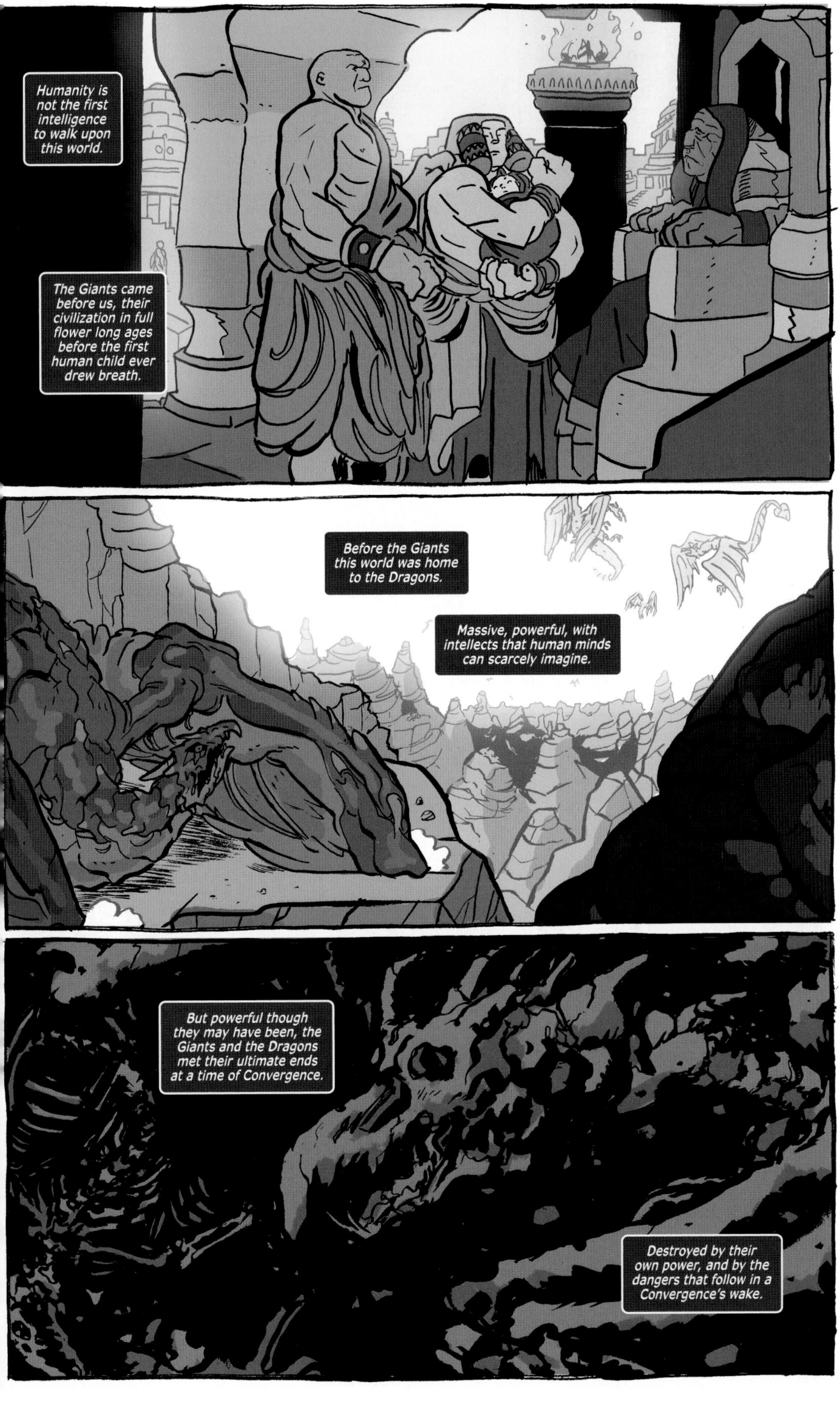
Humanity is not the first intelligence to walk upon this world.
The Giants came before us, their civilization in full flower long ages before the first human child ever drew breath.
Before the Giants this world was home to the Dragons.
Massive, powerful, with intellects that human minds can scarcely imagine.
But powerful though they may have been, the Giants and the Dragons met their ultimate ends at a time of Convergence.
Destroyed by their own power, and by the dangers that follow in a Convergence's wake.

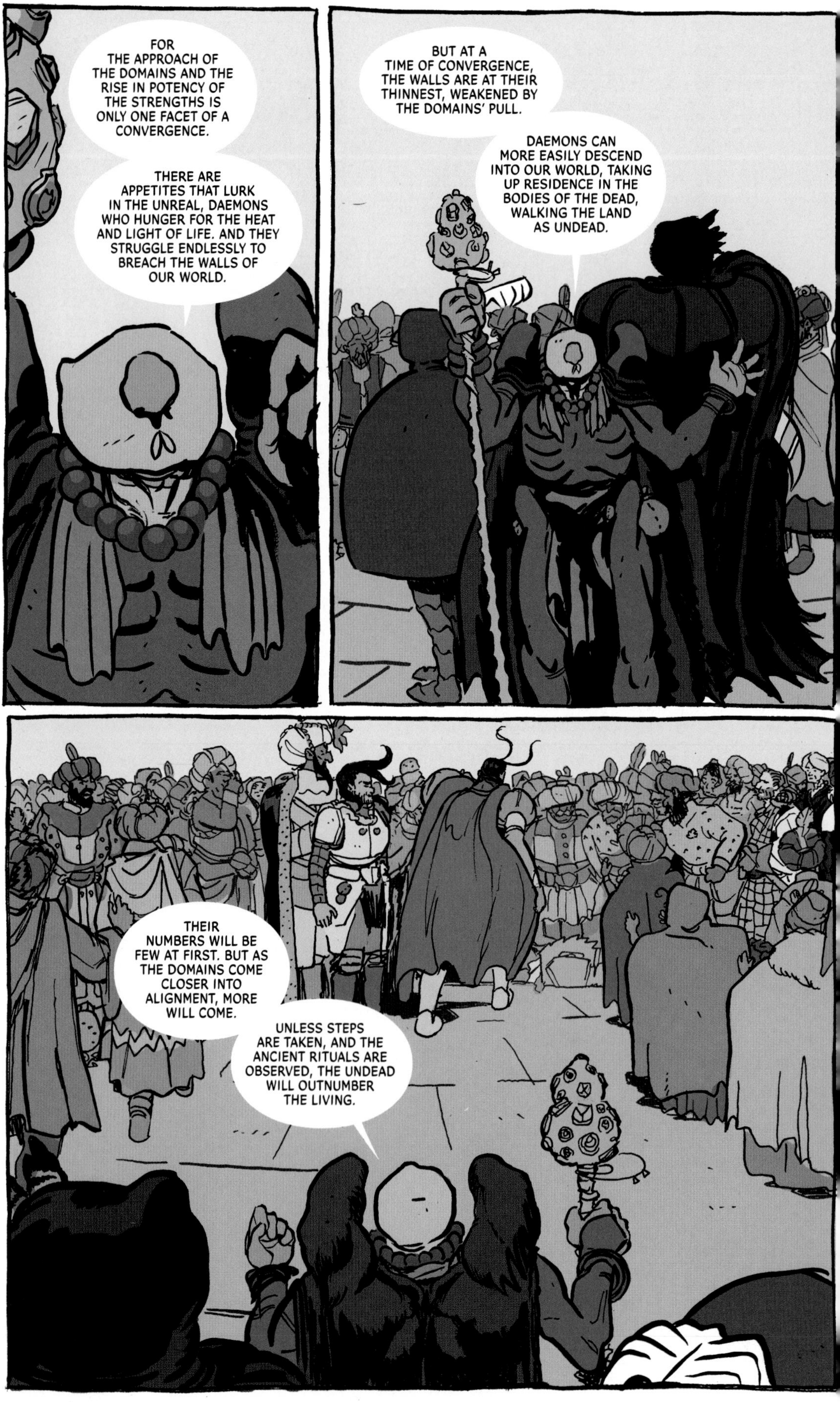
FOR THE APPROACH OF THE DOMAINS AND THE RISE IN POTENCY OF THE STRENGTHS IS ONLY ONE FACET OF A CONVERGENCE.
THERE ARE APPETITES THAT LURK IN THE UNREAL, DAEMONS WHO HUNGER FOR THE HEAT AND LIGHT OF LIFE. AND THEY STRUGGLE ENDLESSLY TO BREACH THE WALLS OF OUR WORLD.
BUT AT A TIME OF CONVERGENCE, THE WALLS ARE AT THEIR THINNEST, WEAKENED BY THE DOMAINS' PULL.
DAEMONS CAN MORE EASILY DESCEND INTO OUR WORLD, TAKING UP RESIDENCE IN THE BODIES OF THE DEAD, WALKING THE LAND AS UNDEAD.
THEIR NUMBERS WILL BE FEW AT FIRST. BUT AS THE DOMAINS COME CLOSER INTO ALIGNMENT, MORE WILL COME.
UNLESS STEPS ARE TAKEN, AND THE ANCIENT RITUALS ARE OBSERVED, THE UNDEAD WILL OUTNUMBER THE LIVING.

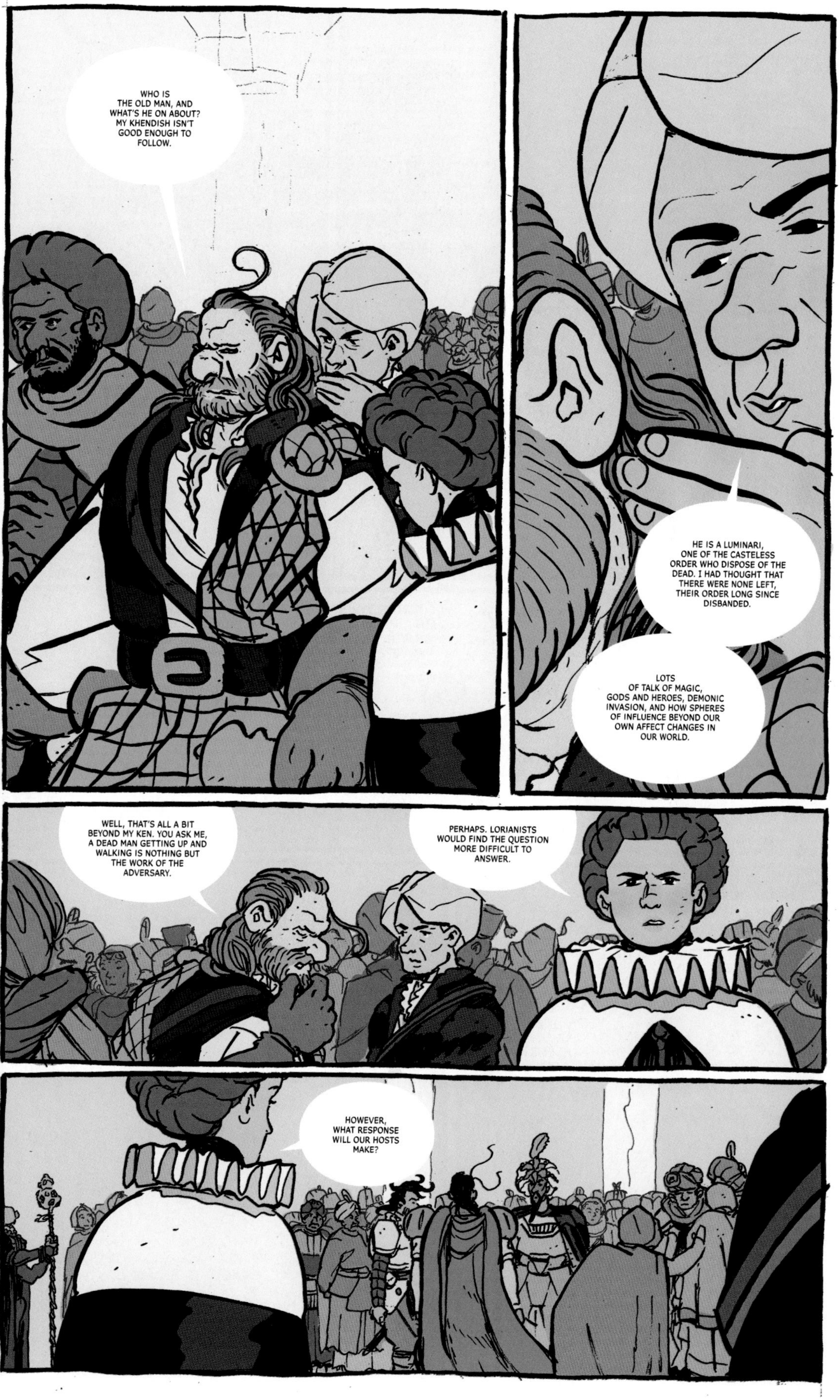
WHO IS THE OLD MAN, AND WHAT'S HE ON ABOUT? MY KHENDISH ISN'T GOOD ENOUGH TO FOLLOW.
HE IS A LUMINARI, ONE OF THE CASTELESS ORDER WHO DISPOSE OF THE DEAD. I HAD THOUGHT THAT THERE WERE NONE LEFT, THEIR ORDER LONG SINCE DISBANDED.
LOTS OF TALK OF MAGIC, GODS AND HEROES, DEMONIC INVASION, AND HOW SPHERES OF INFLUENCE BEYOND OUR OWN AFFECT CHANGES IN OUR WORLD.
WELL, THAT'S ALL A BIT BEYOND MY KEN. YOU ASK ME, A DEAD MAN GETTING UP AND WALKING IS NOTHING BUT THE WORK OF THE ADVERSARY.
PERHAPS. LORIANISTS WOULD FIND THE QUESTION MORE DIFFICULT TO ANSWER.
HOWEVER, WHAT RESPONSE WILL OUR HOSTS MAKE?

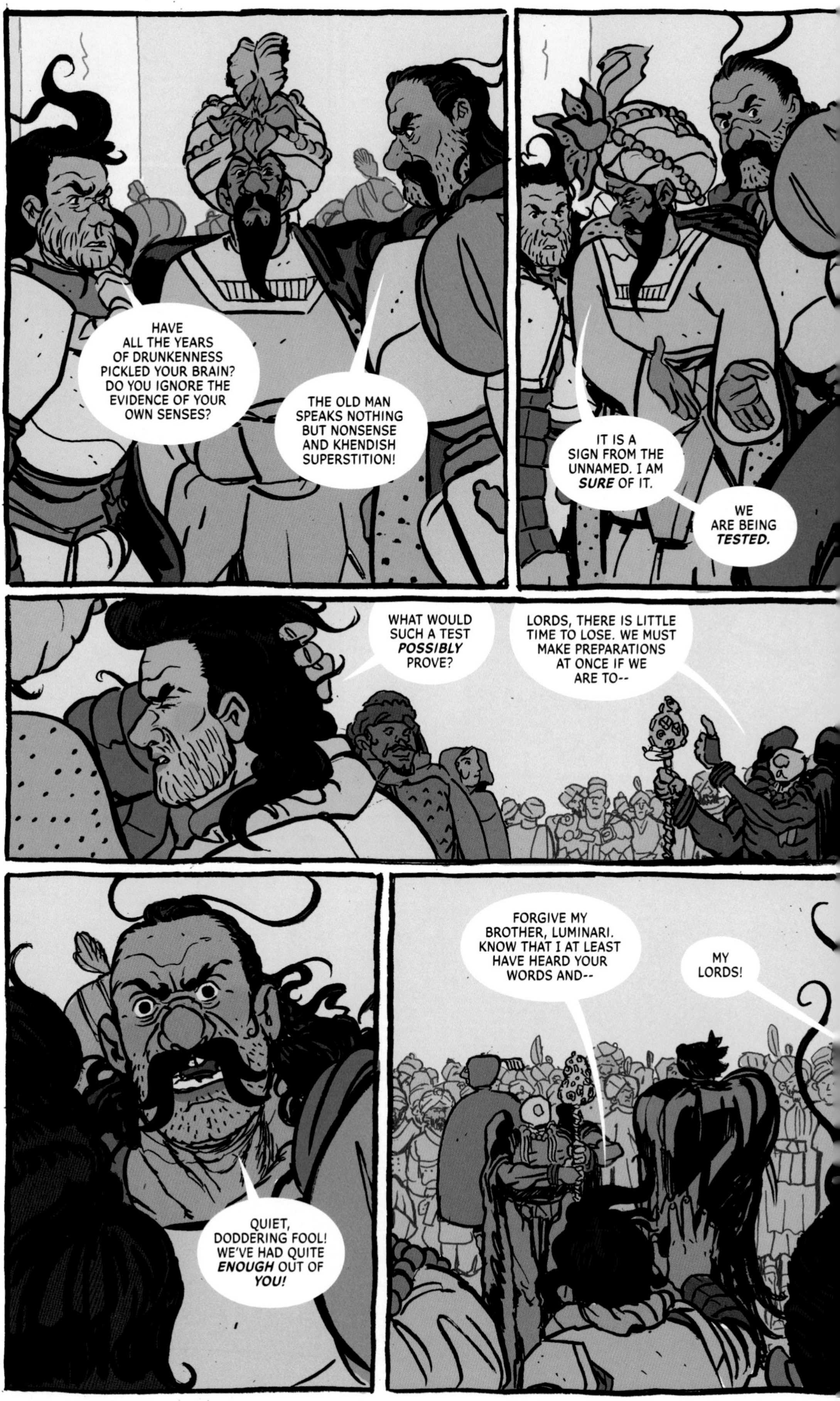
HAVE ALL THE YEARS OF DRUNKENNESS PICKLED YOUR BRAIN? DO YOU IGNORE THE EVIDENCE OF YOUR OWN SENSES?
THE OLD MAN SPEAKS NOTHING BUT NONSENSE AND KHENDISH SUPERSTITION!
IT IS A SIGN FROM THE UNNAMED. I AM *SURE* OF IT.
WE ARE BEING *TESTED.*
WHAT WOULD SUCH A TEST *POSSIBLY* PROVE?
LORDS, THERE IS LITTLE TIME TO LOSE. WE MUST MAKE PREPARATIONS AT ONCE IF WE ARE TO--
QUIET, DODDERING FOOL! WE'VE HAD QUITE *ENOUGH* OUT OF *YOU!*
FORGIVE MY BROTHER, LUMINARI. KNOW THAT I AT LEAST HAVE HEARD YOUR WORDS AND--
MY LORDS!

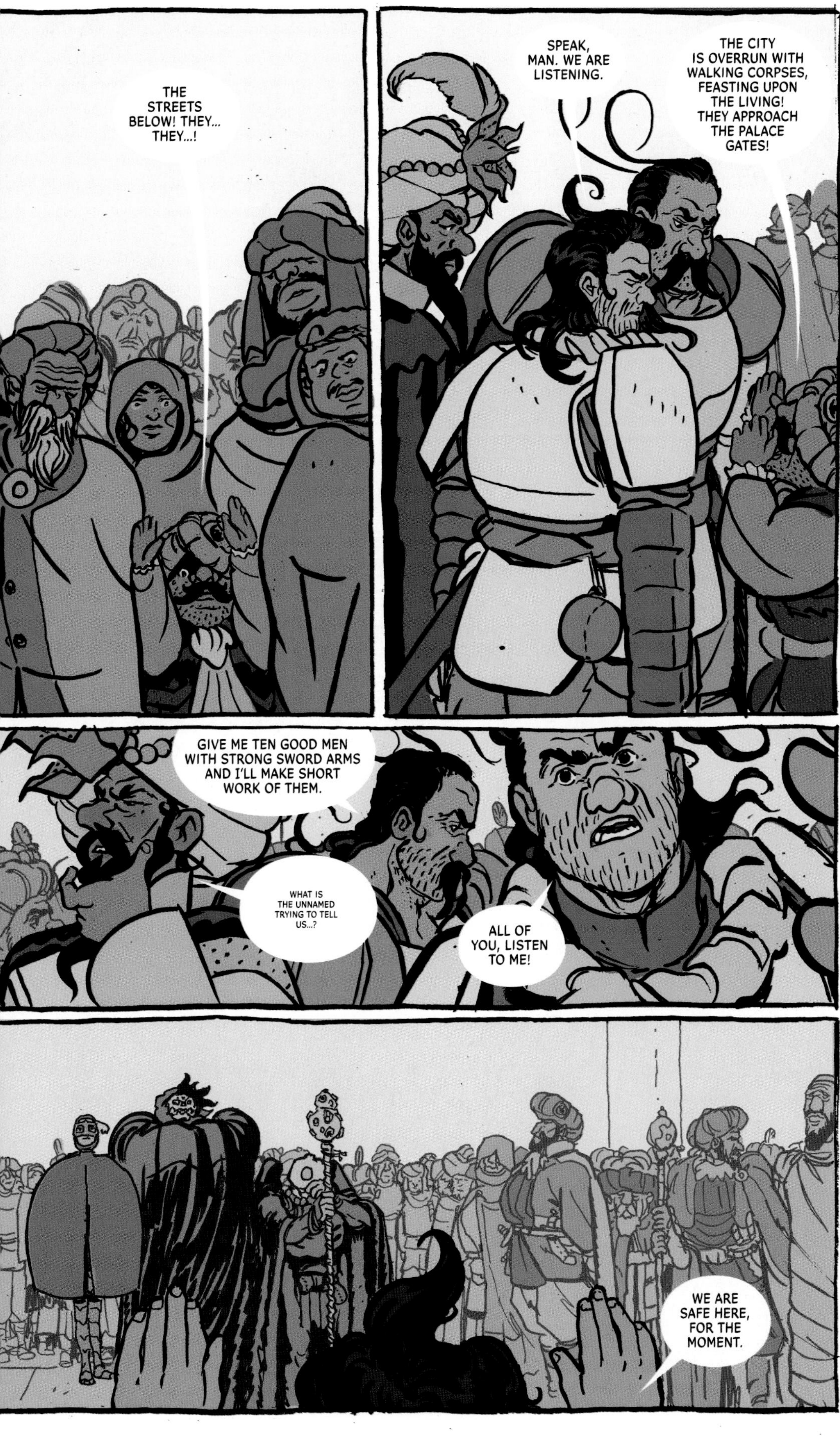
THE STREETS BELOW! THEY... THEY...!
SPEAK, MAN. WE ARE LISTENING.
THE CITY IS OVERRUN WITH WALKING CORPSES, FEASTING UPON THE LIVING! THEY APPROACH THE PALACE GATES!
GIVE ME TEN GOOD MEN WITH STRONG SWORD ARMS AND I'LL MAKE SHORT WORK OF THEM.
WHAT IS THE UNNAMED TRYING TO TELL US...?
ALL OF YOU, LISTEN TO ME!
WE ARE SAFE HERE, FOR THE MOMENT.

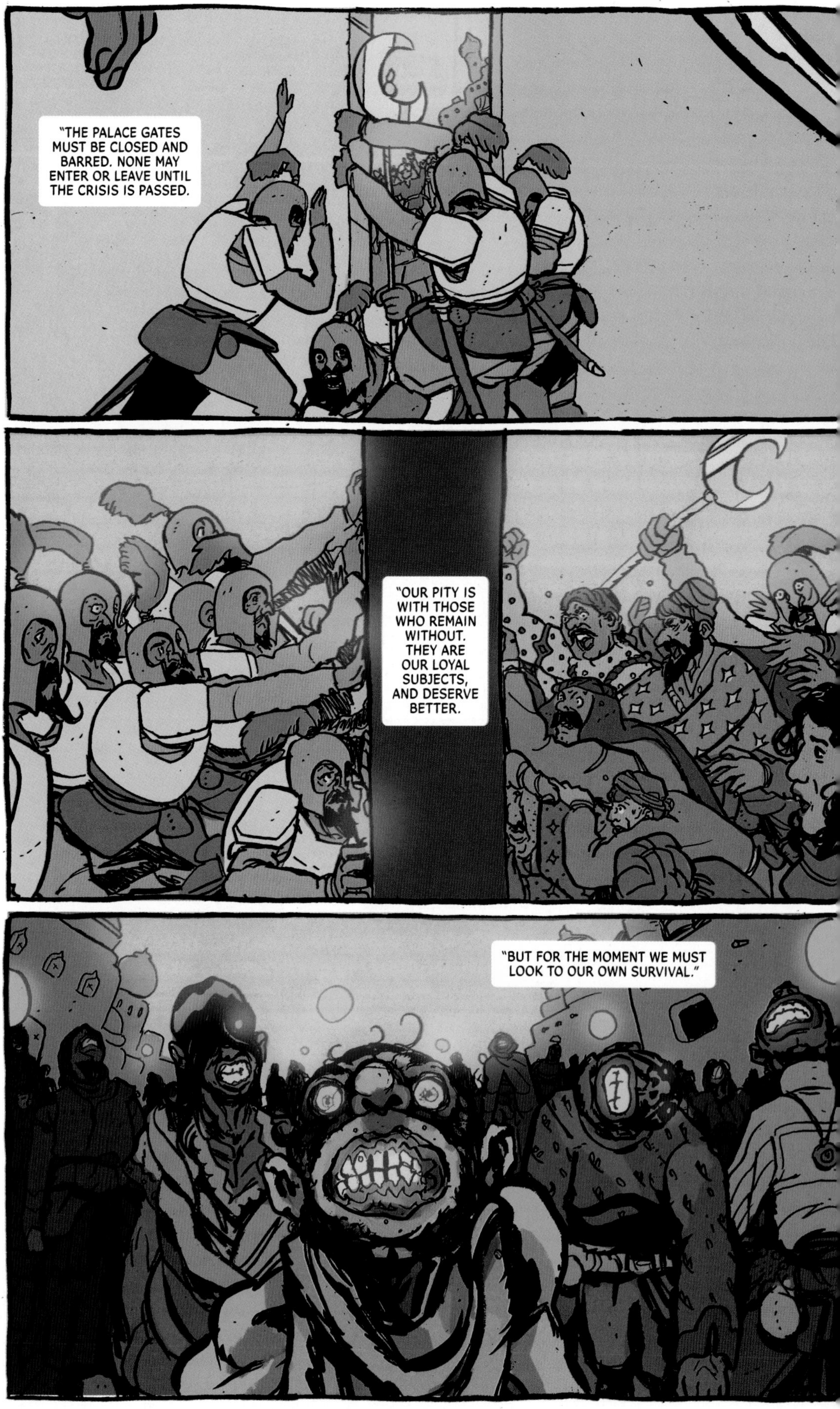
"THE PALACE GATES MUST BE CLOSED AND BARRED. NONE MAY ENTER OR LEAVE UNTIL THE CRISIS IS PASSED.
"OUR PITY IS WITH THOSE WHO REMAIN WITHOUT. THEY ARE OUR LOYAL SUBJECTS, AND DESERVE BETTER.
"BUT FOR THE MOMENT WE MUST LOOK TO OUR OWN SURVIVAL."

invaders

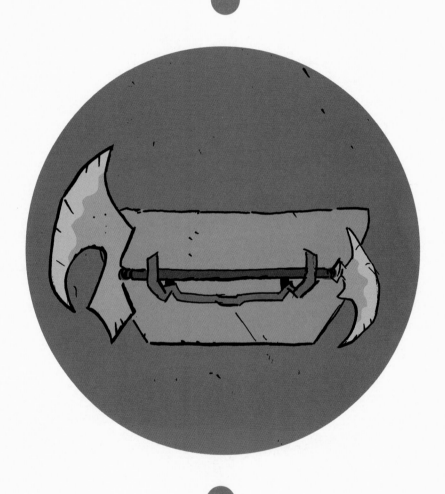

The Unnamed blessed us with victory that
we might serve Its greater glory, and to rule the
people of Khend wisely as The Messenger commands.
The Khendish are our responsibility, every bit as much
as the shepherd is responsible for his flock.

—Zalamgir the Conqueror

YOU CAN HEAR THEM SCREAMING, EVEN FROM UP HERE. WE CANNOT HIDE BEHIND THESE WALLS FOREVER.

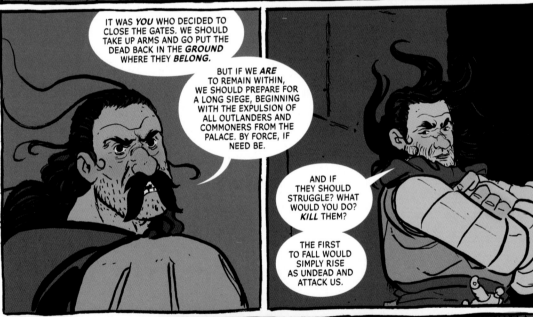

IT WAS *YOU* WHO DECIDED TO CLOSE THE GATES. WE SHOULD TAKE UP ARMS AND GO PUT THE DEAD BACK IN THE *GROUND* WHERE THEY *BELONG.*

BUT IF WE *ARE* TO REMAIN WITHIN, WE SHOULD PREPARE FOR A LONG SIEGE, BEGINNING WITH THE EXPULSION OF ALL OUTLANDERS AND COMMONERS FROM THE PALACE. BY FORCE, IF NEED BE.

AND IF THEY SHOULD STRUGGLE? WHAT WOULD YOU DO? *KILL* THEM?

THE FIRST TO FALL WOULD SIMPLY RISE AS UNDEAD AND ATTACK US.

THE PROPER RESPONSE SHOULD BE *PRAYER,* ENTREATING THE UNNAMED TO AID US.

SURELY *SOMEWHERE* IN THE WRITINGS OF BAQHIR THERE IS JUST THE INVOCATION THAT WE NEED, SOMETHING IN THE RITES OF BURIAL PERHAPS?

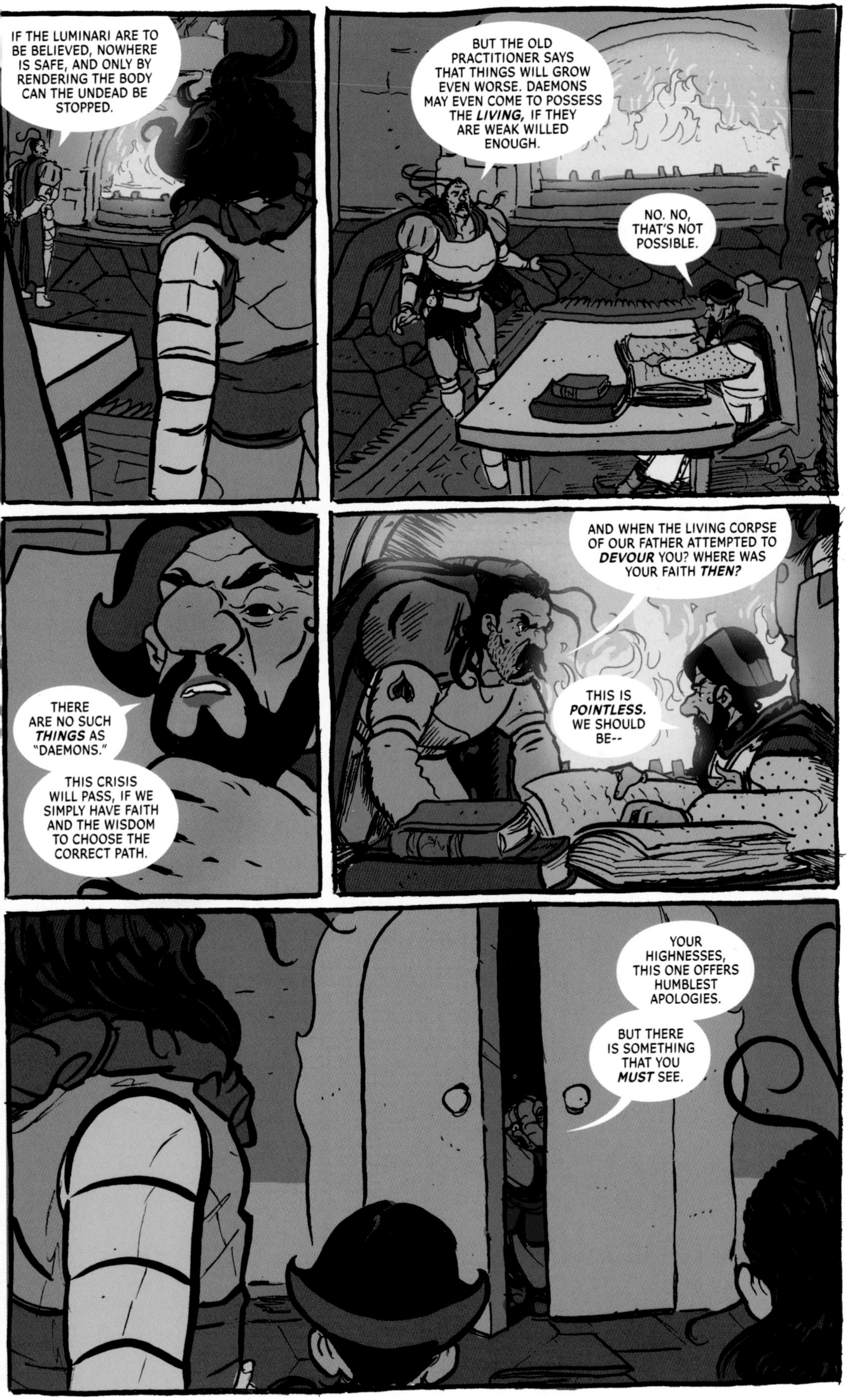
IF THE LUMINARI ARE TO BE BELIEVED, NOWHERE IS SAFE, AND ONLY BY RENDERING THE BODY CAN THE UNDEAD BE STOPPED.
BUT THE OLD PRACTITIONER SAYS THAT THINGS WILL GROW EVEN WORSE. DAEMONS MAY EVEN COME TO POSSESS THE *LIVING,* IF THEY ARE WEAK WILLED ENOUGH.
NO. NO, THAT'S NOT POSSIBLE.
THERE ARE NO SUCH *THINGS* AS "DAEMONS."
THIS CRISIS WILL PASS, IF WE SIMPLY HAVE FAITH AND THE WISDOM TO CHOOSE THE CORRECT PATH.
AND WHEN THE LIVING CORPSE OF OUR FATHER ATTEMPTED TO *DEVOUR* YOU? WHERE WAS YOUR FAITH *THEN?*
THIS IS *POINTLESS.* WE SHOULD BE--
YOUR HIGHNESSES, THIS ONE OFFERS HUMBLEST APOLOGIES.
BUT THERE IS SOMETHING THAT YOU *MUST* SEE.

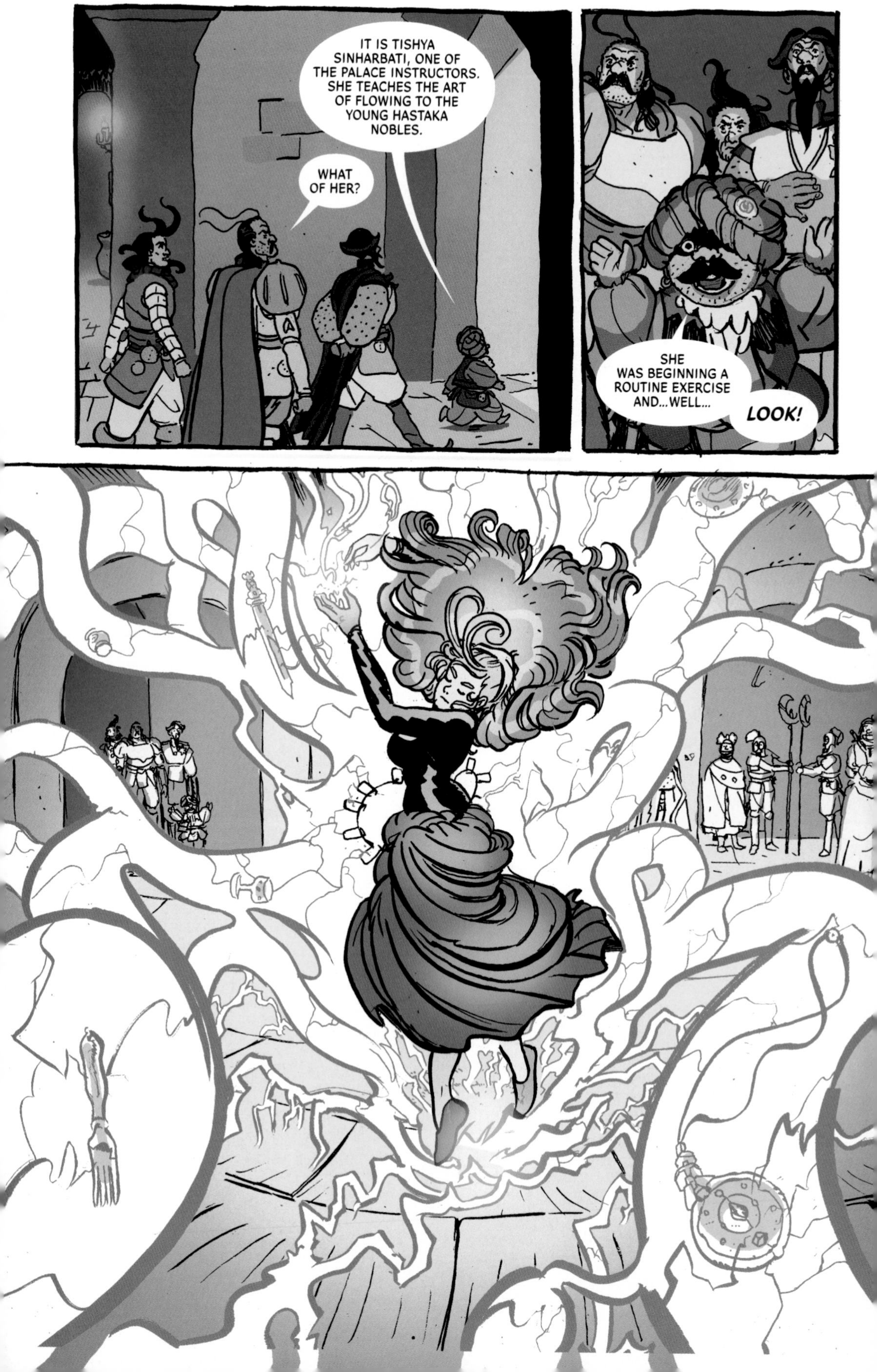
IT IS TISHYA SINHARBATI, ONE OF THE PALACE INSTRUCTORS. SHE TEACHES THE ART OF FLOWING TO THE YOUNG HASTAKA NOBLES.
WHAT OF HER?
SHE WAS BEGINNING A ROUTINE EXERCISE AND...WELL...
LOOK!

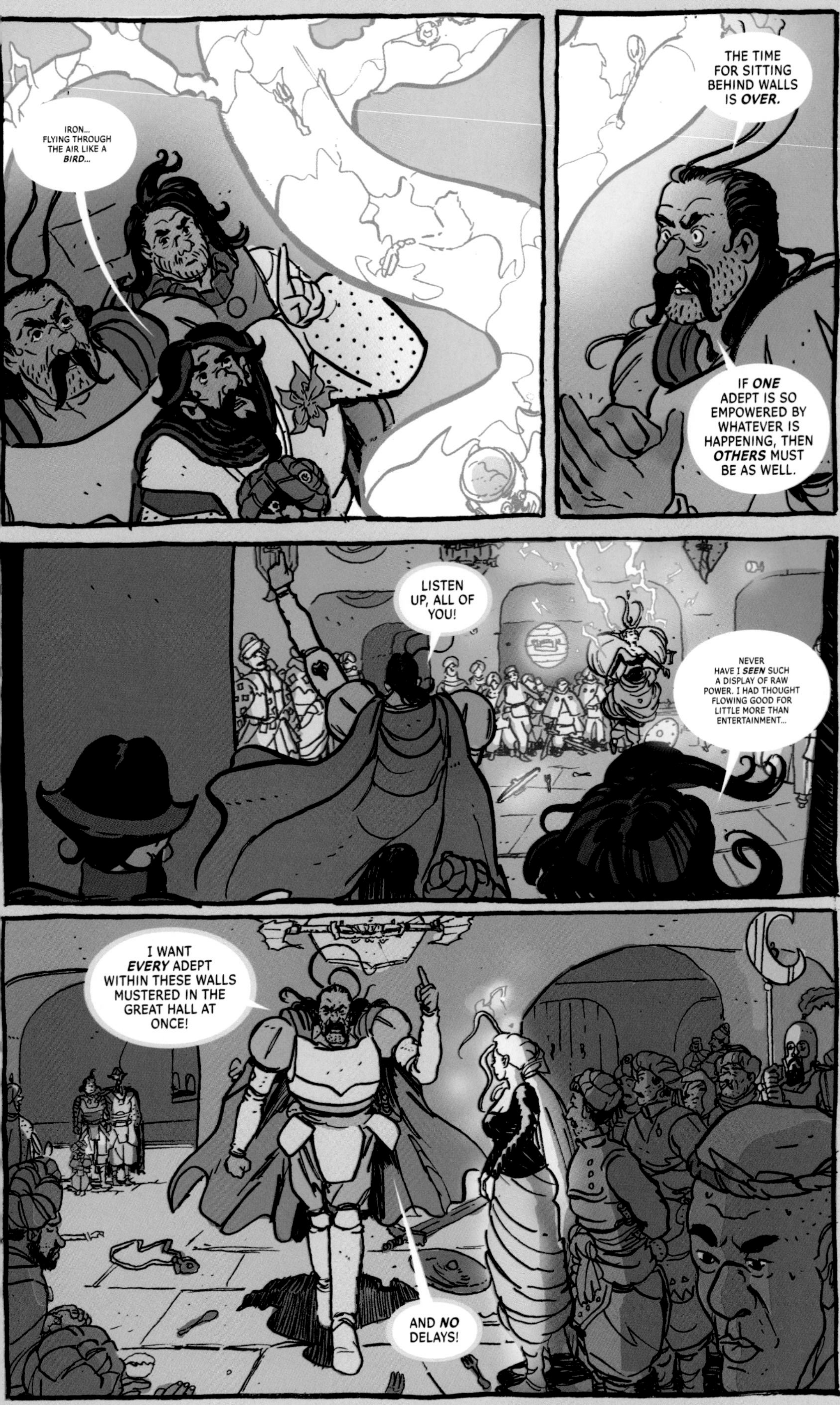
IRON... FLYING THROUGH THE AIR LIKE A *BIRD...*
THE TIME FOR SITTING BEHIND WALLS IS ***OVER.***
IF ***ONE*** ADEPT IS SO EMPOWERED BY WHATEVER IS HAPPENING, THEN ***OTHERS*** MUST BE AS WELL.
LISTEN UP, ALL OF YOU!
NEVER HAVE I ***SEEN*** SUCH A DISPLAY OF RAW POWER. I HAD THOUGHT FLOWING GOOD FOR LITTLE MORE THAN ENTERTAINMENT...
I WANT ***EVERY*** ADEPT WITHIN THESE WALLS MUSTERED IN THE GREAT HALL AT ONCE!
AND ***NO*** DELAYS!

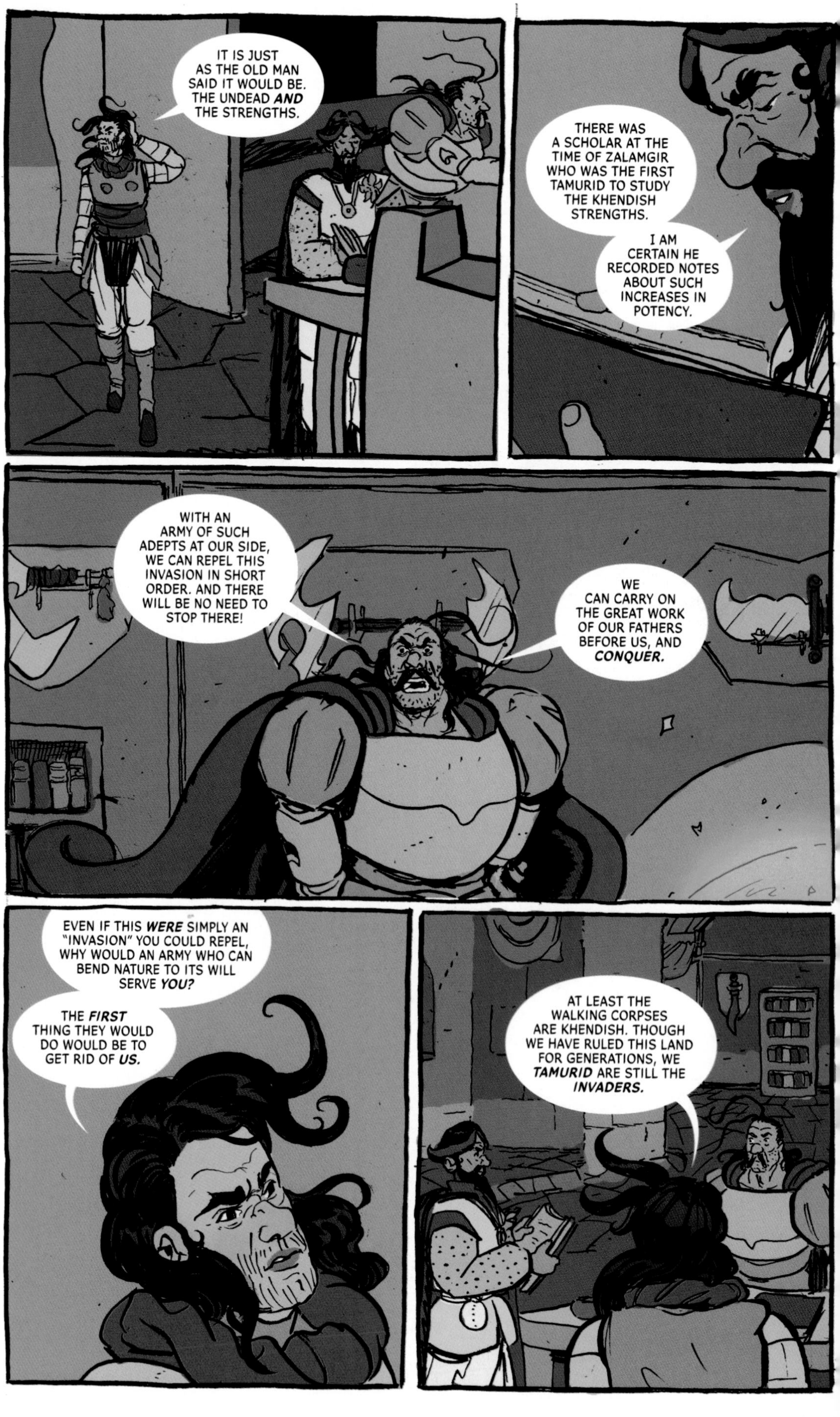
IT IS JUST AS THE OLD MAN SAID IT WOULD BE. THE UNDEAD AND THE STRENGTHS.
THERE WAS A SCHOLAR AT THE TIME OF ZALAMGIR WHO WAS THE FIRST TAMURID TO STUDY THE KHENDISH STRENGTHS.
I AM CERTAIN HE RECORDED NOTES ABOUT SUCH INCREASES IN POTENCY.
WITH AN ARMY OF SUCH ADEPTS AT OUR SIDE, WE CAN REPEL THIS INVASION IN SHORT ORDER. AND THERE WILL BE NO NEED TO STOP THERE!
WE CAN CARRY ON THE GREAT WORK OF OUR FATHERS BEFORE US, AND CONQUER.
EVEN IF THIS WERE SIMPLY AN "INVASION" YOU COULD REPEL, WHY WOULD AN ARMY WHO CAN BEND NATURE TO ITS WILL SERVE YOU?
THE FIRST THING THEY WOULD DO WOULD BE TO GET RID OF US.
AT LEAST THE WALKING CORPSES ARE KHENDISH. THOUGH WE HAVE RULED THIS LAND FOR GENERATIONS, WE TAMURID ARE STILL THE INVADERS.

heights

I need to gain new perspectives if I'm to make any sense of what is happening here.

—Pol Ravenstone's
private journal

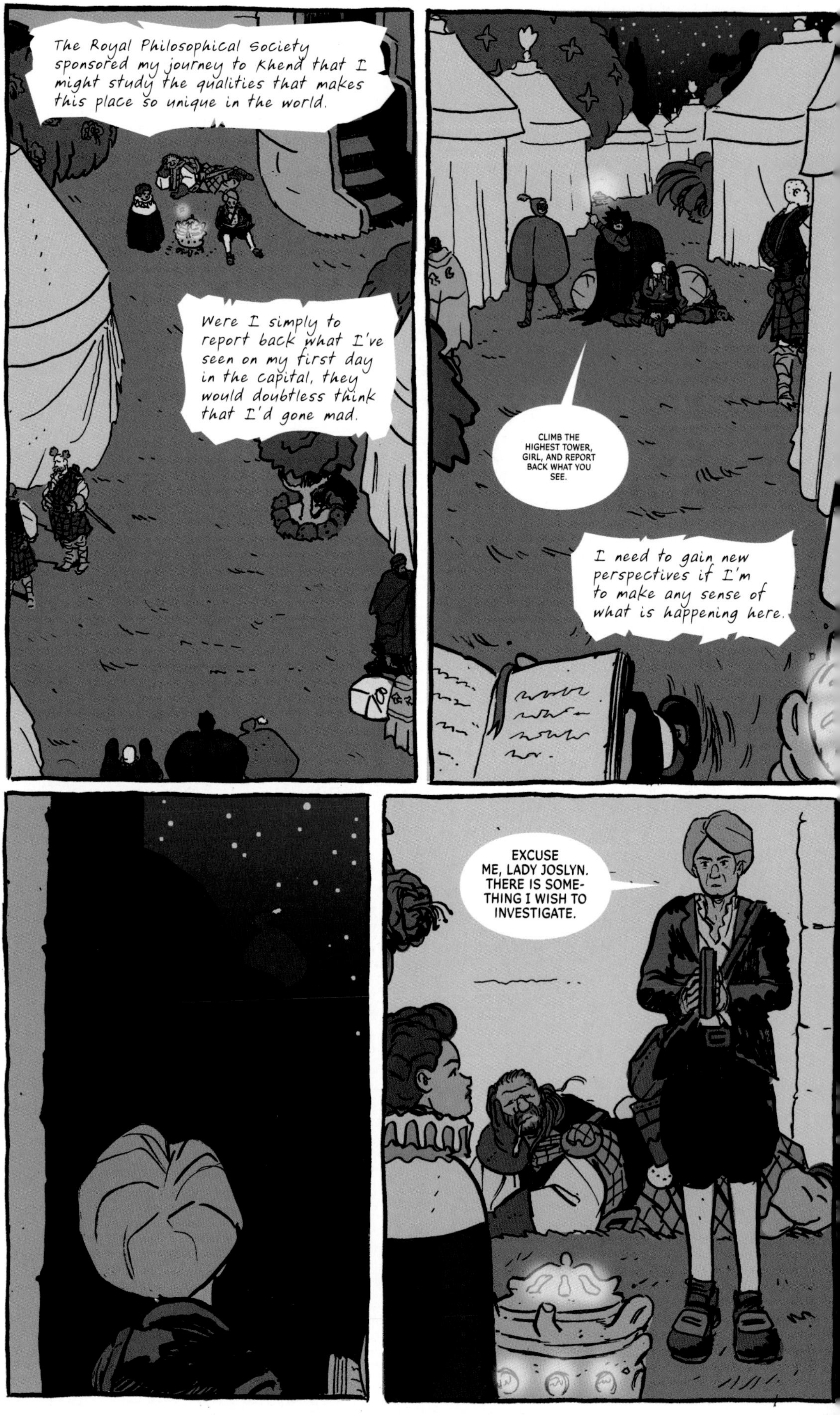

The Royal Philosophical Society sponsored my journey to Khend that I might study the qualities that makes this place so unique in the world.
Were I simply to report back what I've seen on my first day in the capital, they would doubtless think that I'd gone mad.
CLIMB THE HIGHEST TOWER, GIRL, AND REPORT BACK WHAT YOU SEE.
I need to gain new perspectives if I'm to make any sense of what is happening here.
EXCUSE ME, LADY JOSLYN. THERE IS SOMETHING I WISH TO INVESTIGATE.

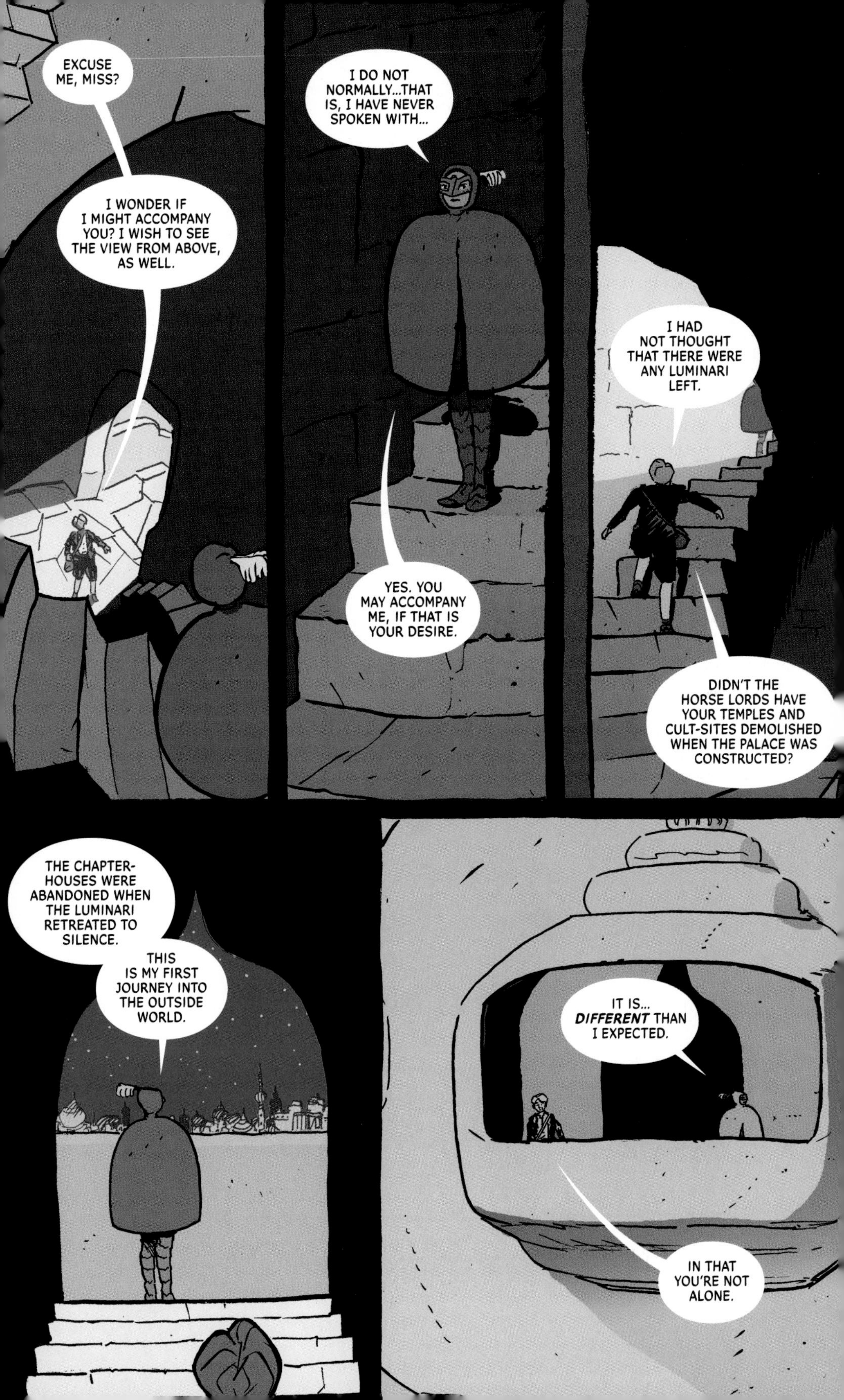
EXCUSE ME, MISS?
I WONDER IF I MIGHT ACCOMPANY YOU? I WISH TO SEE THE VIEW FROM ABOVE, AS WELL.
I DO NOT NORMALLY...THAT IS, I HAVE NEVER SPOKEN WITH...
YES. YOU MAY ACCOMPANY ME, IF THAT IS YOUR DESIRE.
I HAD NOT THOUGHT THAT THERE WERE ANY LUMINARI LEFT.
DIDN'T THE HORSE LORDS HAVE YOUR TEMPLES AND CULT-SITES DEMOLISHED WHEN THE PALACE WAS CONSTRUCTED?
THE CHAPTER-HOUSES WERE ABANDONED WHEN THE LUMINARI RETREATED TO SILENCE.
THIS IS MY FIRST JOURNEY INTO THE OUTSIDE WORLD.
IT IS... ***DIFFERENT*** THAN I EXPECTED.
IN THAT YOU'RE NOT ALONE.

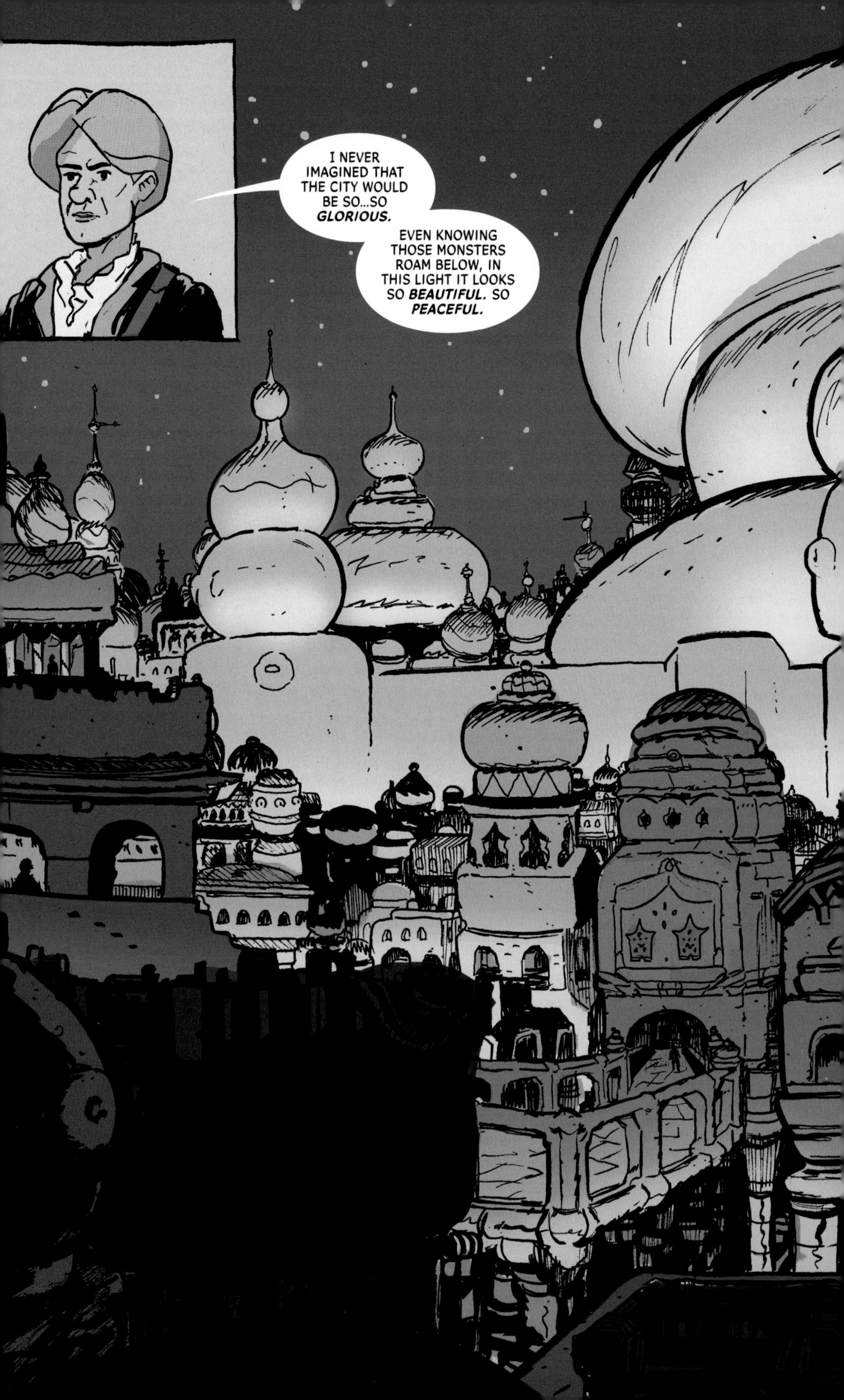
I NEVER IMAGINED THAT THE CITY WOULD BE SO...SO *GLORIOUS.*
EVEN KNOWING THOSE MONSTERS ROAM BELOW, IN THIS LIGHT IT LOOKS SO *BEAUTIFUL.* SO *PEACEFUL.*

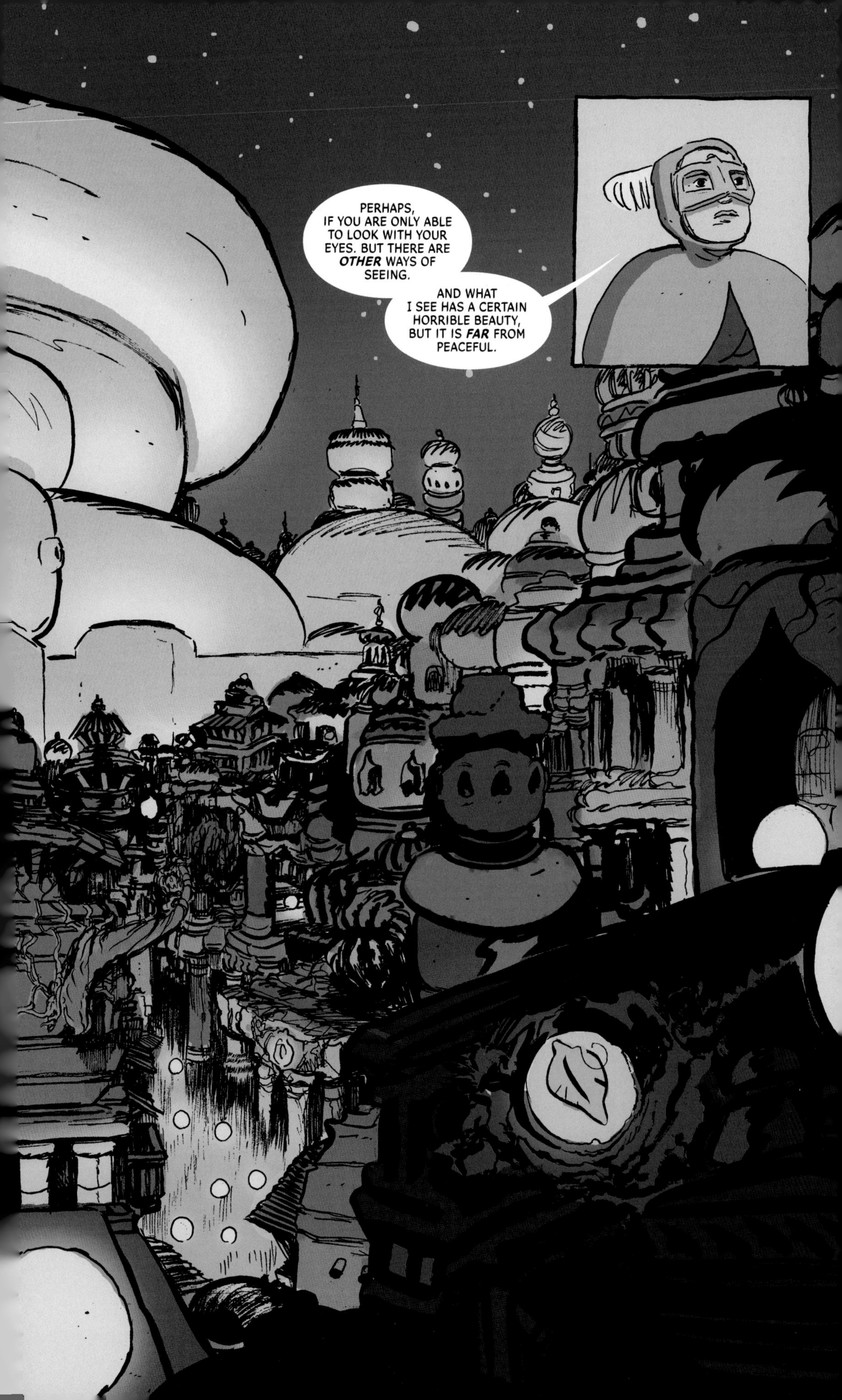

PERHAPS, IF YOU ARE ONLY ABLE TO LOOK WITH YOUR EYES. BUT THERE ARE *OTHER* WAYS OF SEEING.
AND WHAT I SEE HAS A CERTAIN HORRIBLE BEAUTY, BUT IT IS *FAR* FROM PEACEFUL.

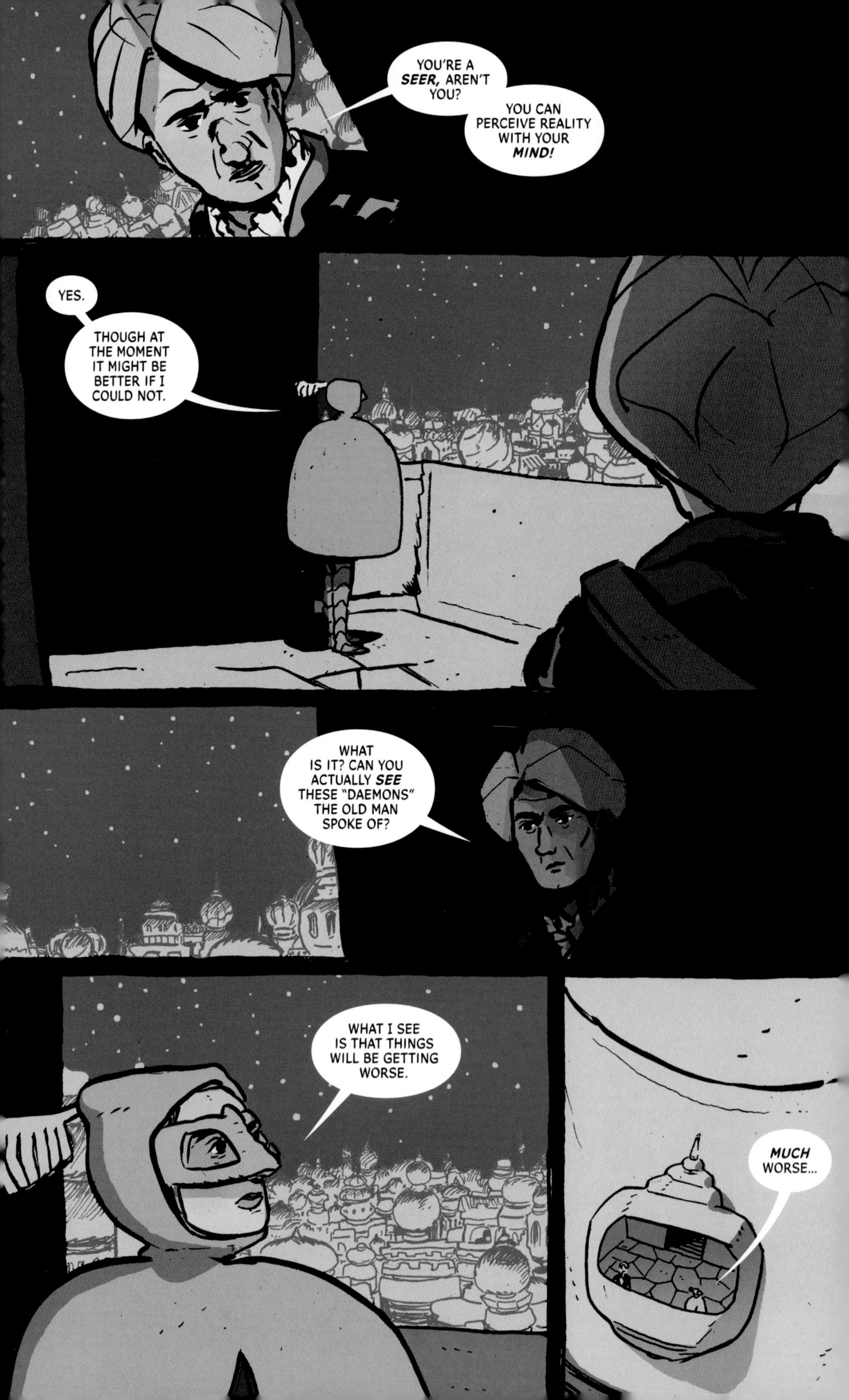
YOU'RE A *SEER,* AREN'T YOU?
YOU CAN PERCEIVE REALITY WITH YOUR *MIND!*
YES.
THOUGH AT THE MOMENT IT MIGHT BE BETTER IF I COULD NOT.
WHAT IS IT? CAN YOU ACTUALLY *SEE* THESE "DAEMONS" THE OLD MAN SPOKE OF?
WHAT I SEE IS THAT THINGS WILL BE GETTING WORSE.
MUCH WORSE...

incarnate

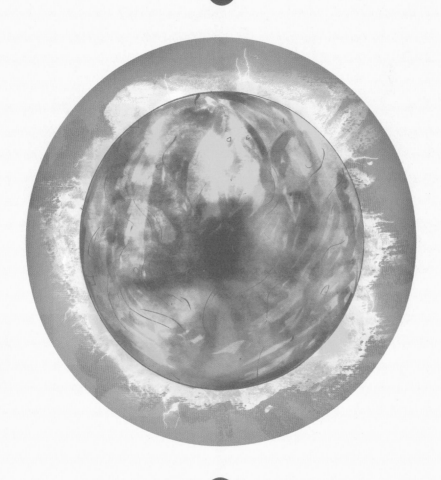

To build, it is often necessary first to destroy.

—Traditional Padara
caste saying

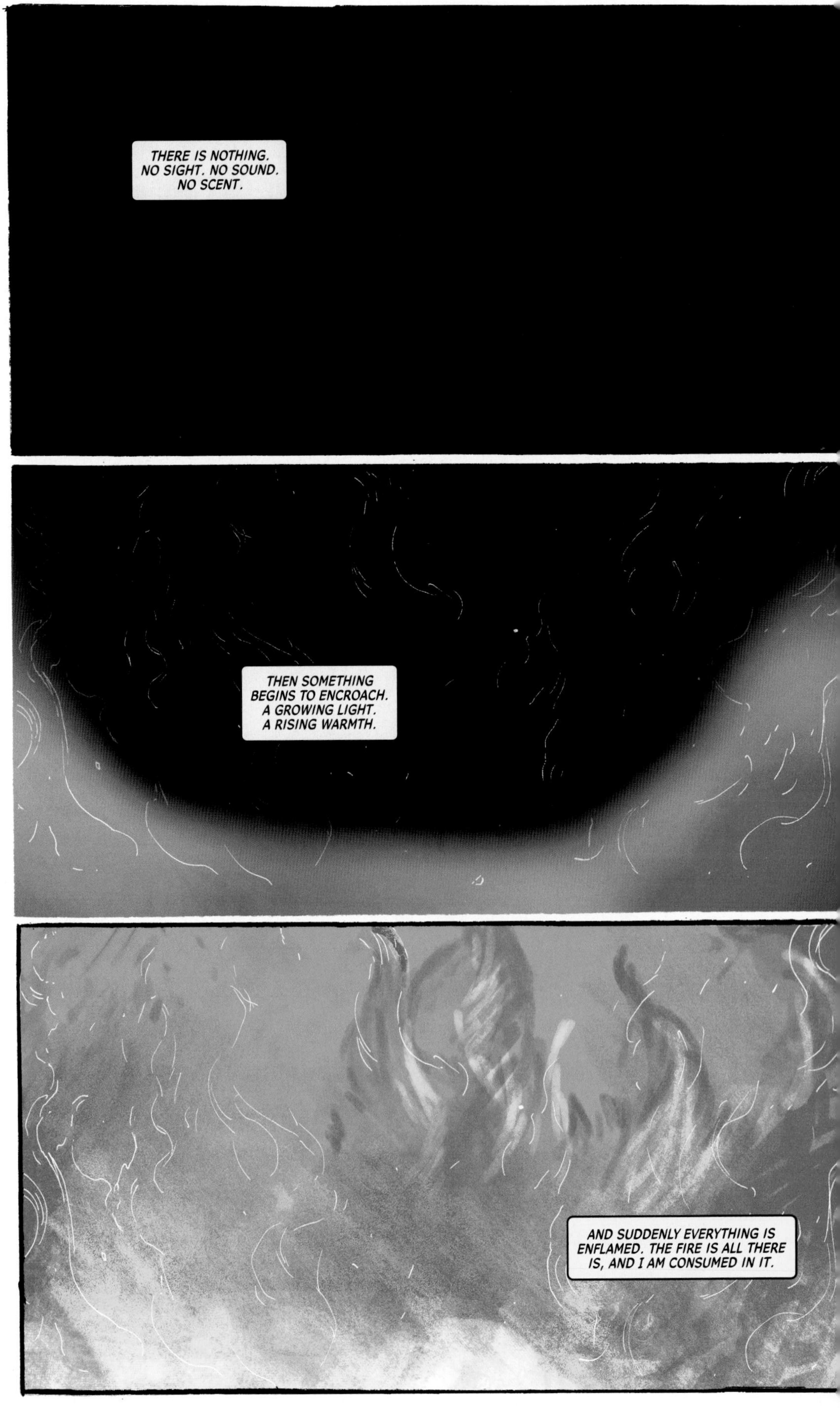
THERE IS NOTHING. NO SIGHT. NO SOUND. NO SCENT.
THEN SOMETHING BEGINS TO ENCROACH. A GROWING LIGHT. A RISING WARMTH.
AND SUDDENLY EVERYTHING IS ENFLAMED. THE FIRE IS ALL THERE IS, AND I AM CONSUMED IN IT.

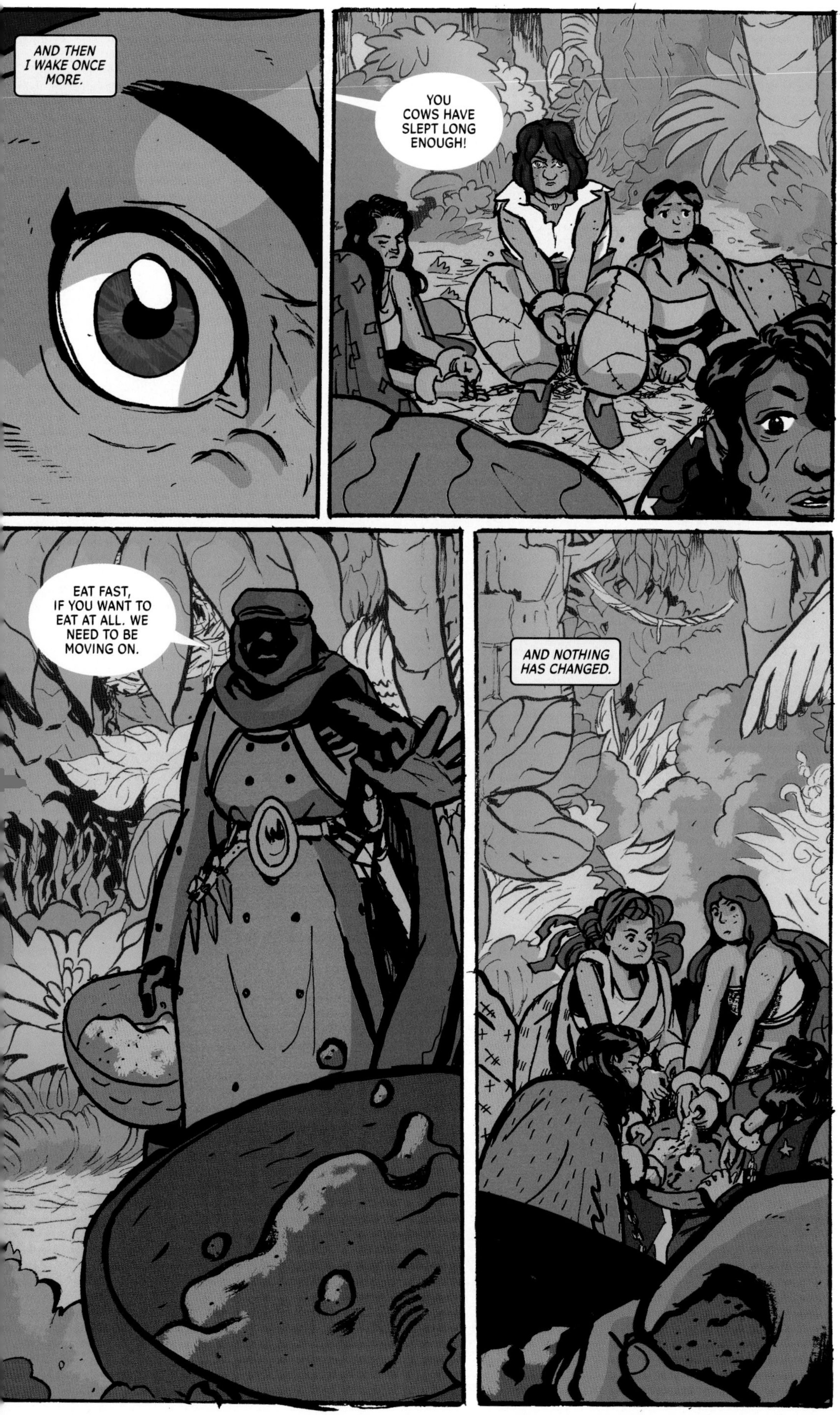
AND THEN I WAKE ONCE MORE.
YOU COWS HAVE SLEPT LONG ENOUGH!
EAT FAST, IF YOU WANT TO EAT AT ALL. WE NEED TO BE MOVING ON.
AND NOTHING HAS CHANGED.

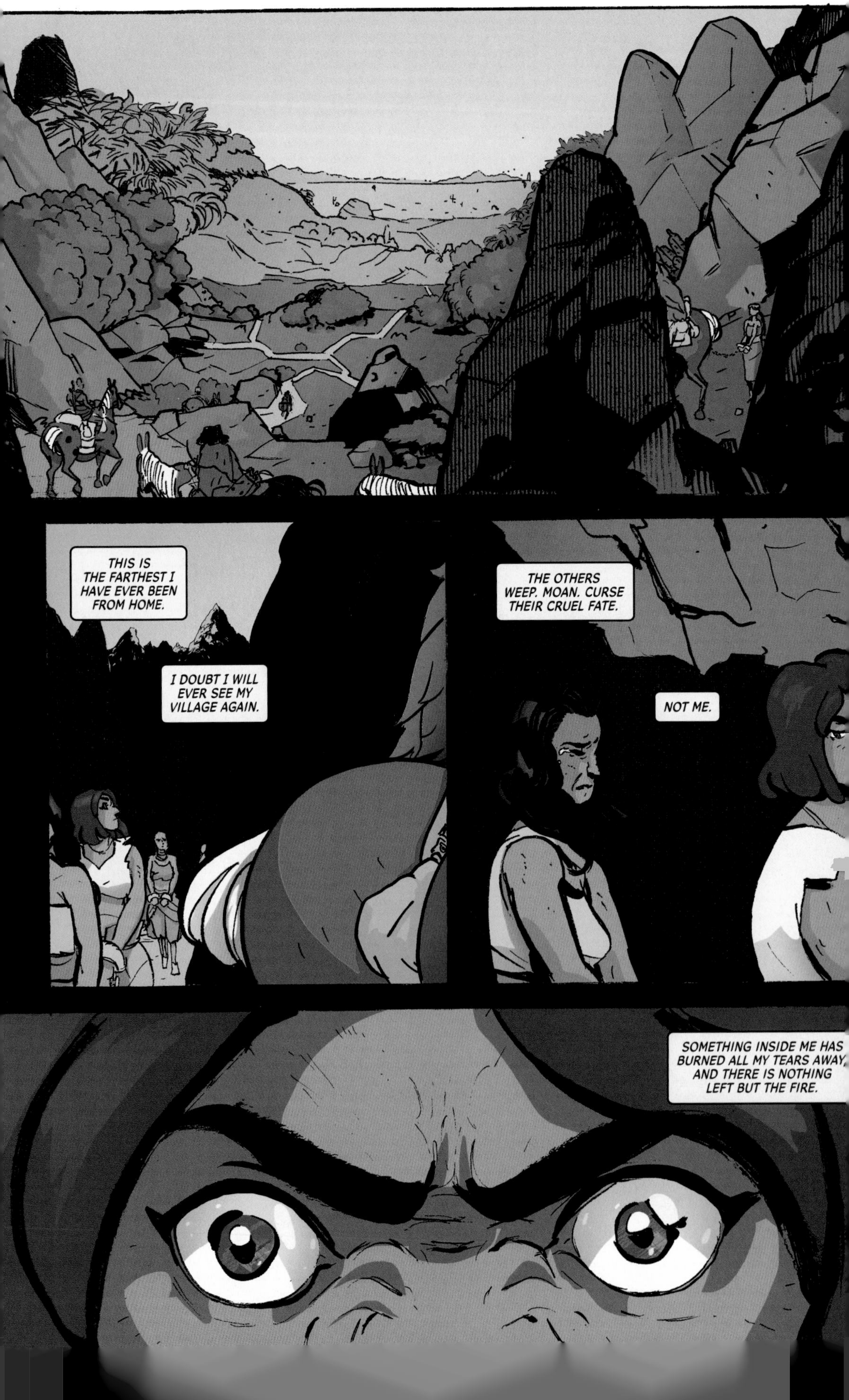

THIS IS THE FARTHEST I HAVE EVER BEEN FROM HOME.
I DOUBT I WILL EVER SEE MY VILLAGE AGAIN.
THE OTHERS WEEP. MOAN. CURSE THEIR CRUEL FATE.
NOT ME.
SOMETHING INSIDE ME HAS BURNED ALL MY TEARS AWAY, AND THERE IS NOTHING LEFT BUT THE FIRE.

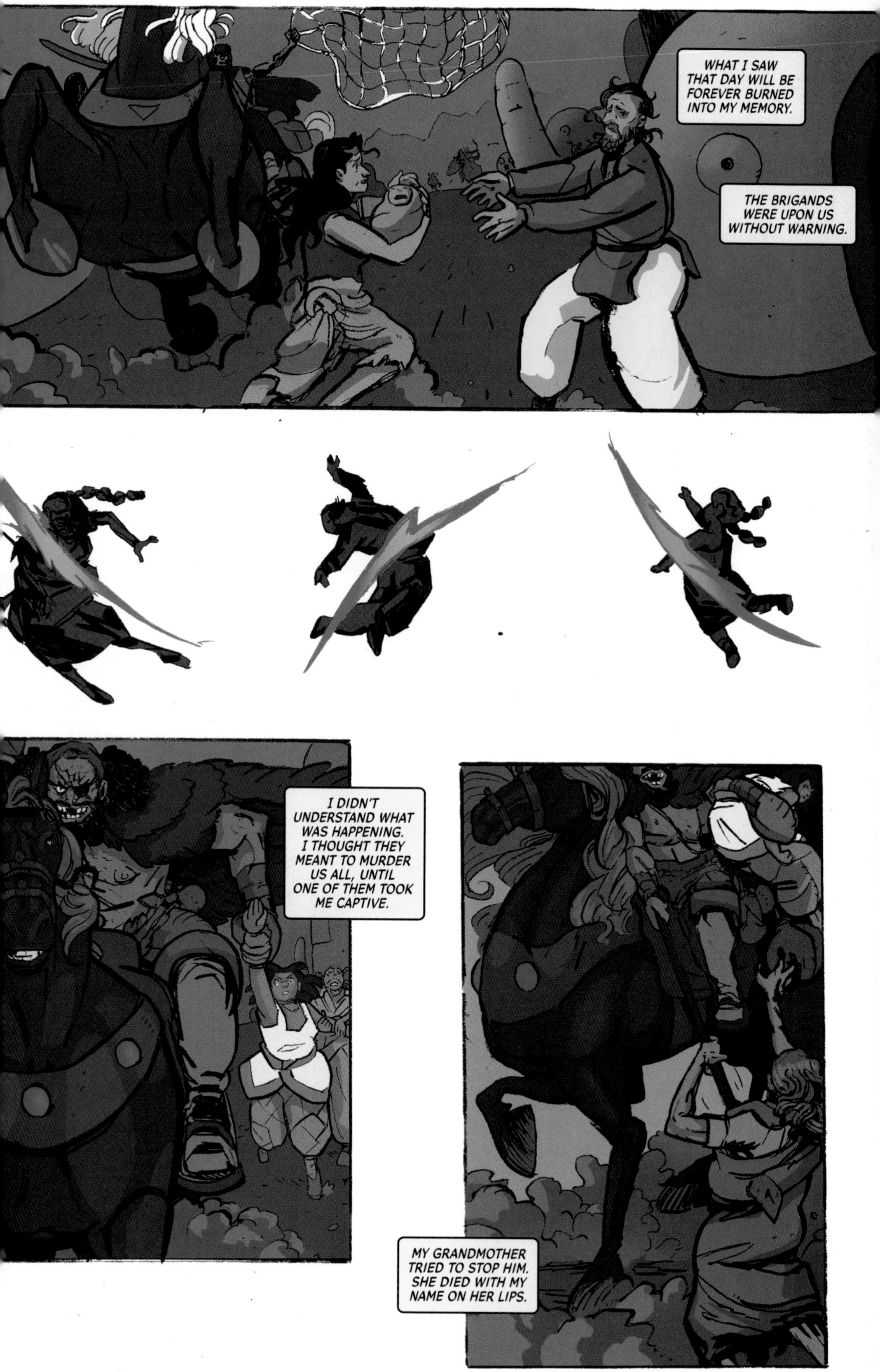
WHAT I SAW THAT DAY WILL BE FOREVER BURNED INTO MY MEMORY.
THE BRIGANDS WERE UPON US WITHOUT WARNING.
I DIDN'T UNDERSTAND WHAT WAS HAPPENING. I THOUGHT THEY MEANT TO MURDER US ALL, UNTIL ONE OF THEM TOOK ME CAPTIVE.
MY GRANDMOTHER TRIED TO STOP HIM. SHE DIED WITH MY NAME ON HER LIPS.

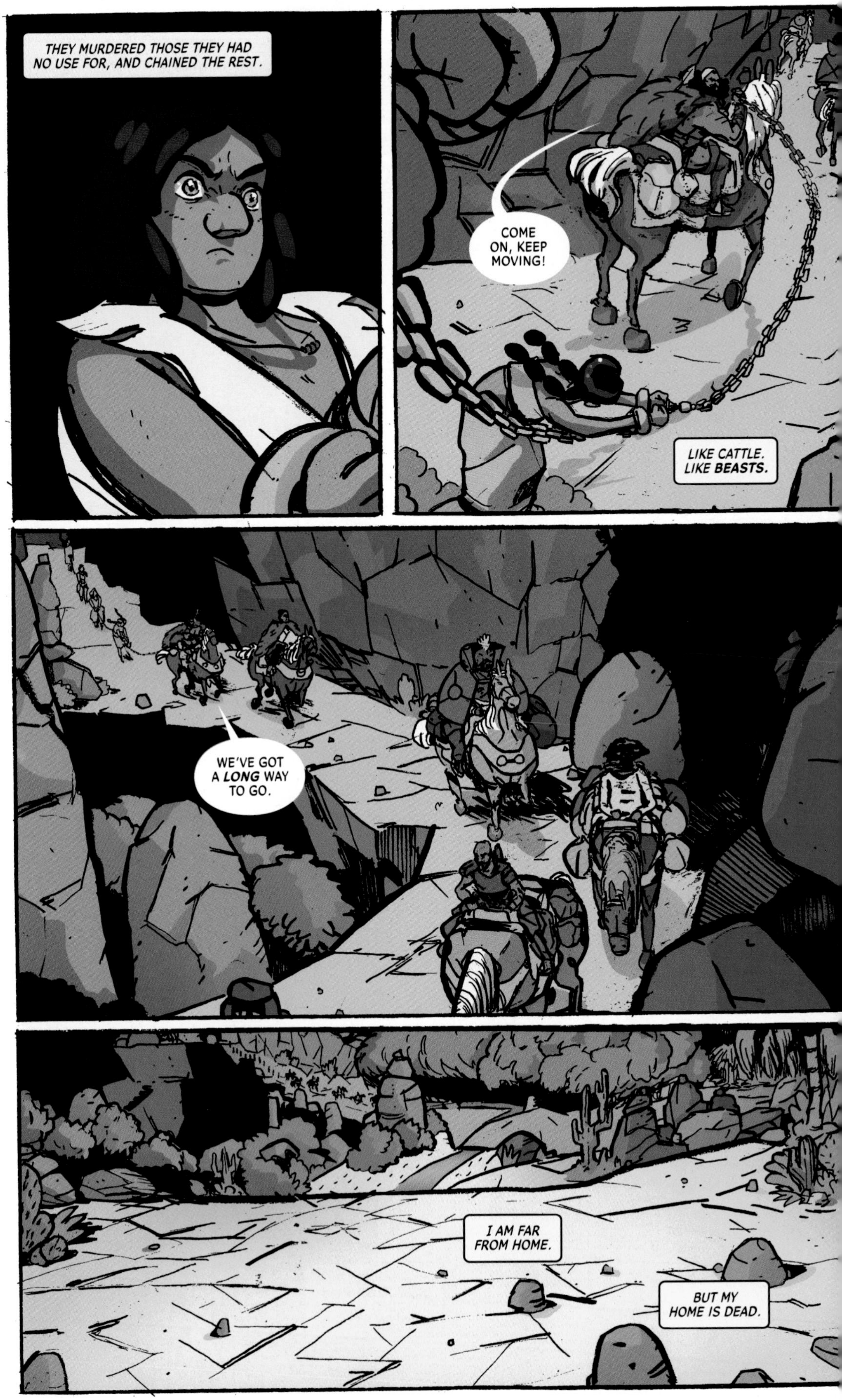

THEY MURDERED THOSE THEY HAD NO USE FOR, AND CHAINED THE REST.
COME ON, KEEP MOVING!
LIKE CATTLE. LIKE **BEASTS.**
WE'VE GOT A **LONG** WAY TO GO.
I AM FAR FROM HOME.
BUT MY HOME IS DEAD.

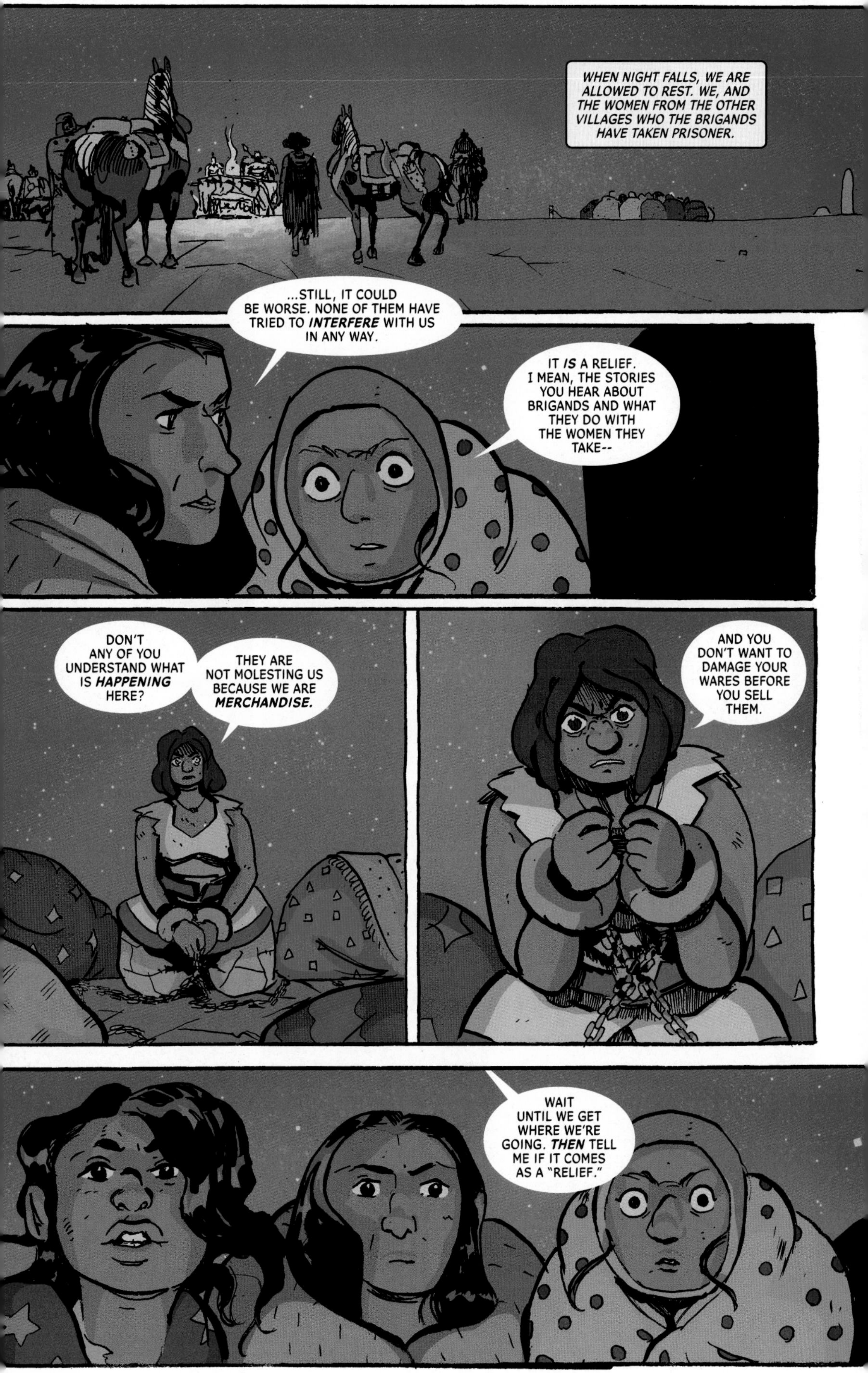
WHEN NIGHT FALLS, WE ARE ALLOWED TO REST. WE, AND THE WOMEN FROM THE OTHER VILLAGES WHO THE BRIGANDS HAVE TAKEN PRISONER.
...STILL, IT COULD BE WORSE. NONE OF THEM HAVE TRIED TO *INTERFERE* WITH US IN ANY WAY.
IT *IS* A RELIEF. I MEAN, THE STORIES YOU HEAR ABOUT BRIGANDS AND WHAT THEY DO WITH THE WOMEN THEY TAKE--
DON'T ANY OF YOU UNDERSTAND WHAT IS *HAPPENING* HERE?
THEY ARE NOT MOLESTING US BECAUSE WE ARE *MERCHANDISE.*
AND YOU DON'T WANT TO DAMAGE YOUR WARES BEFORE YOU SELL THEM.
WAIT UNTIL WE GET WHERE WE'RE GOING. *THEN* TELL ME IF IT COMES AS A "RELIEF."

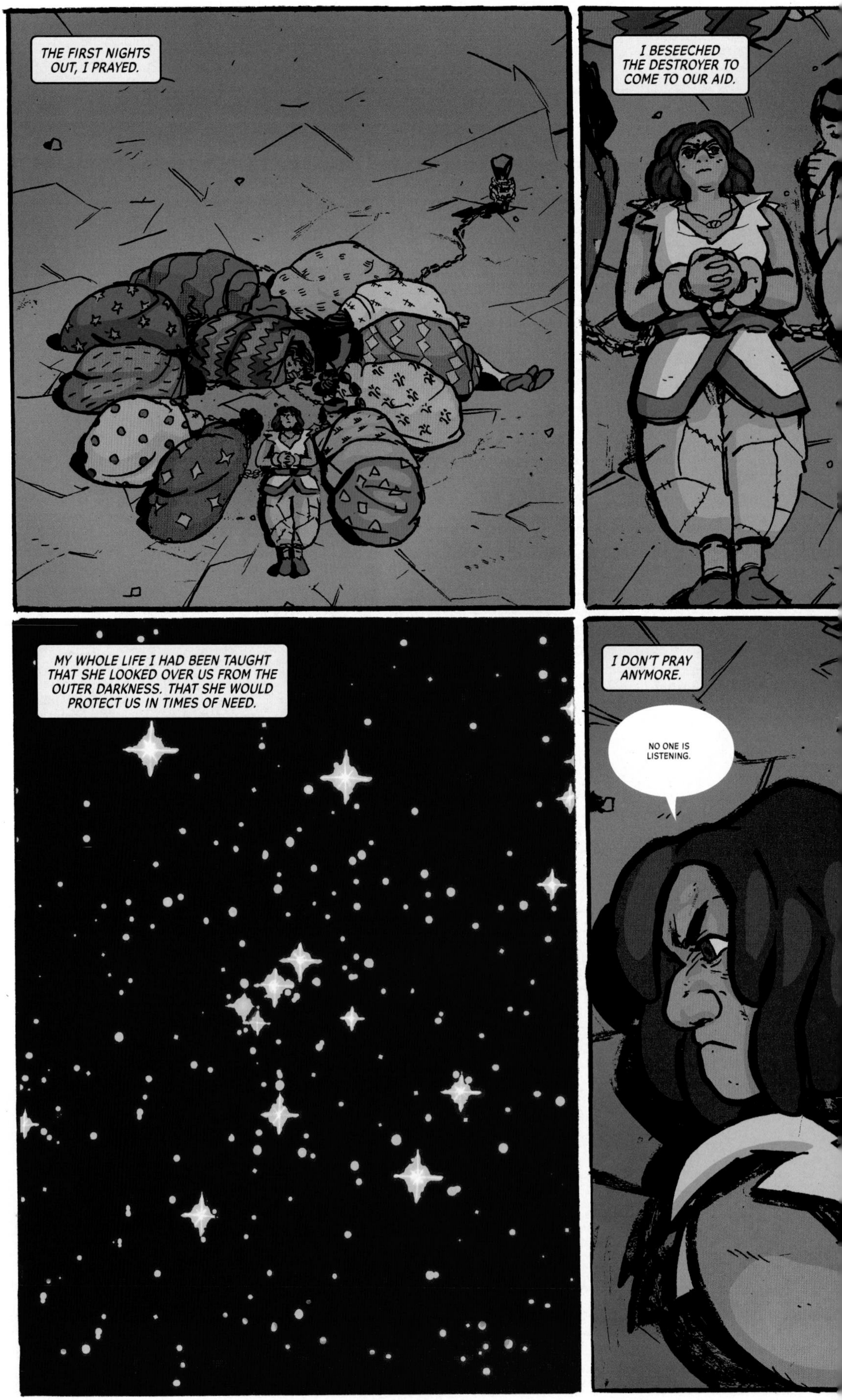
THE FIRST NIGHTS OUT, I PRAYED.
I BESEECHED THE DESTROYER TO COME TO OUR AID.
MY WHOLE LIFE I HAD BEEN TAUGHT THAT SHE LOOKED OVER US FROM THE OUTER DARKNESS. THAT SHE WOULD PROTECT US IN TIMES OF NEED.
I DON'T PRAY ANYMORE.
NO ONE IS LISTENING.

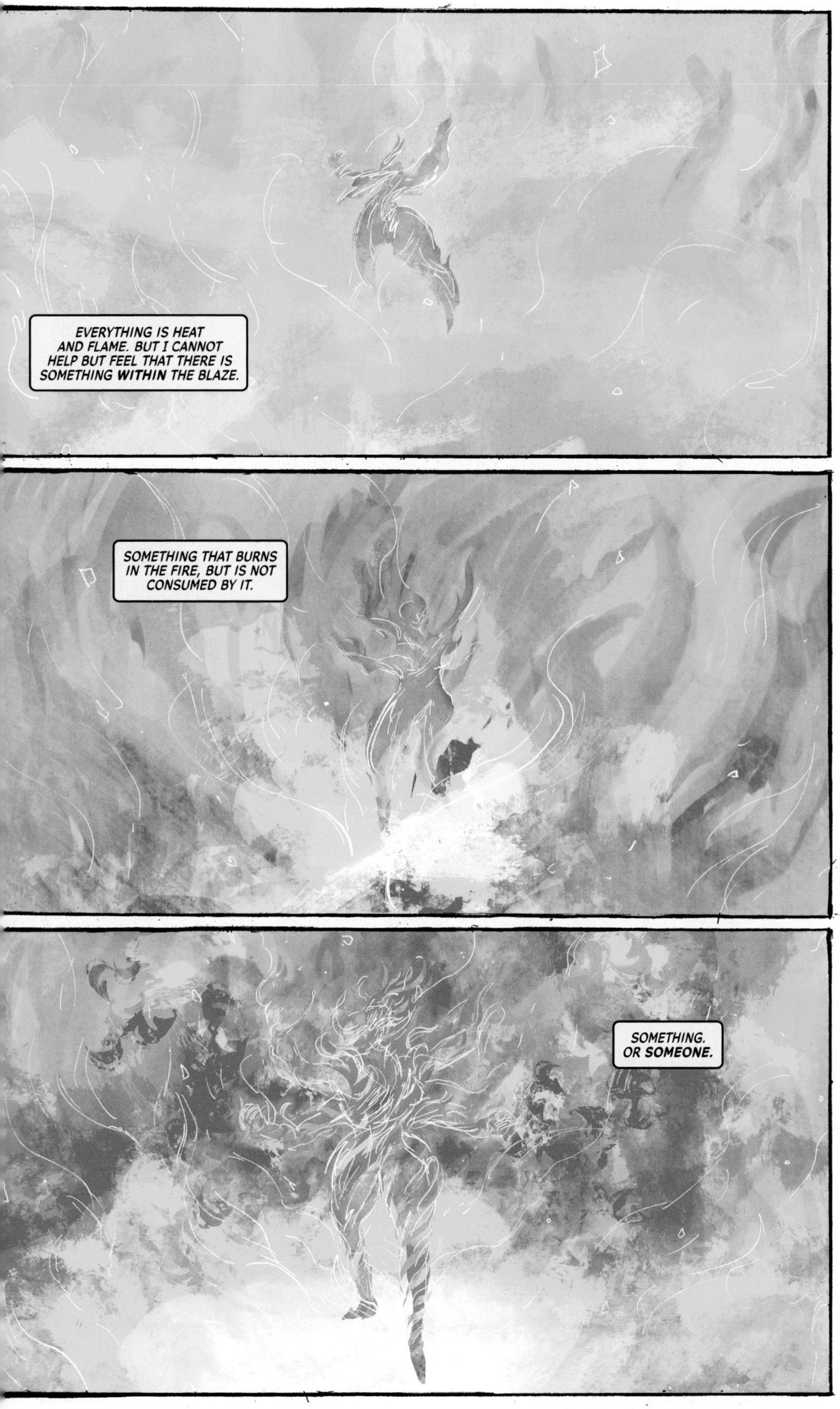

EVERYTHING IS HEAT AND FLAME. BUT I CANNOT HELP BUT FEEL THAT THERE IS SOMETHING **WITHIN** THE BLAZE.
SOMETHING THAT BURNS IN THE FIRE, BUT IS NOT CONSUMED BY IT.
SOMETHING. OR **SOMEONE.**

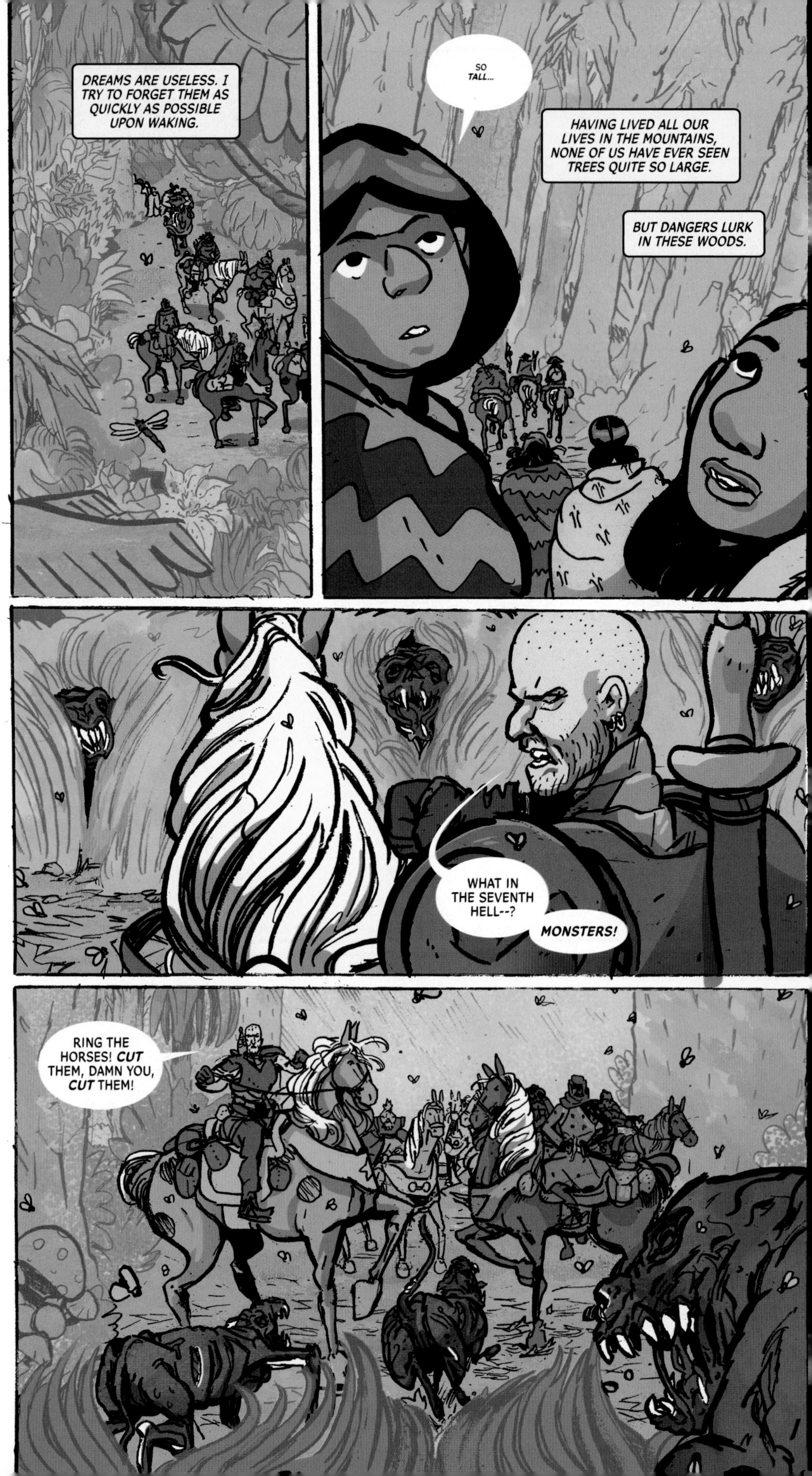
DREAMS ARE USELESS. I TRY TO FORGET THEM AS QUICKLY AS POSSIBLE UPON WAKING.
SO TALL...
HAVING LIVED ALL OUR LIVES IN THE MOUNTAINS, NONE OF US HAVE EVER SEEN TREES QUITE SO LARGE.
BUT DANGERS LURK IN THESE WOODS.
WHAT IN THE SEVENTH HELL--?
MONSTERS!
RING THE HORSES! CUT THEM, DAMN YOU, CUT THEM!

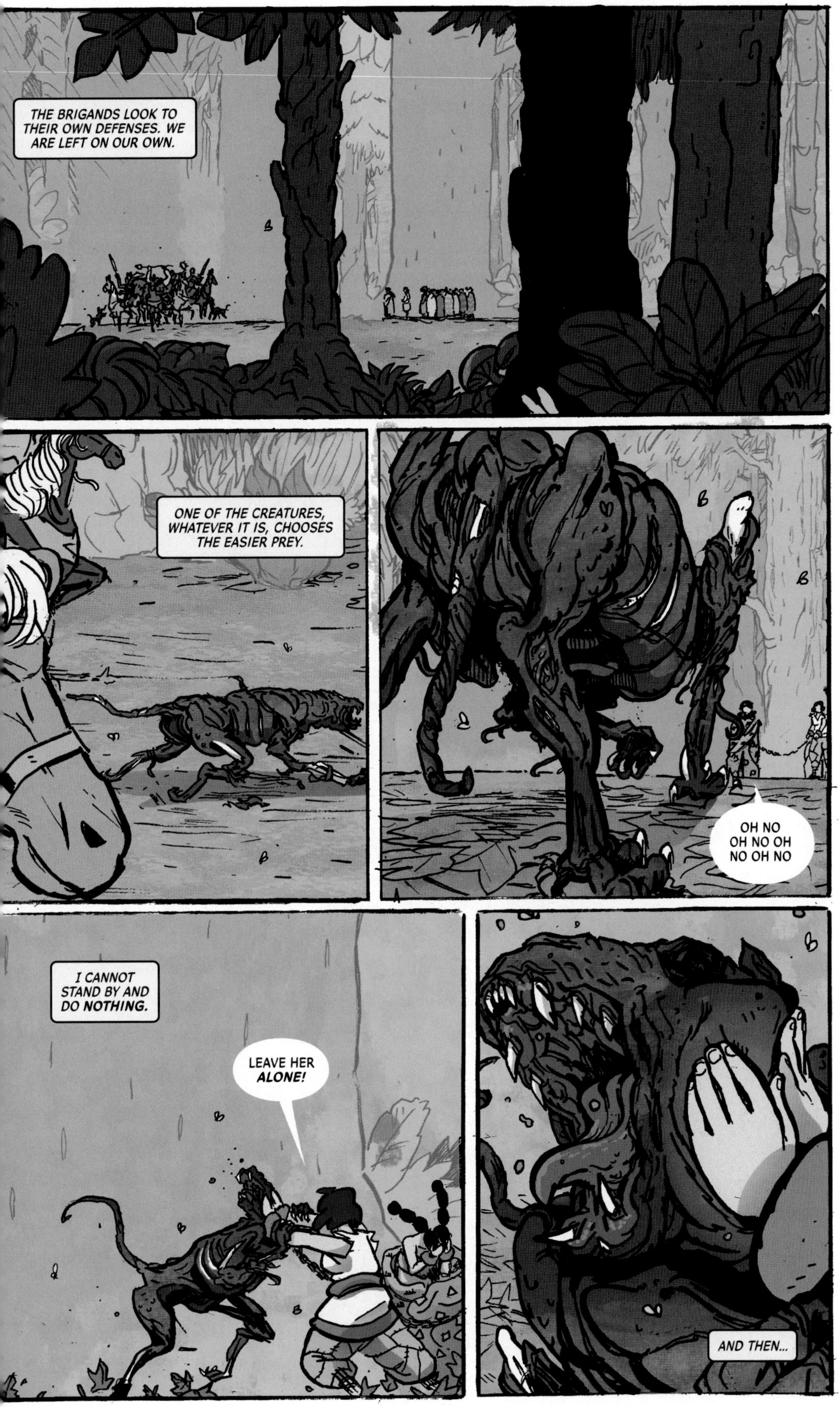
THE BRIGANDS LOOK TO THEIR OWN DEFENSES. WE ARE LEFT ON OUR OWN.
ONE OF THE CREATURES, WHATEVER IT IS, CHOOSES THE EASIER PREY.
OH NO OH NO OH NO OH NO
I CANNOT STAND BY AND DO NOTHING.
LEAVE HER ALONE!
AND THEN...

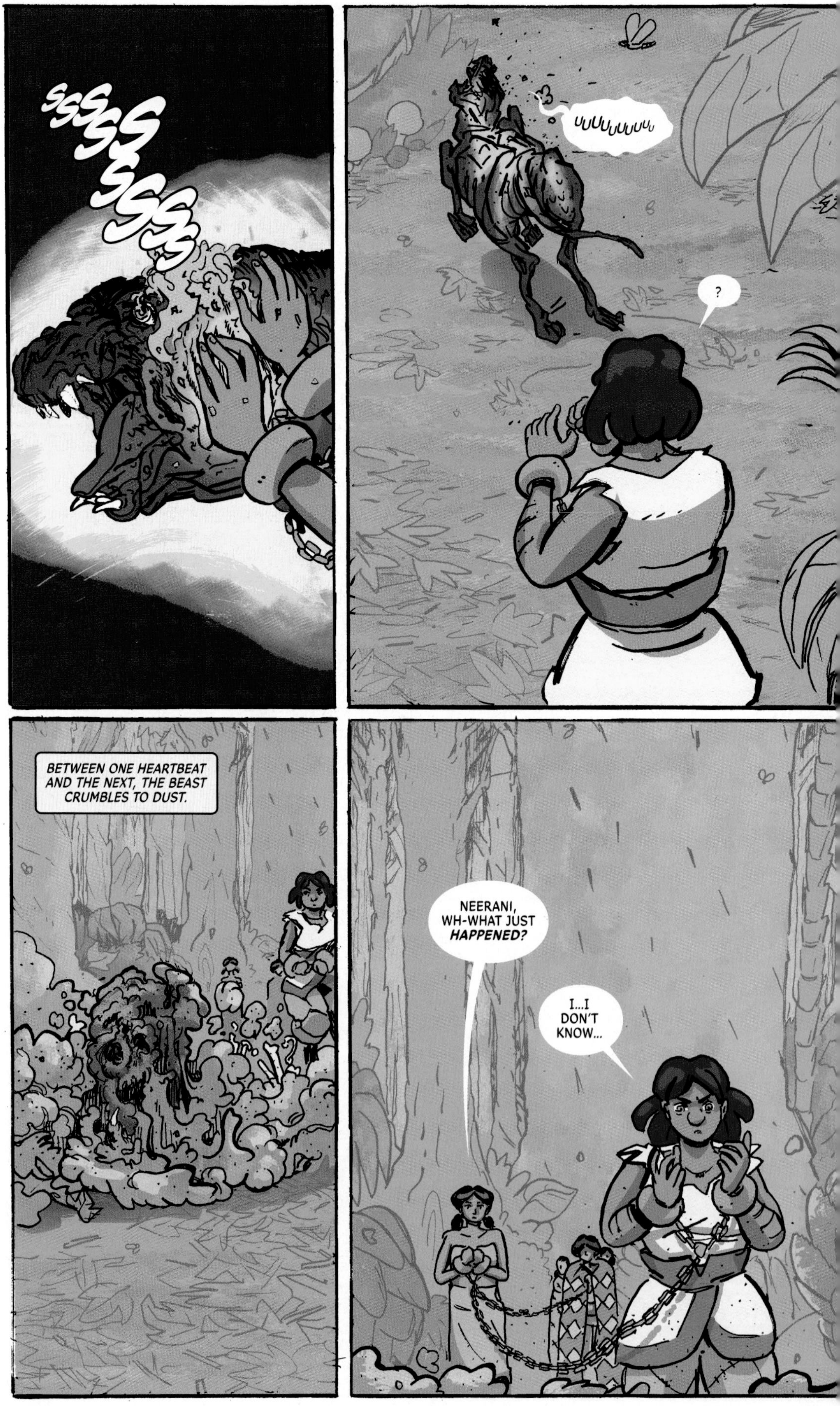
SSSSSSSSS
UUUUUUUUU
?
BETWEEN ONE HEARTBEAT AND THE NEXT, THE BEAST CRUMBLES TO DUST.
NEERANI, WH-WHAT JUST ***HAPPENED?***
I...I DON'T KNOW...

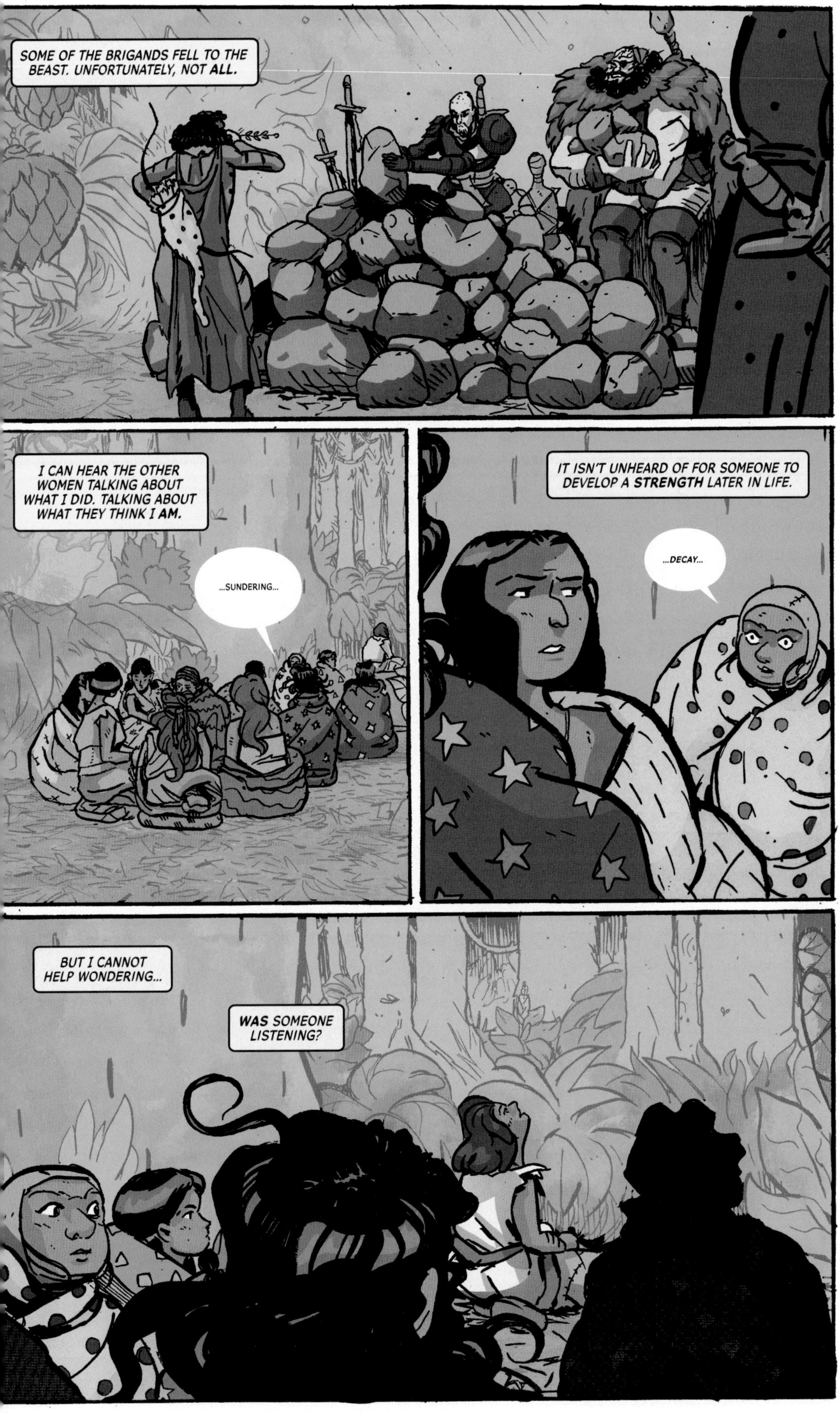
SOME OF THE BRIGANDS FELL TO THE BEAST. UNFORTUNATELY, NOT ALL.
I CAN HEAR THE OTHER WOMEN TALKING ABOUT WHAT I DID. TALKING ABOUT WHAT THEY THINK I AM.
...SUNDERING...
IT ISN'T UNHEARD OF FOR SOMEONE TO DEVELOP A STRENGTH LATER IN LIFE.
...DECAY...
BUT I CANNOT HELP WONDERING...
WAS SOMEONE LISTENING?

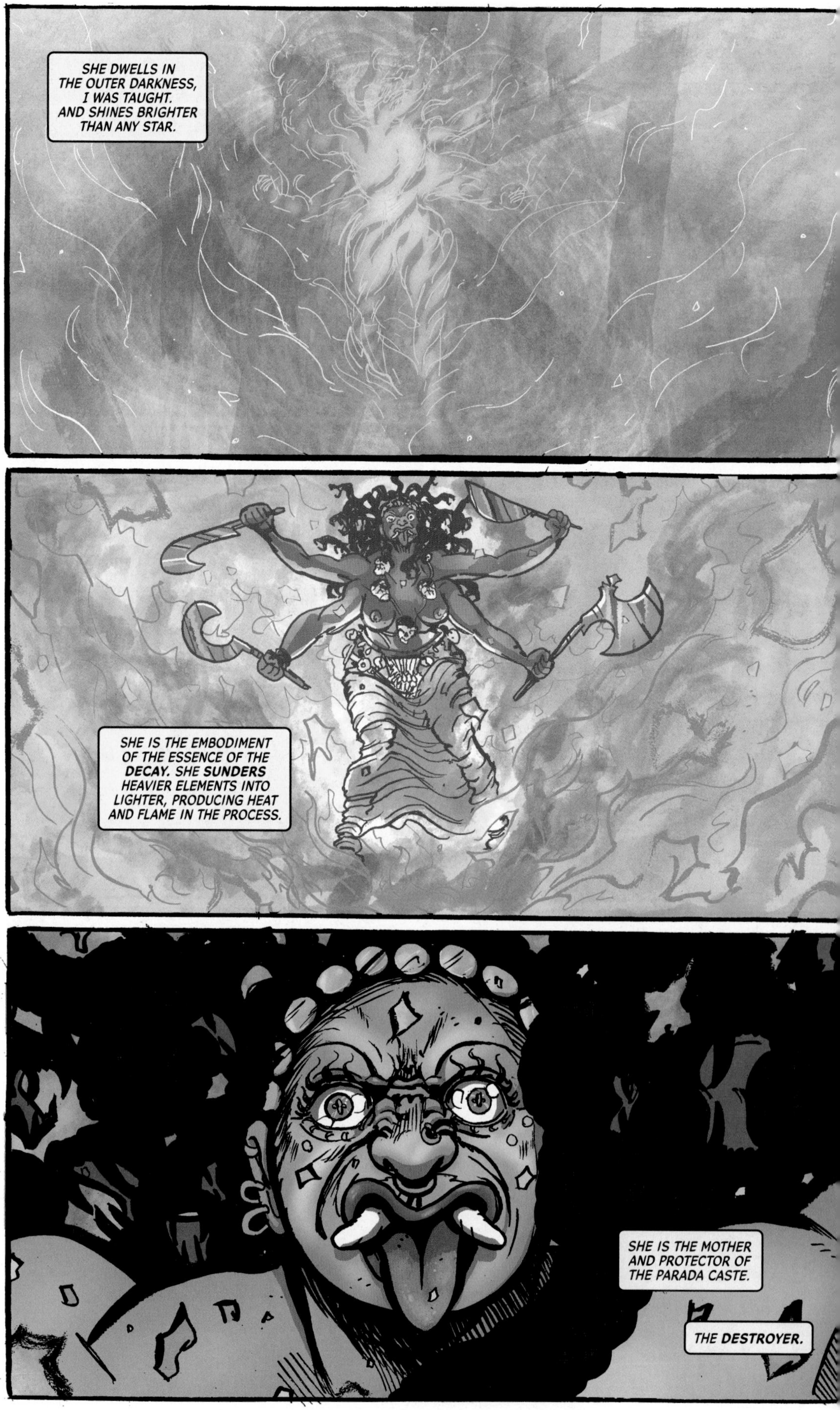
SHE DWELLS IN THE OUTER DARKNESS, I WAS TAUGHT. AND SHINES BRIGHTER THAN ANY STAR.
SHE IS THE EMBODIMENT OF THE ESSENCE OF THE DECAY. SHE SUNDERS HEAVIER ELEMENTS INTO LIGHTER, PRODUCING HEAT AND FLAME IN THE PROCESS.
SHE IS THE MOTHER AND PROTECTOR OF THE PARADA CASTE.
THE DESTROYER.

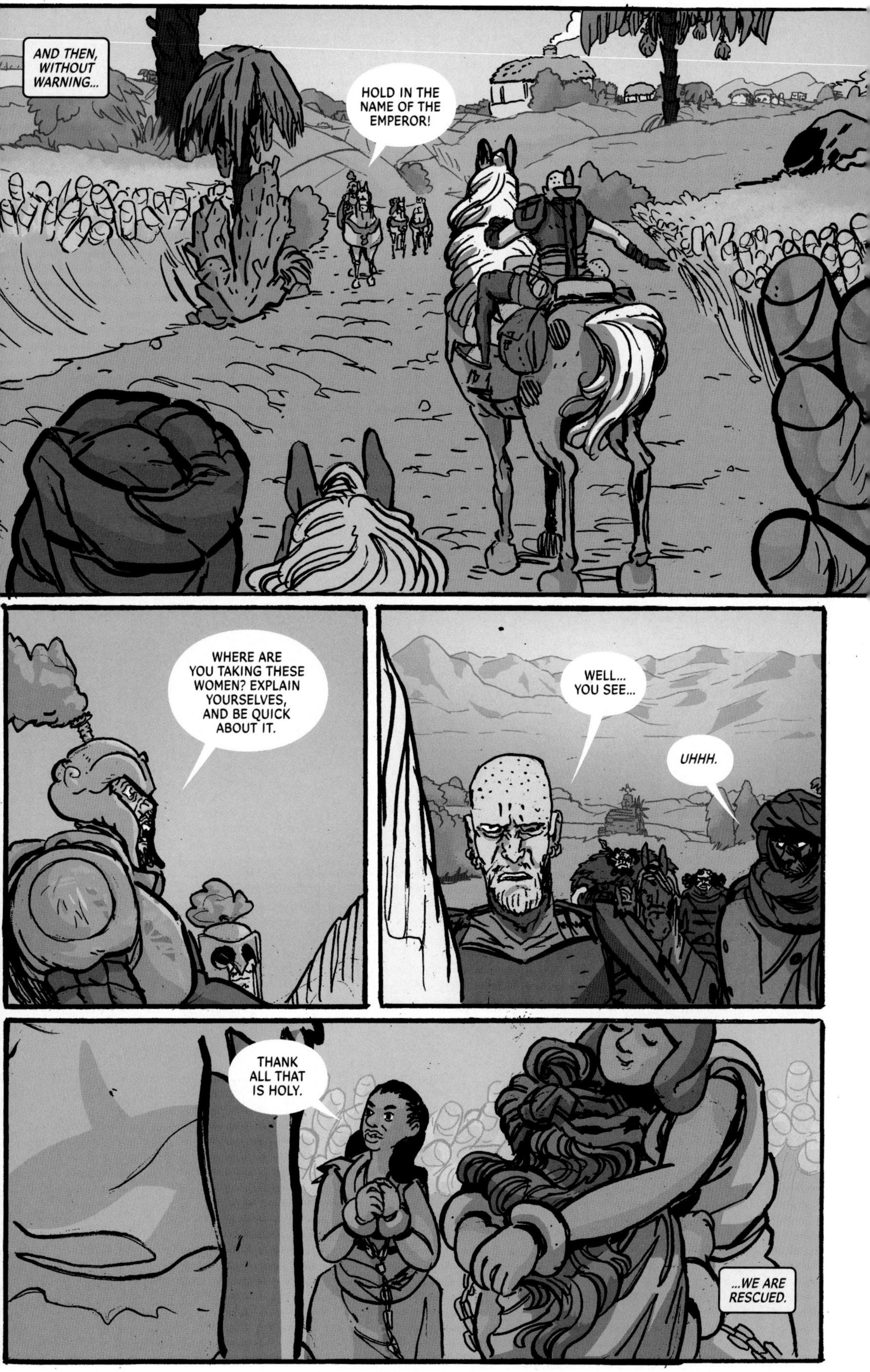
AND THEN, WITHOUT WARNING...
HOLD IN THE NAME OF THE EMPEROR!
WHERE ARE YOU TAKING THESE WOMEN? EXPLAIN YOURSELVES, AND BE QUICK ABOUT IT.
WELL... YOU SEE...
UHHH.
THANK ALL THAT IS HOLY.
...WE ARE RESCUED.

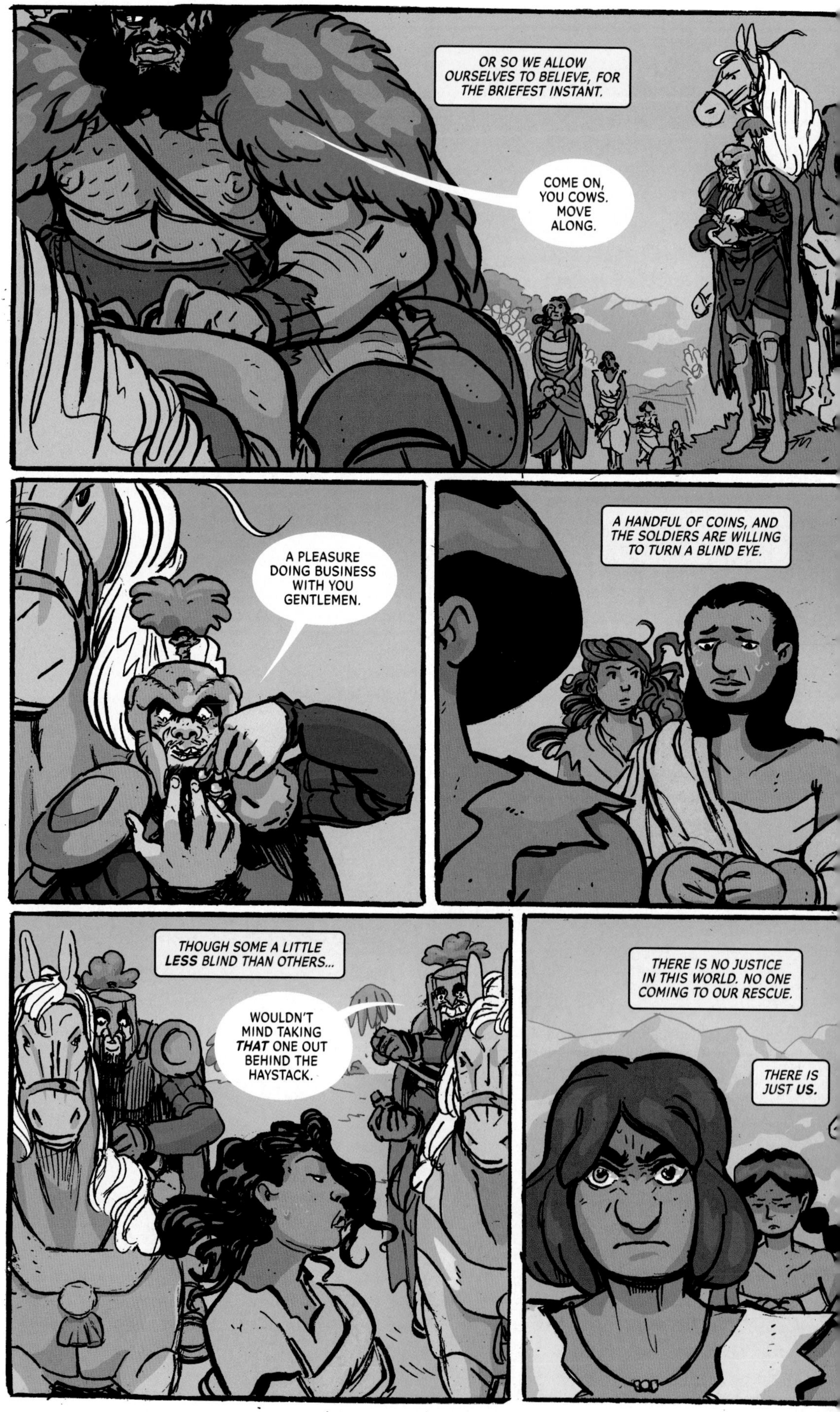

OR SO WE ALLOW OURSELVES TO BELIEVE, FOR THE BRIEFEST INSTANT.
COME ON, YOU COWS. MOVE ALONG.
A PLEASURE DOING BUSINESS WITH YOU GENTLEMEN.
A HANDFUL OF COINS, AND THE SOLDIERS ARE WILLING TO TURN A BLIND EYE.
THOUGH SOME A LITTLE LESS BLIND THAN OTHERS...
WOULDN'T MIND TAKING THAT ONE OUT BEHIND THE HAYSTACK.
THERE IS NO JUSTICE IN THIS WORLD. NO ONE COMING TO OUR RESCUE.
THERE IS JUST US.

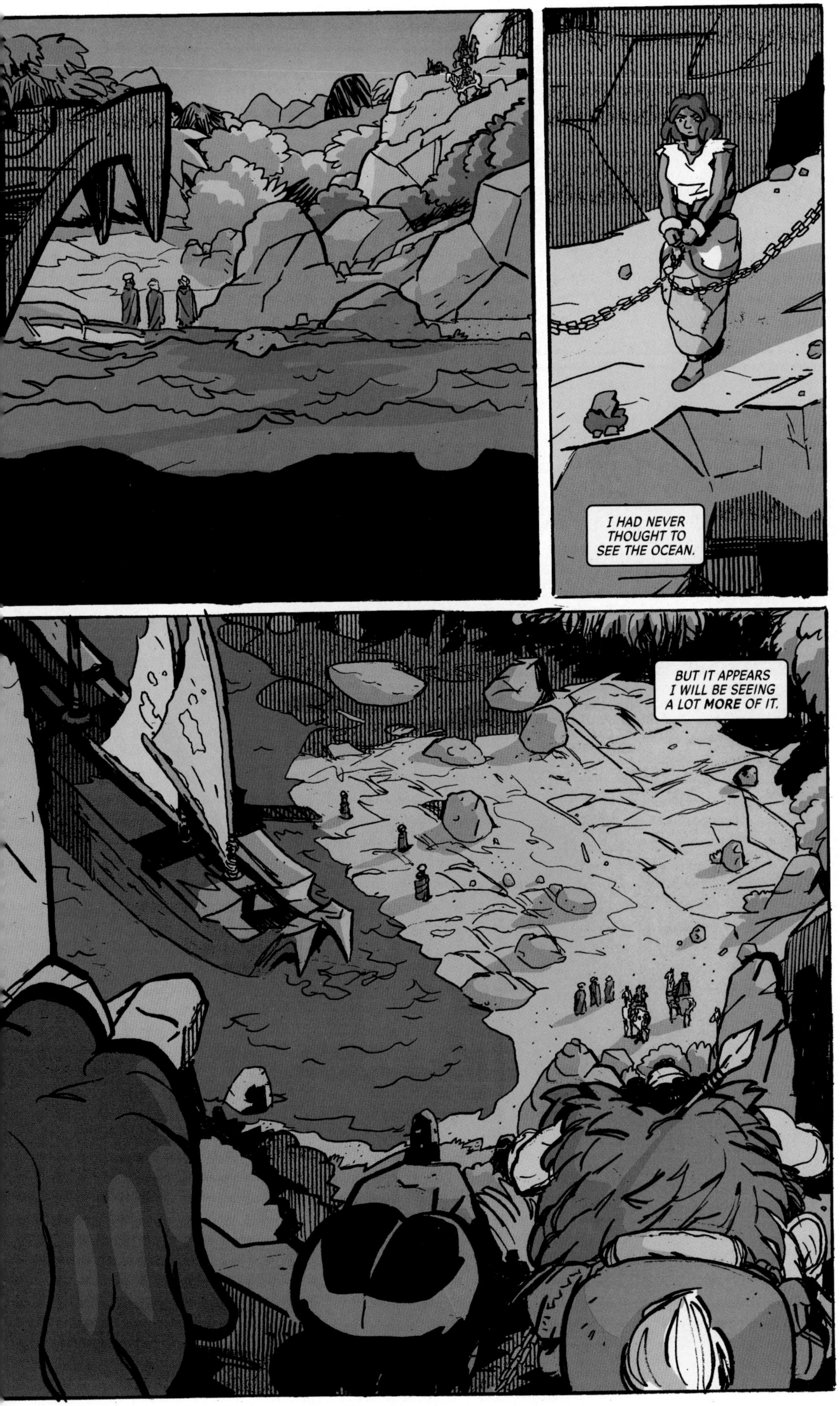
I HAD NEVER THOUGHT TO SEE THE OCEAN.
BUT IT APPEARS I WILL BE SEEING A LOT MORE OF IT.

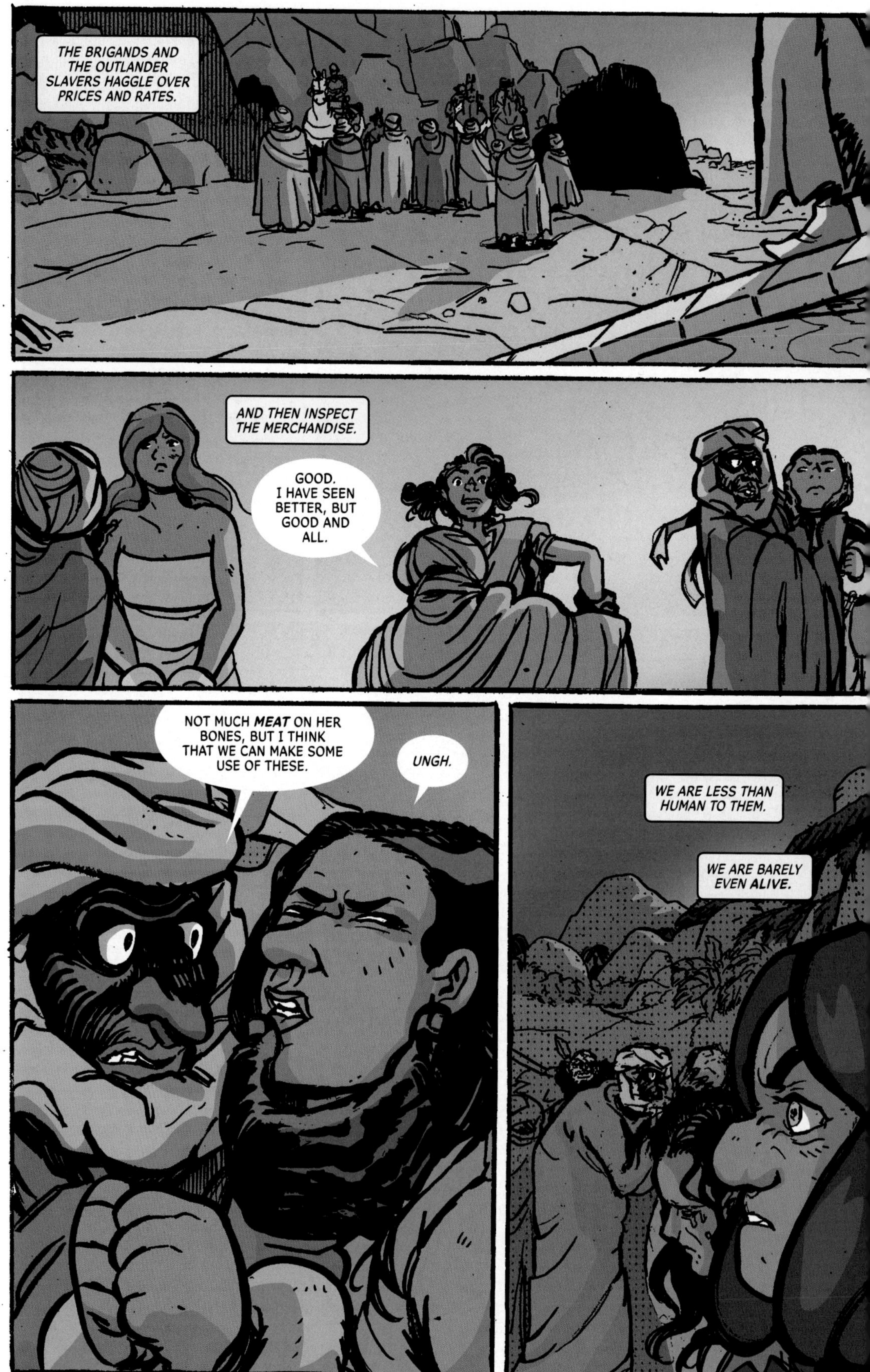
THE BRIGANDS AND THE OUTLANDER SLAVERS HAGGLE OVER PRICES AND RATES.
AND THEN INSPECT THE MERCHANDISE.
GOOD. I HAVE SEEN BETTER, BUT GOOD AND ALL.
NOT MUCH MEAT ON HER BONES, BUT I THINK THAT WE CAN MAKE SOME USE OF THESE.
UNGH.
WE ARE LESS THAN HUMAN TO THEM.
WE ARE BARELY EVEN ALIVE.

THERE IS NO SORROW IN ME. ONLY RAGE.

ALL OF MY TEARS HAVE BEEN BURNED AWAY, AND ONLY FIRE REMAINS.

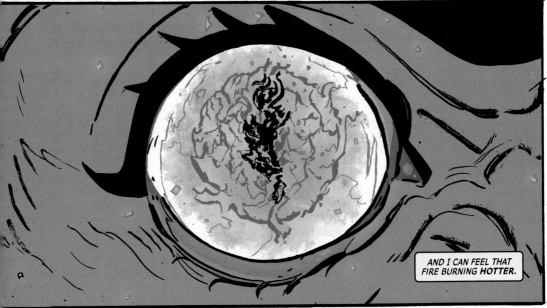

AND I CAN FEEL THAT FIRE BURNING **HOTTER.**

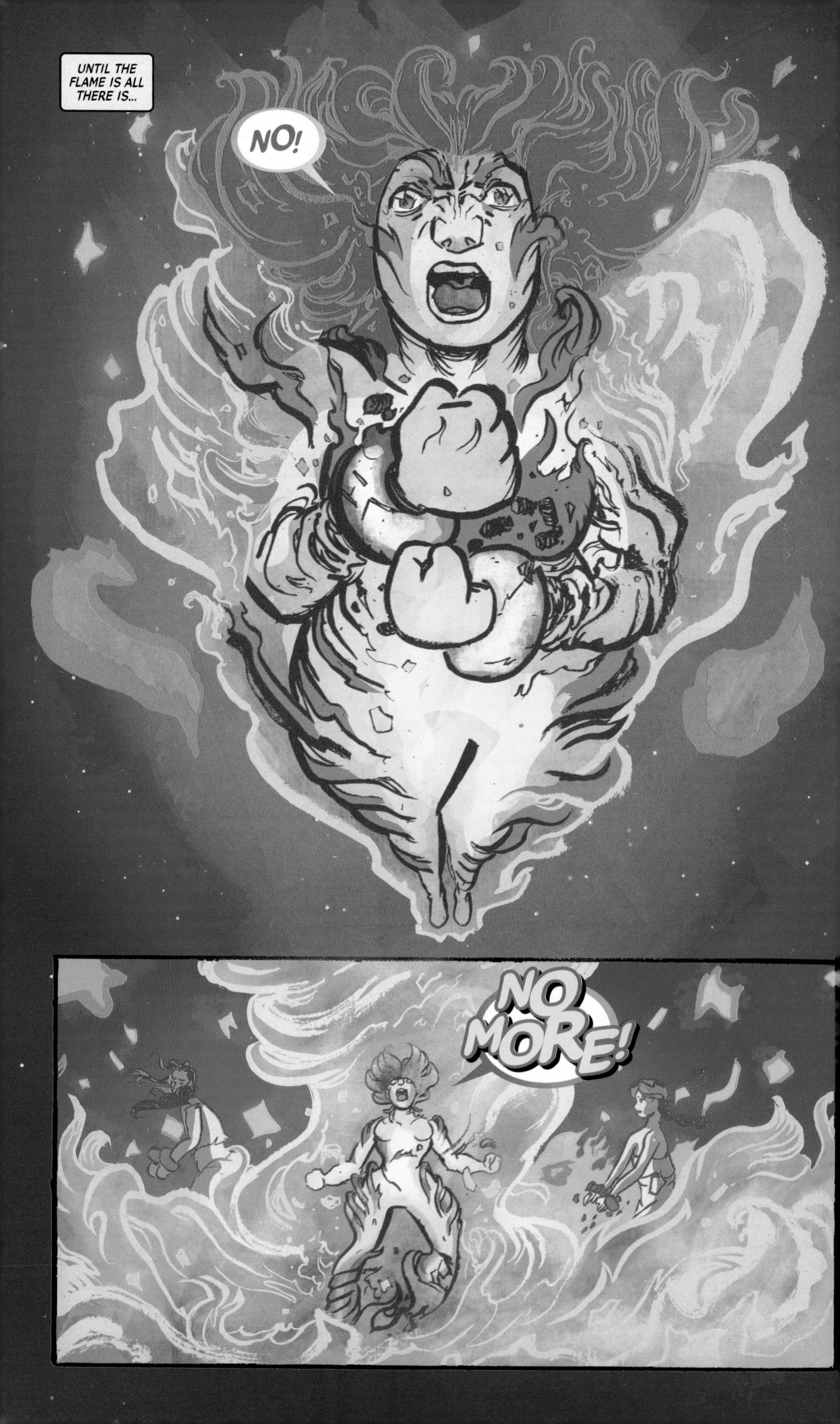
UNTIL THE FLAME IS ALL THERE IS...
NO!
NO MORE!

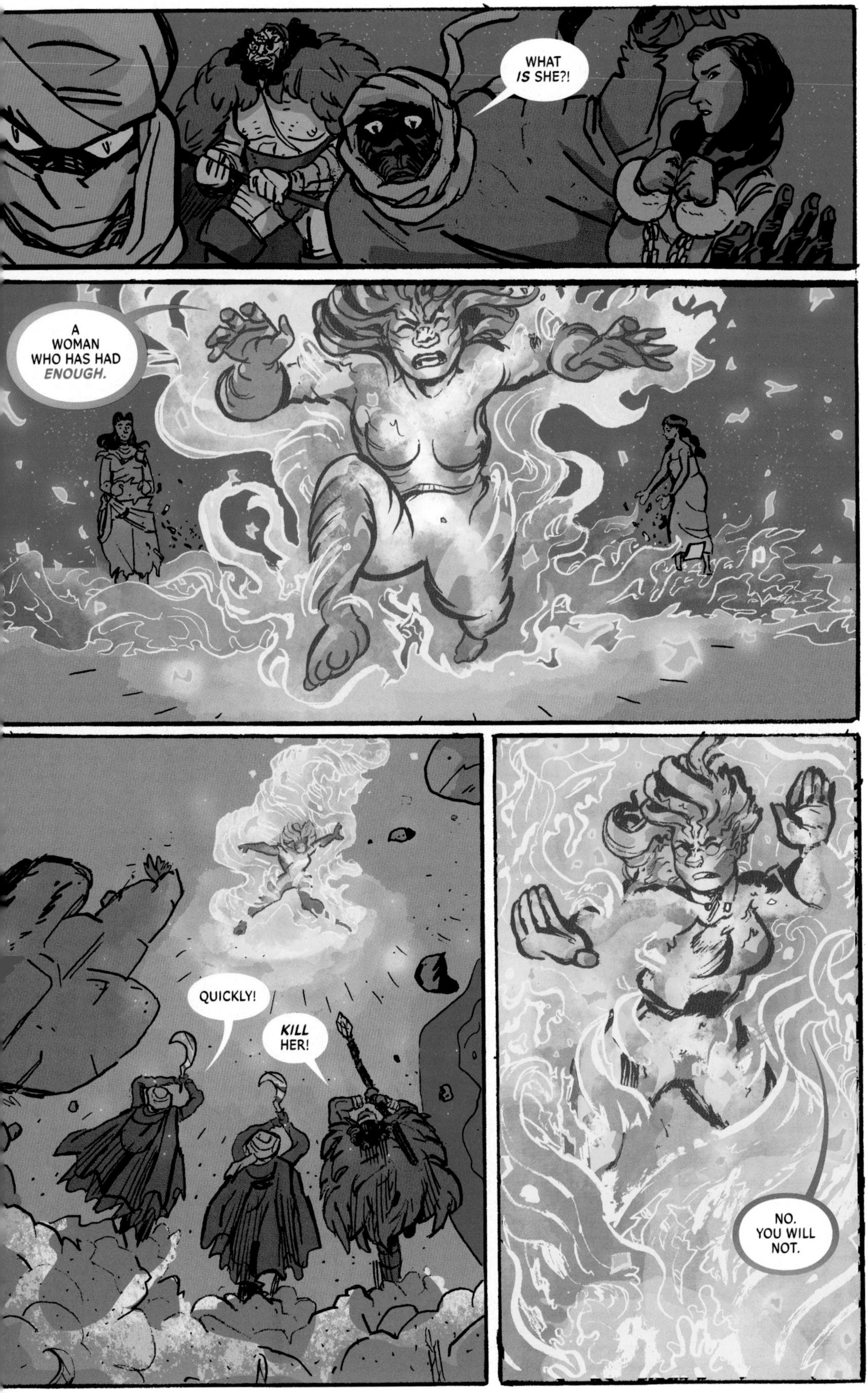
WHAT *IS* SHE?!
A WOMAN WHO HAS HAD *ENOUGH.*
QUICKLY!
KILL HER!
NO. YOU WILL NOT.

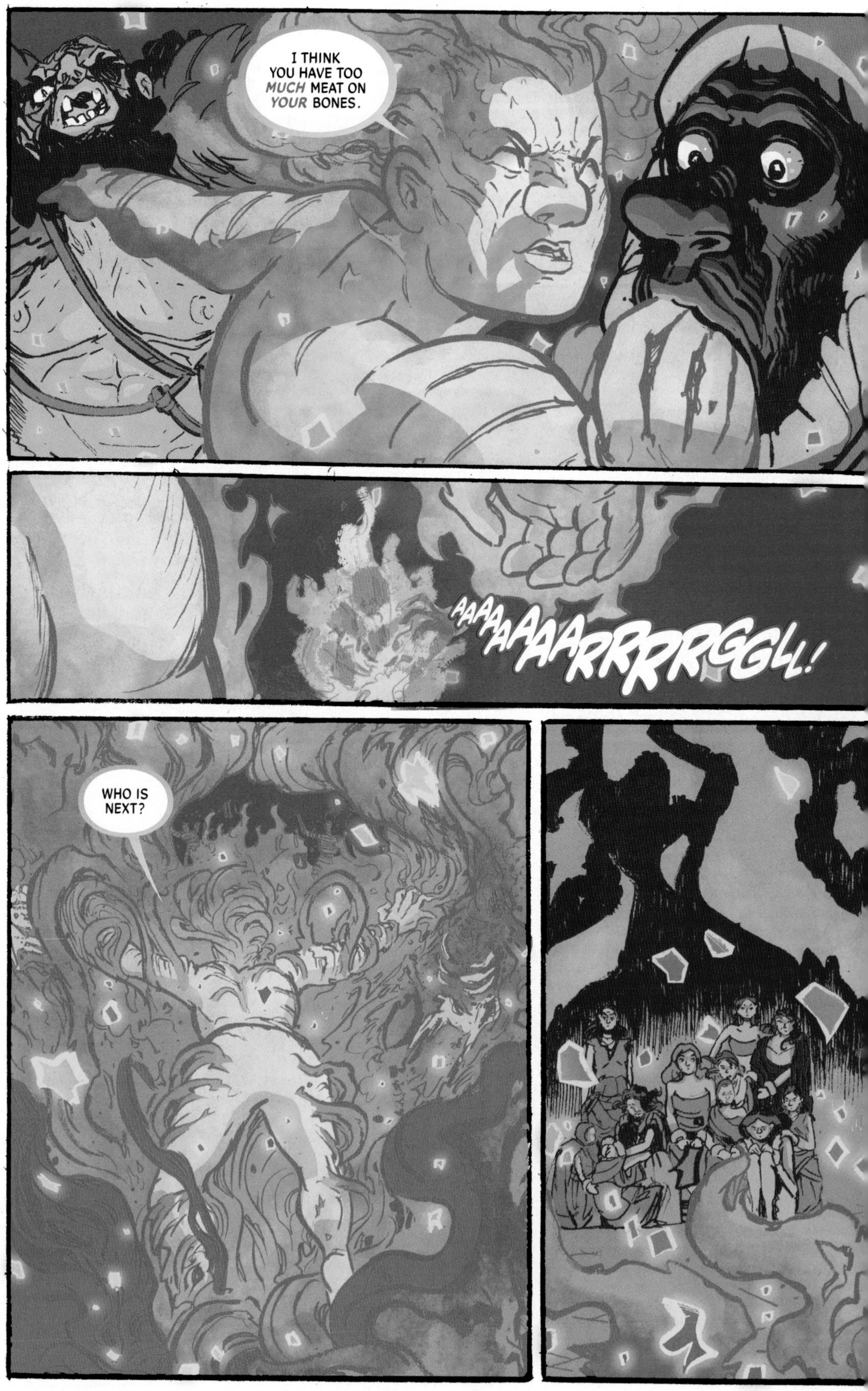
I THINK YOU HAVE TOO *MUCH* MEAT ON *YOUR* BONES.
AAAAAAARRRRRGGLL!
WHO IS NEXT?

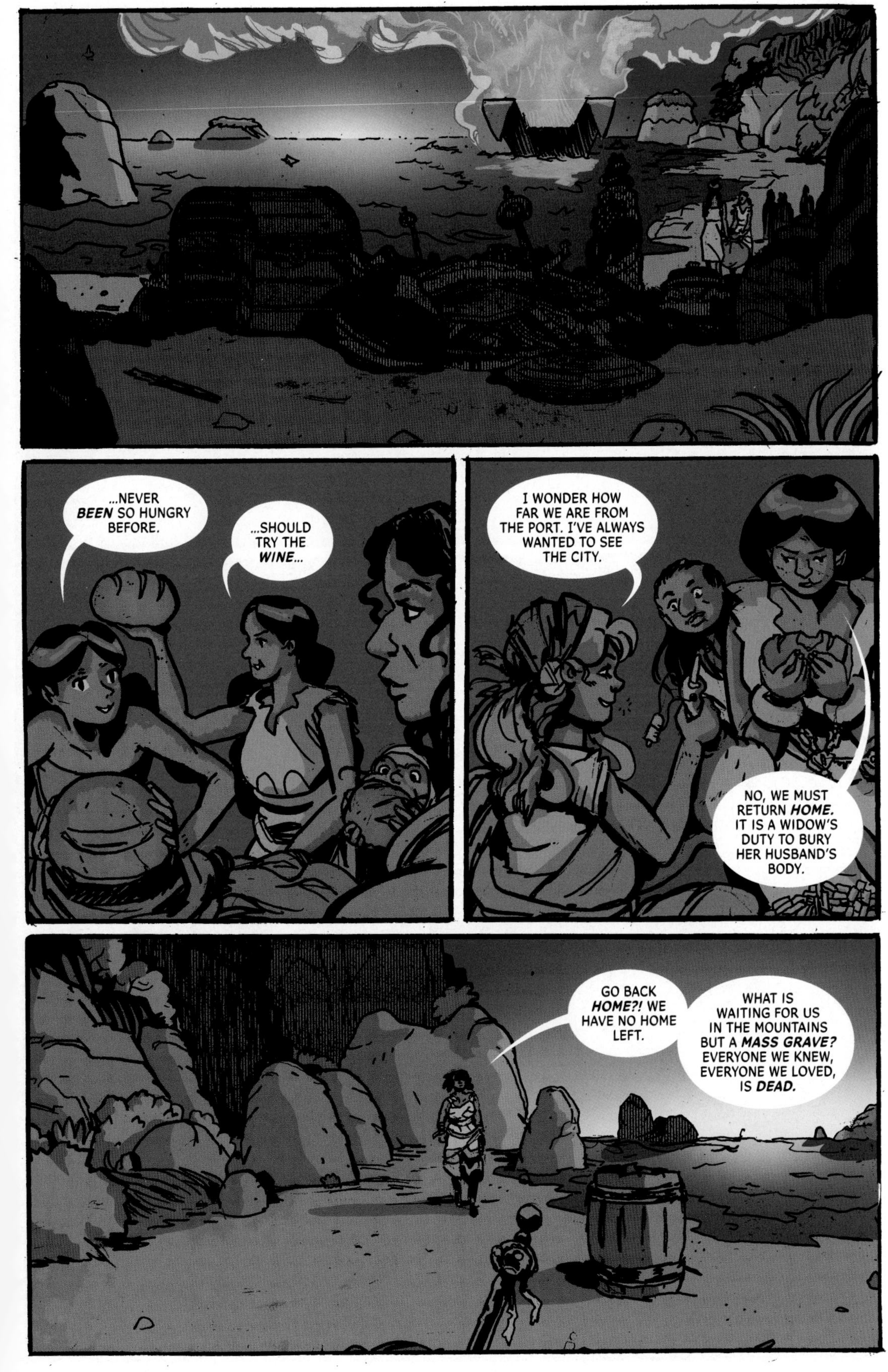
...NEVER BEEN SO HUNGRY BEFORE.
...SHOULD TRY THE WINE...
I WONDER HOW FAR WE ARE FROM THE PORT. I'VE ALWAYS WANTED TO SEE THE CITY.
NO, WE MUST RETURN HOME. IT IS A WIDOW'S DUTY TO BURY HER HUSBAND'S BODY.
GO BACK HOME?! WE HAVE NO HOME LEFT.
WHAT IS WAITING FOR US IN THE MOUNTAINS BUT A MASS GRAVE? EVERYONE WE KNEW, EVERYONE WE LOVED, IS DEAD.

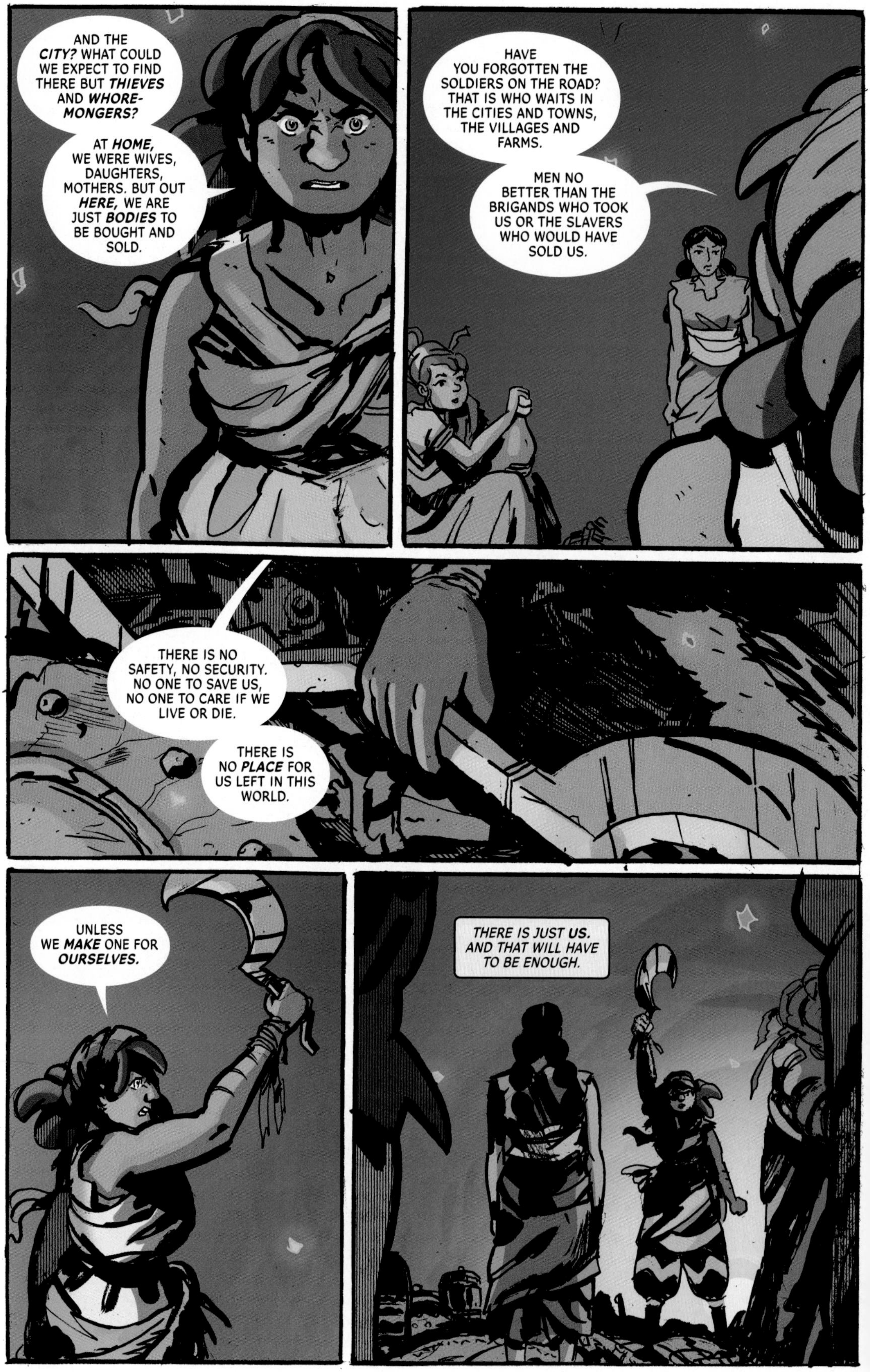
AND THE *CITY?* WHAT COULD WE EXPECT TO FIND THERE BUT ***THIEVES*** AND ***WHORE-MONGERS?***
AT ***HOME,*** WE WERE WIVES, DAUGHTERS, MOTHERS. BUT OUT ***HERE,*** WE ARE JUST ***BODIES*** TO BE BOUGHT AND SOLD.
HAVE YOU FORGOTTEN THE SOLDIERS ON THE ROAD? THAT IS WHO WAITS IN THE CITIES AND TOWNS, THE VILLAGES AND FARMS.
MEN NO BETTER THAN THE BRIGANDS WHO TOOK US OR THE SLAVERS WHO WOULD HAVE SOLD US.
THERE IS NO SAFETY, NO SECURITY. NO ONE TO SAVE US, NO ONE TO CARE IF WE LIVE OR DIE.
THERE IS NO ***PLACE*** FOR US LEFT IN THIS WORLD.
UNLESS WE ***MAKE*** ONE FOR ***OURSELVES.***
*THERE IS JUST **US.** AND THAT WILL HAVE TO BE ENOUGH.*

OUT FROM SILENCE.

The Luminari are the "Defiled" of Khendish culture, caste-less outcasts who are employed in debasing occupations which, the Khendish believe, stain the hands and soul alike. Their principle responsibility is the disposal of the dead, but they have also been called in the past to act as executioners and assassins on occasion, and in ancient times were sometimes employed as bodyguards to kings.

The Luminari get their name from "lumina," a mountain-growing plant that, either dried and smoke or prepared as a tea, is used by the Luminari to enhance and sharpen their sense of Sight, the Talent most crucial to their holy work.

When Luminari are abroad or at their tasks, they cover their faces with cowls, hoods that save others the "disgrace" of looking upon a Defiled.

There are many holy offices held by the Luminari in Silence, the holy city high in the Roof Mountains at the top of the world that serves as the center for Luminari society. But the two principal paths a Luminari may follow, the two sacred offices key to their traditional role in Khendish society, are that of the Practician and the Paladin.

The Practician, whose function is to address the remains of the dead, preparing the body for cremation or sky-burial, wears a white cowl, which with the dark robes of the Luminari often gives them the appearance of bare-headed carrion-eating griffons. Practicians ring the funeral site with a barrier of salt before they begin the work of rendering the remains.

The Paladin, whose function is to protect the Practician and the remains from any threat, whether from the Real or the Unreal, wears a black cowl, often covered with a skull-shaped silver helmet for protection, and carries the paired swords, both with forward-curving blades—the scythe-like kartika sword (or "cutter") and the shorter, heavier sawback svadhiti (or "chopper"), a combination of knife, axe, and saw. Paladins ritually spill their own blood to act as a lure for any daemons who might be near, drawing them away from the funeral site until the Practician's work is done.

Novice Luminari, students who have not yet completed their studies in the Five Halls, are called Proficients.

Luminari in ancient times oversaw the funeral rites of all in Khend, from the lowest to the highest, scrupulously ensuring that the bodies of the fallen—man and animal alike—could not pay host to daemons or other intelligences from the Unreal. Since the coming of the horse-lords, though, burial by internment has become more and more common in the lowlands, and for more than a generation, since Sanram Rhan ordered the destruction of all Khendish temples and cult-sites, ordering them replaced with Bahqirist temples, the Luminari have been sealed within the city of Silence.

Once there were outposts of Luminari all across the length and breadth of Khend, in chapter-houses located on the western approaches to every large village and town. Even by the coming of the horse-lords, though, many in the lowlands had put aside the old ways, and refused the services of the Luminari, preferring instead to entomb their honored dead in crypts, or bury them beneath the ground. Many lowlanders rejected the Luminari warnings about the threat of the Unreal and of daemons as mere superstition, and accused the Luminari themselves of being atavistic holdouts from a simpler age.

Many of the Luminari chapter-houses in the north were lost when Zalamgir ordered the Khendish temples and holy sites in his new-won kingdom demolished, so that he could build his new house of worship with its tower dedicated to the Messenger Baqhir. In the generations that followed, many more chapter-houses fell into disuse as more and more Khendish adopted the Tamurid

practice of interring their dead in tombs.

By the time Sanram Rhan called for the destruction of all Khendish temples and cult-sites across Khend, most of the chapter-houses had already been abandoned, left to disuse and ruin. The remaining Luminari had retreated to the Roof Mountains and to the holy city of Silence, turning their backs on the ungrateful lowlands.

Before the current emperor Sanram Rhan came to the throne, Father Griffon had been among the Luminari who followed the calls of Sant Koel, who argued for a greater involvement in lowland politics and power-struggles. When still a young Practician, when he still had the use of his eyes, he followed Sant Koel as part of a contingent of Luminari who journeyed south to join the faction that supported the claim of Raghir Rhan's son Zirhandar for the Golden Throne.

Zirhandar pledged to carry on the reforms begun by his grandfather Ikandar, who had preached the Faliq principle of "universal tolerance." But Zirhandar's father had already seized the throne from Ikandar and had himself named Raghir Rhan, or Universal Ruler in the Tamur tongue, impatient for Ikandar to die. Ikandar soon died, some said of a broken heart, others said of poison.

Zirhandar was married to a Khendish princess, whose father supplied Zirhandar with an army, and with the Luminari contingent lead by Sant Koel at their side, they confidently marched towards the palace to seize the throne and restore Ikandar's reforms. But Raghir Rhan had the full might of the Tamurid imperial army at his side, and was able to put down his son's uprising with ease. Zirhandar was imprisoned in the capital city, and left to rot while Raghir Rhan systematically tortured and then executed Zirhandar's followers.

(Zirhandar remained imprisoned for years, until he finally died under mysterious circumstances. Many whispered that he'd been poisoned, perhaps like his grandfather was said to have been, particularly when Zirhandar's younger brother Rafir died in similarly suspicious circumstances.)

Sant Koel was a Shifter, and could have escaped at any time, but refused to flee, pledging instead to stand with his allies and with his sibling Luminari. The young Brother Griffon was a Slider, but only with the aid of lumina to help enhance his Sight. Imprisoned in the dungeons of Raghir Rhan without even the option of fleeing, Griffon was finally selected for the torturer's chamber. He was blinded, his eyes put out, and in his mindless pain and panic he Slid from his bonds and beyond the dungeon walls, finding himself sightless and bleeding in the streets of the capital city.

He survived, but it was a pitiable existence, living as a beggar for months, subsisting on nothing but refuse and scraps. Finally, nearly two full years later, he managed to make his way to the city of Silence in the north. In the time it took him to return, he learned that Sant Koel had met his end at the blade of Raghir Rhan's torturer, and that a new Sant had been selected. But even as a Paladin Barbet had been one who insisted that defense was the truer calling and that the lowlands should be left to look after their own defenses, and after the death of Koel and the others the now Sant Barbet had called for a full-scale retreat to Silence, the holy city all but sealed off from any contact with the lowlands.

THE HORSELORDS

The Tamur dynasty has ruled Khend for generations. The first Tamurid ruler of Khend was Zalamgir the Conqueror. Before coming to Khend, Zalamgir was just one of a number of clanleaders among the horselords of steppes north of the Roof Mountains. Zalamgir could trace his descent from Vorghiz Rhan, first and greatest of the Tamurid horselords. But while he was a formidable warrior and superior tactician, Zalamgir was unsuccessful in conquering their homeland, unable to overcome the other clans. Seeking an easier prize, Zalamgir instead lead his people west and south, around the mountains and into the plains of northern Khend.

Zalamgir led his people to victory, carving out a small kingdom in northern Khend, conquering local princes, kings, and warlords. But while he had found success, Zalamgir did not care for his new home, and always looked north to the steppes. He tried several times in his remaining years to take the steppes by force, but failed each time.

Instead, Zalamgir had elaborate gardens constructed in his new capital, and spent much of his time there. A fine warrior, Zalamgir was a poor administrator.

Zalamgir, as a sign of his devotion to the faith of his fathers, had countless Khendish temples destroyed, the stones used to build a new house of worship surmounted by an enormous spire, dedicated in the name of the Messenger, Baqhir. Those Baqhirists already living in Khend, Tafiya and Karimi alike, praised Zalamgir for his devotion, but Khendist pantheists looked on with grave concern.

When Zalamgir died, he was succeeded by his eldest son, Jaluhaddin. A poor warrior, better suited to keeping account ledgers than holding a kingdom, Jaluhaddin was driven from his capital by a revolt lead by a Khendish prince, and for some years after was a king without a kingdom.

A devout man, Jaluhaddin died when he fell to his death from a high tower. He had gone up to view the stars, and when he heard the call to prayer he tried to kneel, got tangled in his robes, and tumbled out into empty air.

With Jaluhaddin's death, his successor and son Ikandar took the throne. Having grown up haunted by memories of his father as a king without a kingdom, Ikandar was determined that the same fate would not befall him. He led the armies of the Tamurid against their Khendish enemies, recapturing his grandfather Zalamgir's capital, and expanding the kingdom farther, conquering more and more kingdoms each year, until nearly all of Khend was in his control, all except the upper reaches of the Roof Mountains, and the unruly south. The Tamurids had now established a true empire in Khend.

Ikandar had been born in a fort at the edge of a desert, one of his father's last holdings. In later years, a stele was erected there, proclaiming it the birthplace of the "conqueror and refuge of the world," the first true Tamurid emperor of Khend.

Raised a devout Tafiya, in later life Ikandar became enchanted with the mystic teachings of the Faliq orders, and decreed ever greater degrees of religious tolerance. This served to unsettle orthodox Tafiya and Karimi alike. Nevertheless, Ikandar was a firm believer in the Faliq principle of "universal tolerance." Even so, Ikandar firmly believed that the emperor was the shadow of the Unnamed in the mortal world.

Ikandar practiced matrimonial politics where military might would not suffice. He married a string of Khendish princesses, as did several of his sons and nephews. And he invited to his court princes of other kingdoms, to be educated in the arts and trained in combat, to serve ultimately in Ikandar's armies. Ikandar had sufficient military might to punish any kingdom who refused his invitation or proposal of marriage, and while he could not have attacked them all, none knew what the other kingdoms might do, and so with the strength to conquer but one kingdom at a time, he brought dozens under his banner, without a drop of blood spilled.

Ikandar undertook an aggressive campaign of reform. He divided the empire into provinces, and appointed a governor to head each, along with an official to collect taxes and another to oversee religion. None of these positions were hereditary, and all reported directly to the emperor. Typically, officials were brought in from other provinces, to prevent the concentration of power.

Suspicious, and having difficulty chosing between his son Badahur, and Badahur's son Zirhandar as his successor, Ikandar has the two men each send to court an elephant. Then, at the end of a grand celebration, Ikandar had the elephants goaded into a fight to the death. Badahur's elephant was victorious, and he was named Ikandar's successor.

Several years later, with the aging Ikandar still on the throne and in good health, the now forty-year-old Badahur grew too impatient to wait any longer, and had himself proclaimed emperor. He took the new name Raghir Rhan, or "Universal Leader." The former emperor Ikandar died a short time later, heartbroken by the betrayal. Raghir Rhan was opposed by a faction who favored his son Zirhandar for the throne. Zirhandar had married a Khendish princess, and her father supplied Zirhandar with an army. Leading the empire's armies, Raghir Rhan put down his son's revolt.

Zirhandar was imprisoned in the capital city, and his followers cruelly tortured and executed. Raghir Rhan ruled for some years, neither expanding the empire built by his father, nor allowing any kingdoms to slip away. His reign was opulent, apathetic, and cruel.

In the last years of Raghir Rhan's reign, one of his youngest wives, Pakrhani Dey, nicknamed "the Light of the World," ruled the empire from behind the painted screens of the harem, defending Baqhirism and holding the reins of power. It was her portrait stamped on the reverse of the empire's silver coins in those years, not the emperor's. Pakrhani Dey supported the emperor's youngest son, Kussayn, for succession. Kussayn was a devout Karimi, and was supported by orthodox Baqhirists, who were critical of the more liberal attitudes of Zirhandar who, though still imprisoned after his failed revolt of years before, was still the designated heir.

Zirhandar died while still imprisoned, and it was whispered that he had been poisoned. When his younger brother Rafir died in similarly suspicious circumstances, some suspected Kussayn of complicity. But few suspected the emperor's fourth son, the studious Dalaut.

When Raghir Rhan died, Kussayn had himself named emperor. Dalaut had been in the south, leading the emperor's army in another attempting at conquest. When he heard of his father's death and brother's succession, Dalaut marched north, with the support of the army behind his own claim to the throne. His own father-in-law was brother to Raghir Rhan's widow, Pakrhani Dey, but Dalaut's father-in-law's loyalties were with his son-in-law, rather than his sister. At Dalaut's urging, his father-in-law lead his personal guard into the palace and executed Kussayn on the spot. When Dalaut arrived he had himself named Sanram Rhan, the new emperor of Khen.

Sanram Rhan was a strong ruler and accomplished warrior. However, he was forced to contend with other forces. The orthodox Baqhirists, who had supported Kussayn's bid for the throne, were discontented with the manner of Sanram Rhan's succession, and to appease them the new emperor found himself compelled to order the destruction of Khendish temples, and thereafter started a campaign to demolish cult sites and replace them with Bahqirist temples. Khendish were required to wear tunics that buttoned on the left, while Bahqiri buttoned theirs on the right. In addition, Sanram Rhan abolished many of the reforms instituted by Ikandar.

During the early years of Sanram Rhan's reign, a group of soldiers from Estacia, a nation to the north and west, tried to establish a foothold on the Khendish coast, and Sanram Rhan routed them. Thereafter he was always suspicious of the pale-skinned men from the north-west.

KHEND

Called the Land of a Thousand Gods, before the coming of Zalamgir and his Tamurid armies Khend was divided into a vast number of kingdoms and principalities of widely varying size and power. Nearly all of the Khendish kings were either traditional Khendish pantheists, with a small minority being adherents of Baqhirism.

When Zalamgir conquered portions of the north, the rest of the Khendish kingdoms gave the new kingdom little thought. But as the years passed, and Zalamgir and his successor went on to conquer more and more of Khend, the other rulers became increasingly concerned. Eventually only the south remained beyond the Tamurid's control, and these areas were periodically harried by attempted invasions by the emperor's forces.

Khendish society is pantheistic, and stratified into four Castes. The Anika caste are the scholars and doctors, the Hastaka are the warriors and rulers, the Urasa are the artisans and merchants, and the Padara are the laborers.

The Khendish pantheon has four main gods, each ruling over a sub-pantheon of associated demigods, spirits, and heroes. Each of the four is associated with one of the four Strengths, and venerated by one of the four Castes.

Outside of the four castes of Khendish tradition are the untouchables, the Defiled, who perform functions which no casted Khend would consider—butchery, assassination, and burial. Chief among these are the Luminari.

While the Tamurid emperor controls most of Khend, there are still places where his authority does not reach. In the wild places, for example, robbers, highwaymen, dacoits, and thieves rule.

There are Khendish nobles, too, who have bent their knees to the Tamurid emperors, but still harbor dreams of a kingdom of their own. Ambitious men who mouth pledges of loyalty while in the emperor's palace of white marble, but who keep their swords sharpened against the day they might take up arms in their own interests.

THE CONJUNCTION

The adepts of the four Strengths call upon four different Domains, or spheres of being beyond our own. The relations between the Strengths, their relative effectiveness and potency, are set through the entire duration of an epoch, or "ritu." The Strengths wax and wane, through, as the domains move and shift in relation to one another and with the mortal world, just like the movements of the stars and planets in the heavens.

Periodically, though, the domains all draw near at the same time, all growing in potency as one. This Conjunction of the four domains marks the end of one epoch and the beginning of the next. It is a tumultuous, discordant time, as the preeminent adept of each Strength is selected to act as their domain's Champion. When the moment of exact Conjunction arrives, and all four Strengths are at their most potent, the four Champions face one another in single combat, to determine the relation of the Strengths in the epoch to follow. And since the castes are ordered by the relative potency of their associated Strengths, the resulting ranking also determines the structure of Khendish society in the following epoch.

Man is not the first intelligence to walk upon the world of Avani. The giants preceded him, as did the dragons. But all of the races before man destroyed themselves eventually during epochs in which all of the Strengths were at their most potent following a Conjunction.

Unfortunately, there are greater threats during a Conjunction than unchecked adepts alone. There are intelligences out in the darkness of the Unreal, in the void between worlds. Demons, devils, and monsters, insane gods and outcast mages. All of them hungry for life, light, and heat. The Conjunction of the four domains weakens the walls between the worlds, making it easier for the intelligences to break through. At first, only their thoughts are able to bridge the rifts, influencing and even controlling the weak-willed, and animating the dead. Then the lesser beings being to squeeze their way in, and later the greater beings. It is the traditional role of the Luminari to lead the fight against these, disposing of the dead so that they will not serve as vessels, then driving back the invaders from beyond.

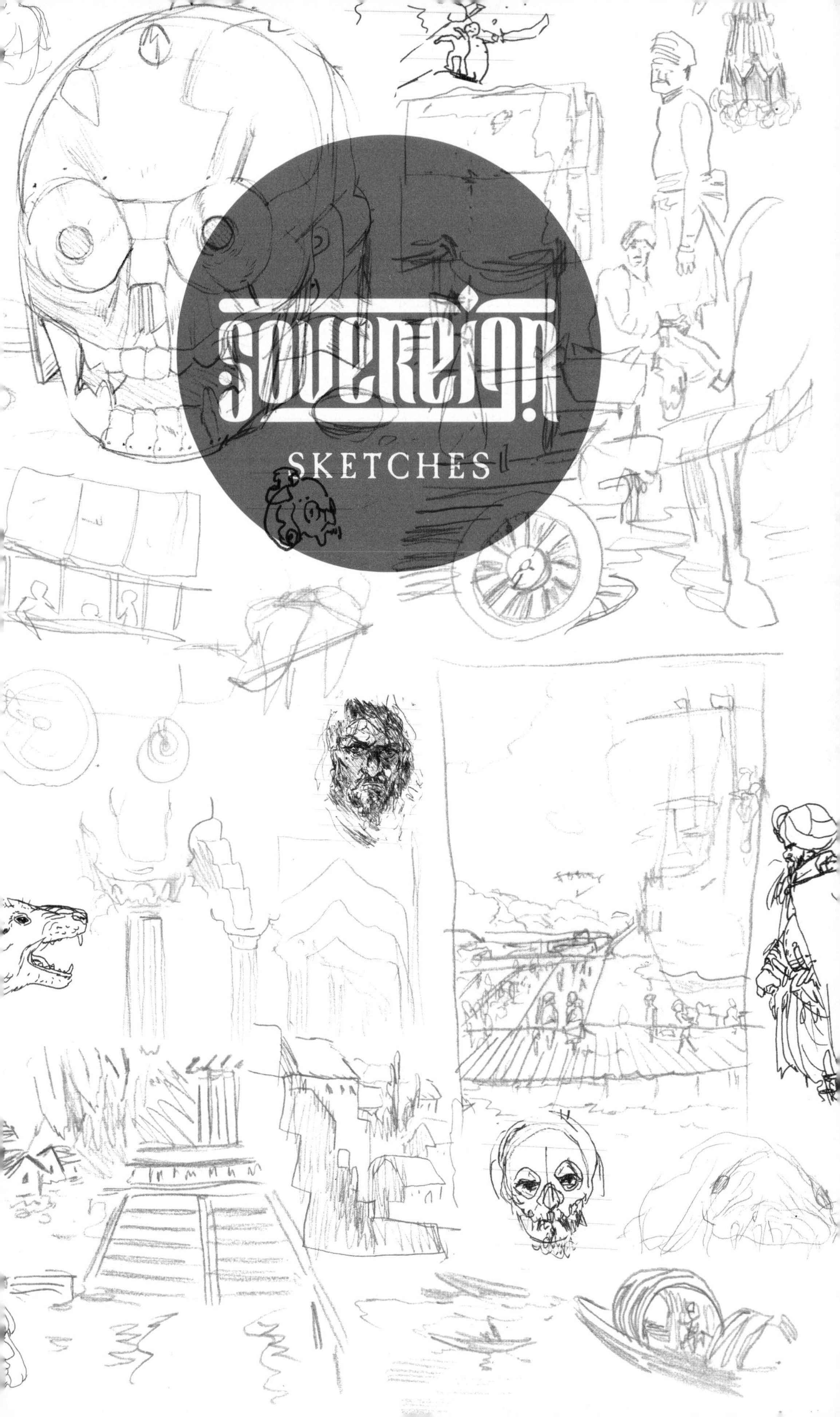
SOVEREIGN
SKETCHES

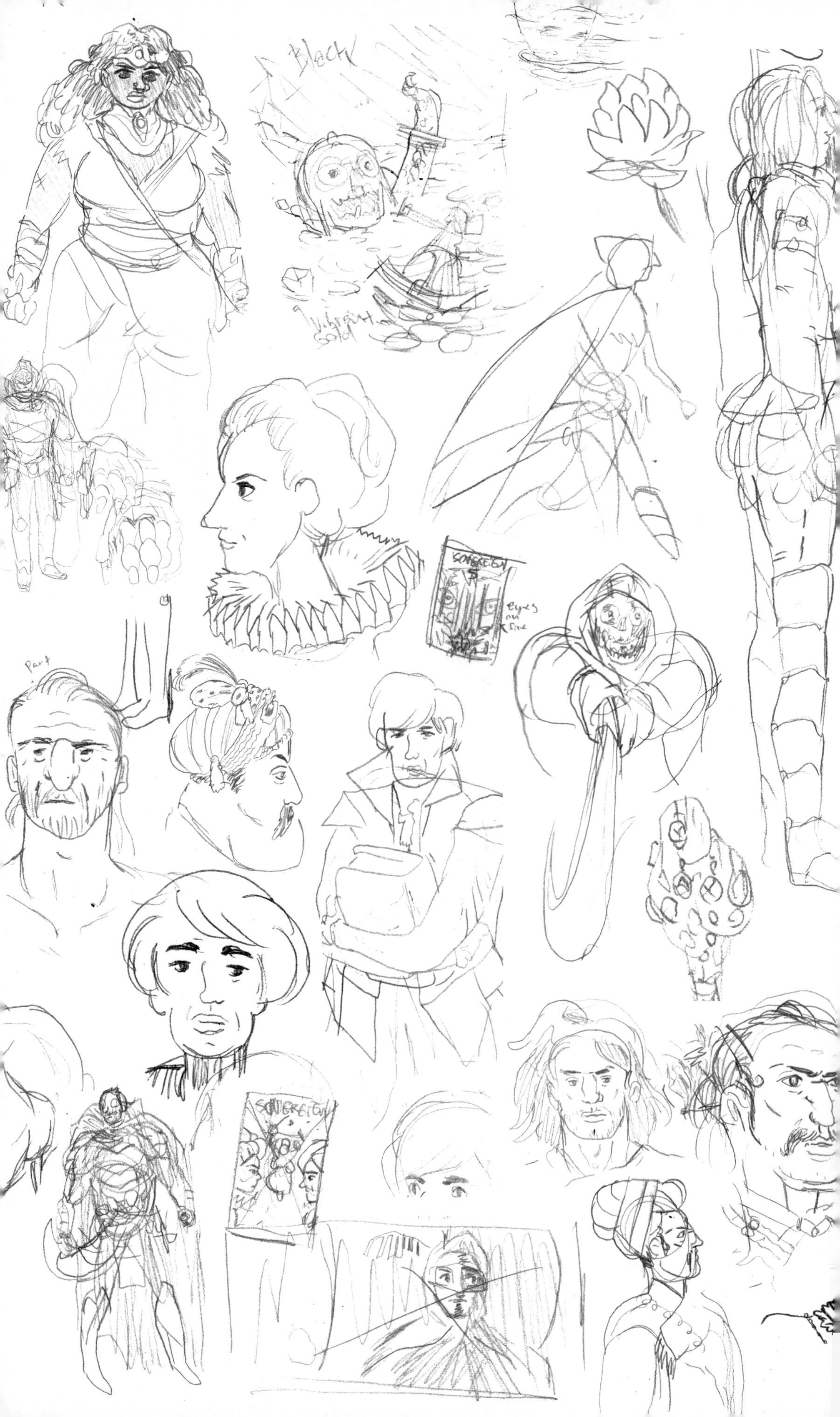
Black
vibrant gold
SOVEREIGN
5
eyes on fire
SOVEREIGN

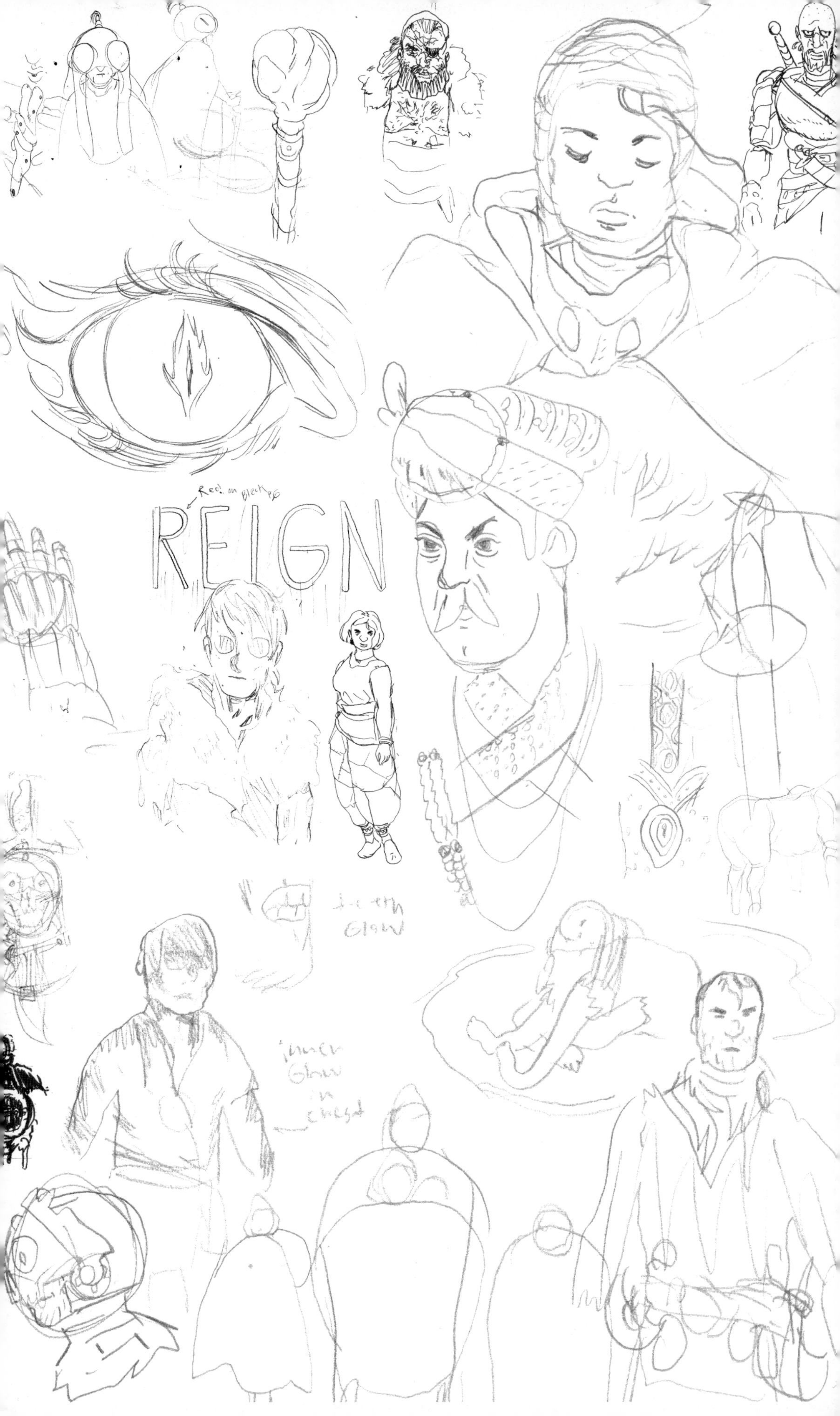
Red on Black BG
REIGN
teeth glow
inner glow in chest

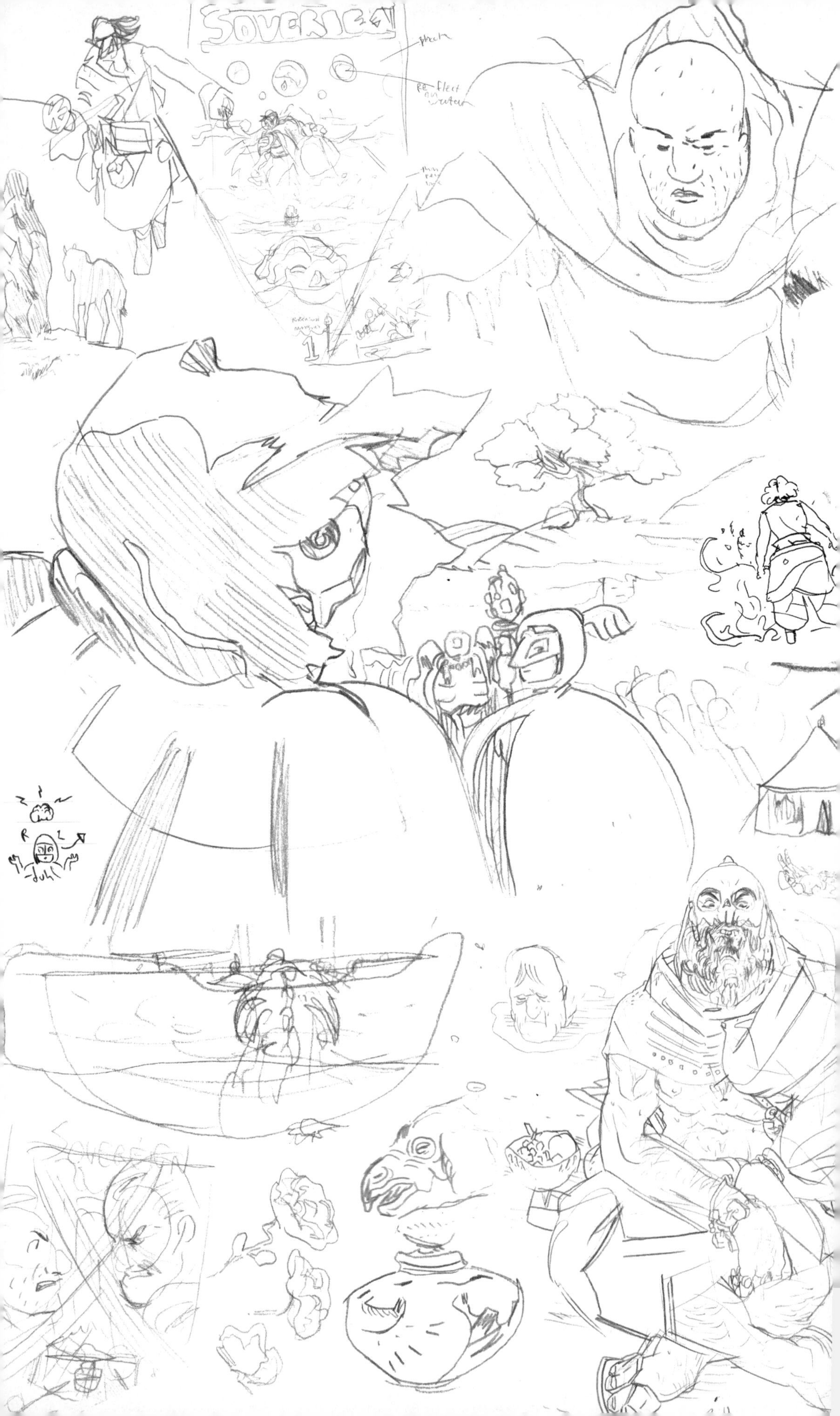
SOVEREIGN
re flect on water
1

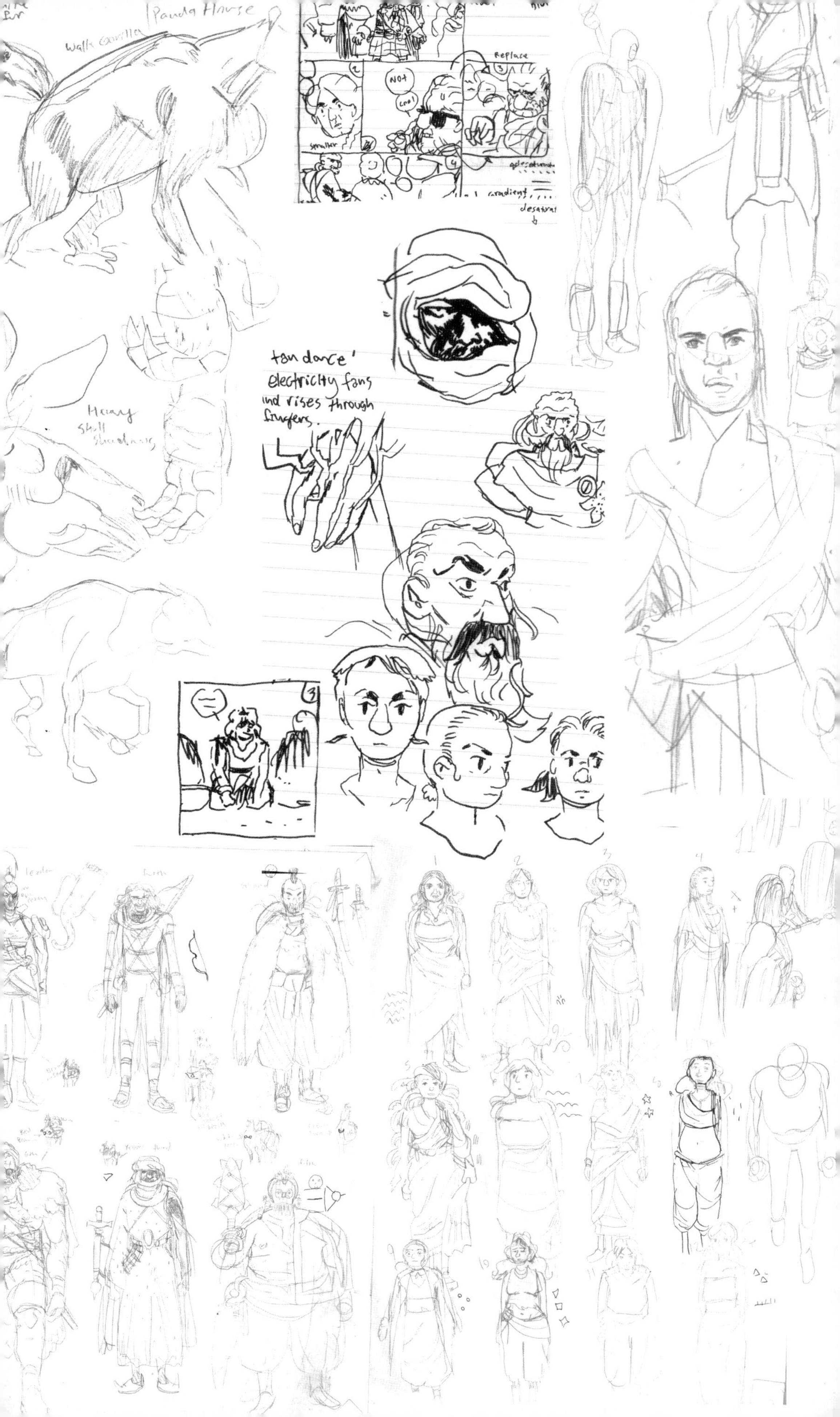
Panda Horse
Walk Gorilla
Replace
Not
cool
smaller
gradient
desaturat
tan dance' electricity fans and rises through fingers.

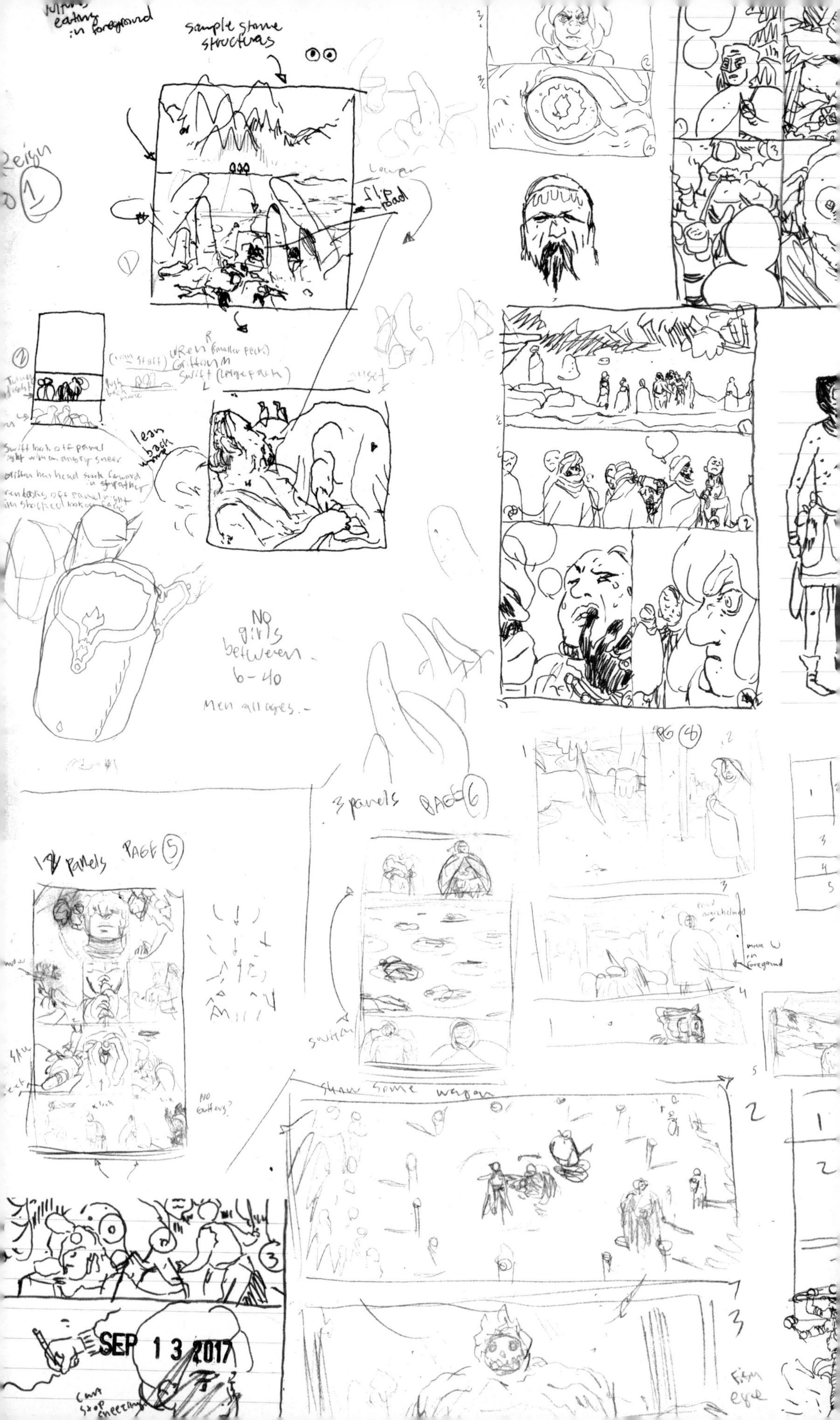

in foreground
Sample stone structures
Wren (smaller pack)
Griffon M
Swift (large pack)
lean back more
Swift looks off of panel right with an angry sneer
Griffon has head sunk forward in sympathy
No girls between 6-40
Men all ages.
PG 4
3 panels PAGE 6
14 panels PAGE 5
No gutters?
Switch
Show some wagon
SEP 13 2017
Fish eye